SOMEWHERE ON THE BORDER ■ ANTHONY AKERMAN

A unit of whites-only artillery trainees in basic camp before and during their going over the Border in South Africa's invasion of Angola in 1978. The script of this outspoken anti-war play, banned in South Africa, has nevertheless been performed there during the 1980s, and has twice been directed by the author while he lived in exile from South Africa.

THE HUNGRY EARTH ■ MAISHE MAPONYA

Developed with the Bahumutsi Theatre Company in the late 1970s, *The Hungry Earth* is one of the essential texts of black South African theatre. Many sketches about the lives of victims and underdogs culminate in a hugely moving final chorus of dispossession and outrage. The production toured the U.K. and Europe in 1981.

CURL UP AND DYE ■ SUSAN PAM–GRANT

Five women in a hair salon in Johannesburg's changing flatland face the divisions of apartheid as it drives their common interests into opposition. One of South Africa's longest running comedies, *Curl Up and Dye* had a successful season at the Tricycle Theatre, London, in 1990.

OVER THE HILL ■ PAUL SLABOLEPSZY

A one-acter for three performers, this play was first presented as part of a double-bill at various South African festivals in 1984-85. The performers take a theme and variations through the world of macho sport, satirically undermining apartheid norms.

JUST LIKE HOME ■ PIETER-DIRK UYS

The prolific satirist and playwright Pieter-Dirk Uys's remarkable and poignant play about the victims of South African racism building a life for themselves in the sanctuary of London. Cathy's flat is the scene of explosive replays of old games and eventually of reconciliation. The play enjoyed a run at the King's Head in Islington in 1989.

in the same series

KATHARINE BRISBANE (Ed)
Australia Plays
New Australian Drama
Jack Davis No Sugar; **Alma De Groen** The Rivers of China; **Michael Gow** Away; **Louis Nowra** The Golden Age; **David Williamson** Travelling North
1- 85459-056 -1

ALASDAIR CAMERON (Ed)
Scot-Free
New Scottish Plays
John Byrne Writer's Cramp; **John Clifford** Losing Venice; **Chris Hannan** Elizabeth Gordon Quinn; **Ann Marie Di Mambro** The Letter Box; **Rona Munro** Saturday at the Commodore; **John Mckay** Dead Dad Dog; **Tony Roper** The Steamie
1- 85459-017- 0

MICHAEL GLENNY (Ed)
Stars in the Morning Sky
New Soviet Plays
Alexander Chervinsky Heart of a Dog; **Alexander Galin** Stars in the Morning Sky; **Alexander Gelman** A Man with Connections; **Grigory Gorin** Forget Herostratus!; **Ludmila Petrushevskaya** Three Girls in Blue
1- 85459-020- 0

DAVID GRANT (Ed)
The Crack in the Emerald
New Irish Plays
Dermot Bolger The Lament for Arthur Cleary; **Marina Car** Low in the Dark; **Michael Harding** The Misogynist; **Marie Jones** The Hamster Wheel
1-85459-088-X

KATE HARWOOD (Ed)
First Run
New Plays by New writers
Simon Donald Prickly Heat; **Paul Godfrey** Inventing A New Colour; **Clare McIntyre** Low Level Panic; **Winsome Pinnock** Leave Taking; **Billy Roche** A Handful of Stars
1-85459-010-3

First Run 2
New Plays by New writers
John Clifford Ines De Castro; **Trish Cooke** Back Street Mammy; **Victoria Hardie** Sleeping Nightie; **Michael Harding** Una Pooka; **Stuart Hepburn** Loose Ends; **Stephen Jeffreys** Valued Friends
1-85459-002-2

MATTHEW LLOYD (Ed)
First Run 3
New Plays by New writers
Kathy Burke Mr Thomas; **Julian Garner** The Awakening; **Kevin Hood** Sugar Hill Blues; **Rona Munro** Bold Girls; **Richard Zajdlic** Infidelities
1-85459-059-6

South Africa Plays

SOMEWHERE ON THE BORDER ANTHONY AKERMAN

THE HUNGRY EARTH MAISHE MAPONYA

CURL UP AND DYE SUSAN PAM–GRANT

OVER THE HILL PAUL SLABOLEPSZY

JUST LIKE HOME PIETER-DIRK UYS

EDITED WITH AN INTRODUCTION BY
STEPHEN GRAY

NICK HERN BOOKS   HEINEMANN-CENTAUR

LONDON   SOUTH AFRICA

A Nick Hern Book

South Africa Plays first published in Great Britain in 1993 as an original paperback by Nick Hern Books Limited, 14 Larden Road, London W3 7ST and in South Africa by Heinemann-Centaur Publishers, P. O. Box 2017, Houghton, 2041.

Somewhere on the Border first appeared as a working script from the Thekwini Theatre Foundation, Amsterdam, in 1983; *The Hungry Earth* appeared as a working script from Polyptoton in 1981 during the play's London run.

Typeset, printed and bound in India by Seagull Books, Calcutta.

British Library Cataloguing in Publication Data
A Catalogue record for this book is available from the British Library

ISBN 185459 148 7

Contents

Introduction

Sketching in the background of the plays in this collection is not exactly straightforward. What theatre tradition there is in South Africa has been discontinuous, subject to brief booms when socio-economic circumstances and worthwhile ideas have combined at particular junctures. The inspired moments of South African theatre have always been scratched together seemingly out of nowhere . . . and stayed on to change the direction of the local business.

This volume is a record of unexpected talents grabbing opportunities, because the great teachers, drama schools, companies and even play publishers that have brought about renewals in theatre overseas are largely lacking in South Africa. The theatre consists of only a couple of thousand people, thinly spread, keeping two dozen venues country-wide alight, and each has to perform many jobs, often without training and for poor rewards. We theatregoers inside the country have until very recently had to rely on *their* new directions second-hand. Every new style, technique or even set-fabric and lighting-board developed in the U.K. and the U.S., or more remotely in Western Europe, has in due course been taken on here as well.

But, despite their client status, South African theatre practitioners have not been uncritical in their uses of imported material as it has come down to them. Interesting South African styles of doing the imported thing have always been in evidence. Rather than copycat imitation, a degree of creative adaptation has become usual, in order to meet local audience expectations and to delight them. By the 1980s, a typically South African school of making its own theatre had at last evolved which the contents of this volume reflects. Within the last decade South African theatre may be said to have arrived in its own terms.

Nevertheless, all the scripts here could only be part of Western theatre after 1945: they have absorbed the Absurd, Brecht, Brook, the cinema, Disney, Existentialism . . . through Shaw, Shepard, Walcott, Wesker and Williams. There is no South African playwright who has not come through that climate. The English language in South Africa has for historical reasons been the country's main carrier of the arts and through English it has had access to developments abroad.

English in South Africa is the medium of the powerful culture-broker, just as it is of politics. English is the cloak with which South Africans gird themselves to meet the outside world. Yet within

South Africa English is by no means the only transactable tongue. Afrikaans through Zulu, these languages are spoken by more people in living situations, and substantial, accomplished dramatic literatures have grown up in them as well, fully deserving study in their own right. But English has remained the medium into which and from which the others are translated. In the process over the last two centuries standard Southern English has had to acquire quite a cargo of non-English vocabulary. A glance at the glossary included with this collection will indicate the range of concepts – often raunchy and plain-spoken, usually assertively African – that it is felt our inherited English is too limited, or just too alien, to carry. South Africans of all kinds assert their differences – from non-South Africans and from each other – by gleefully flaunting these linguistic additions. Although this may be difficult for *readers* of the scripts, this is not so in performance; nor are such words italicised here, as they wouldn't be in the mouths of actors. Dialect adds bite and authenticity to dialogue and characterises the work.

The historical background we are speaking of is roughly as follows. With the British Occupation of the Cape at the turn of the nineteenth century came the colony's first African Theatre, a free-standing building in the shade of Table Mountain. It was staffed by the garrison, and the conquered Dutch and French were encouraged to cut their losses and show their loyalty with suitable amateur dramatic performances. Sheridan, Beaumarchais and Shakespeare, with prologues and epilogues appropriate to the circumstances, were introduced to the tip of the continent. Much local alcohol was also sold. (After emancipation the building was turned over to liberated slaves as their church.)

Later in the century patriotic circuses appeared. One entrepreneur managed to re-stage the Frontier Wars more or less as they were happening at the other end of the subcontinent, with casts of thousands and heavy casualties. In the 1880s in the Cape, and also in Natal Colony when it was pacified, saloon theatres gave way to the institution of the music hall, which was introduced complete with the standard design buildings for Tivoli Palaces of Varieties, latest scenic illusions included. Opera Houses alongside, catering for enormous audiences, enjoyed being on the circuit of the more intrepid actor-managers (Cedric Hardwicke was one). Their companies would set off from Southampton for years on end to 'play the Empire': Cape Town, Port Elizabeth, East London, Durban, Mombasa, Bombay, Singapore . . . and, after Australia and New Zealand, China. A fresh West End comedy in their repertoire would, by the end of such a tour, have become a museum piece of British tribal solidarity.

In 1889, within a year of its proclamation, Johannesburg, founded as the world's capital of gold with money from Kimberley, the city of diamonds, could boast an entire prefabricated corrugated iron theatre, complete with gaslit chandelier and colour-spraying organ, which had been rolled out in bits on trusty ox-waggons. This was Searelle's Theatre Royal, the first venue in the Transvaal to be open for entertainment all year round, Sundays excluded. Later, British and American stars like Gracie Fields and Danny Kaye would be accorded ticker-tape welcomes by this outpost, keen to keep on the world entertainment routes.

The first hundred years of this cultural conquest of Africa effectively put paid to any indigenous expressions which may have been construed as rival attractions. Beyond the invading frontier Bushman rain-dance ceremonies, Xhosa or Sotho dance pageants and other highly organised rituals were fatally touched, at first, by the missionaries, who intervened not only with the administrative backup of war, but with more subtle converters like the church service. Then came the slate, the radio, the satellite. The relics are studied under subjects like 'ethnography', but are otherwise extinct. No link exists between the pre-contact performances of Southern Africa and any work labelled 'African' today. Such shows have been too compromised by European notions of what such performances must be. (The hilarious sequence in *The Hungry Earth* about tourists attending a mine-dance says all that needs to be said in this regard.)

The first South African work as such concerns exactly this conflict of interests in the arts. *Kaatje Kekkelbek, or Life among the Hottentots* features the popular 'Hottentot Venus' character in full cry against the indignities heaped on her to obtain her co-operation in the colonial enterprise: brandy, fences, prison . . . The sketch, complete with shrieks and feathers, is a turn that parodies an authentic shuffle-and-chant routine. First performed by an amateur cross-dresser in a Border regiment in 1846, it was for ever after on the bill at smokers and family entertainments. Its real subject is not the intractability of Khoisan subjects, but the po-faced Puritans who forget that theatre must accommodate many (all) South African voices, even if the real world outside systematically excludes them.

With the post-Second Anglo-Boer War unification of the South African provinces due in 1910, and riding the wave of a nation-wide spirit, Stephen Black – the father of South African English drama – devised a play that really did give all types of South African a voice. *Love and the Hyphen* featured just about every facet of the life of the new, unfolding country, hell-bent on peace, prosperity and record box-office returns. The departure of the British garrison from the Cape was actually enacted, as its band marched off to board the ships for Home.

Black's second play, a farcical Edwardian melodrama called *Helena's Hope, Ltd.*, was revived over the next twenty years; it still holds the record as the most performed South Africa piece. Black used broad cross-sections of South African people and presented their predicaments recognisably. From scratch he had to train his performers away from the familiar drawing-room style of comedy – from 'doing cockney' to 'doing Coloured'. His mode remained pre-naturalist, so that you may say his type of theatre was doomed to die a death when the naturalism of the movies supplanted it.

As many theatres were converted to cinemas with the advent of the talking picture, the development of South African drama in English was arrested for most of a generation. In the 1930s there was only one dramatist – H.I.E. Dhlomo. Partly because of his colour, he had had so little access to drama in action that his scripts in English and in Zulu about lost worlds of black history were largely unperformable. At best they received walk-throughs on a Saturday night in the privacy of the Bantu Men's Social Centre in Johannesburg, a cultural club devoted to the uplifting of the Negro. There was no opportunity for him to develop his work on any commercial basis.

But in the years between the World Wars some extraordinary performers were produced and their work was widely acknowledged. André Huguenet is an example. If South Africa had little going for it – was a citrus and mineral-producing Dominion at the end of the Union-Castle Line, afflicted with cultural cringe – at least Huguenet made it from touring the bundu to the West End where he played the lead in James Elroy Flecker's *Hassan!* The esteem he earned was remembered the way matrons in Melbourne recall Dame Nellie Melba's – 'He was *invited*, you know, and to give *Royal* Performances!' Another South African-born star was Marda Vanne who started with Stephen Black and duly returned from metropolitan glory to her home in 1939, more or less to get away from the blackouts and rationing. With her lifelong partner, Gwen ffrangçon-Davies, Vanne *was* South African professional theatre for the duration. With four productions using local talent they went out by train for the Schlesinger entertainment group, triumphantly received at every stop.

After World War II a recognisably modern theatre industry began to emerge in urban South Africa. Despite vicissitudes, this has become established as a legitimate business on a par with that of, say, any other industrialised English-speaking area outside Europe or of an American state outside New York or California. The input came from returning ex-servicemen (like Guy Butler), who were determined to propagate the spread of English as the language of mediation between the newly rising white Afrikaners and black nationalists, while at the same time stressing that English had become an African language as well. Counter to this, Afrikaner cultural workers were equally keen to hold the liberalising tendency of English at bay in order to build a white elitist Afrikaans-medium culture (at the expense of other language and population groups). With the coming to power of the Nationalist government in 1948 the latter movement gained momentum. In due course their 'apartheid' policy of cultural separateness was defined.

At first the truly remarkable National Theatre Organisation was unaffected. Its members were talented and skilful, took theatre to every (not always whites-only) hall in the godforsaken hinterland and used a versatile, bilingual approach – Molière in Afrikaans for the matinée, Fry or Eliot in the original at night. Here Athol Fugard acquired the only training he has ever had, stage-managing the NTO's experimental company, touring Ionesco (in Afrikaans) and Camus (in English).

But in the 1950s the arts in general began to receive the attention of the powers that be, ranged against the evolution of any mixed, representative and multicultural endeavour. This movement towards the formation of a truly national theatre was, in fact, driven underground and thwarted for decades to come. The rising generation of black writers now known as the *Drum* school, for example, had all been driven into exile by the end of the decade, and thereafter all traces of the vibrant, hybridised cultural style they pioneered were erased. The same purge began of whites who were of what was construed as a leftist orientation.

Resistance to government strictures climaxed in 1959 with the musical *King Kong*. (This was not based on the Edgar Wallace story, but on the biography of a South African black boxer, who adopted the title as a gesture of defiance.) When *King Kong* began its lengthy run in the West End, with it went an entire generation, Miriam Makeba included, and the company was a nucleus of South African performers in the diaspora. Those who survived abroad were not to return to their country of birth for all of thirty years.

In 1960 the Sharpeville Massacre by police of demonstrators against the pass laws, together with the implementation of the Group Areas Act (by which both residential and business areas including theatre districts were set aside for the exclusive use of particular racial groups), brought down the curtain between South Africa and the rest of the world. A year later Dr Verwoerd was obliged to withdraw South Africa from the British Commonwealth and the long, punishing isolation of the new Republic began.

At the same time Fugard's *The Blood Knot* was launched . . . a wonderful moment that signalled all the pain of apartheid and the artistry which could be used to combat it. This two-hander played in the dingiest locales for over a year. It is salutary to remember now that that extraordinary play featured two characters who made the Population Registration Act look not only plain evil, but fatuous: they were two blood brothers, one classified 'white' and the other 'non-white'. Also one must recall that the players, Zakes Mokae (black) and Athol Fugard (white), were by then forbidden to share a dressing-room, a toilet or even the stage-area itself. And yet they persisted, as did their audiences in finding them.

In 1962 the easy-going NTO was disbanded in favour of four government-sponsored provincial performing arts councils – five, if

South Africa's colony of South West Africa (now independent Namibia) is included. While existing theatre was driven into private spaces (on university campuses, or into garages, back rooms, distant church or township halls), the councils began erecting what may be called the new 'culture bunkers', fortified buildings, modelled on Stuttgart or Essen, usually underground, where ballet, opera and music could thrive – for whites alone and without controversy. Public protest in Cape Town delayed the opening of one of these, the Nico Malan complex – named after a National Party stalwart rather than anyone in the arts – and even succeeded in getting it 'open' (that is, to all racial groups without discrimination).

For many years there were gains and there were losses. Mostly losses, at first. In 1963 the British Playwrights' Boycott was formed and the country's greatest source of stagework dried up overnight. Although the boycott in principle was targeted at segregated venues, it rapidly became a blanket ban that merely expressed a generalised disapproval of South Africa. That same year inside the country the Publications Control Board was formed to organise and tighten up the already pervasive censorship-system. One of the board's early triumphs was to close the South African premiere – five minutes before the curtain was due to rise before a full house in a non-segregated venue – of *Who's Afraid of Virginia Woolf?* (When the movie was released years later the soundtrack had Burton and Taylor hiccup every time there was a swear word in the original.)

In 1966 the Equity ban on British performers appearing in South Africa came into effect, closing off the last of the old guest appearances. This is the point where British interests and influence begin to wane in South Africa and the less finicky U.S. moved in. From here on the musicals, the movies, the sitcoms and soaps, the jargon, the popular music all rapidly Americanise. The name of the playwright most peformed in South Africa during the apartheid period becomes Arthur Miller.

From the cultural point of view the 1960s in this country was a period of increasing deprivation and loss. Declining educational standards, specifically thanks to the Bantu Education Act system forced on blacks, and the promotion of wider illiteracy made theatrical activity as we know it seem an irrelevant luxury. Theatre had pretty well died from a twin lack of resilience and sense of mission. Fugard's theatre works of the decade were about this: works of claustrophobia, of bare essentials, minimal, tenacious, but without hope. All the characters in the plays presented here, if we are to imagine them having real and extended lives outside the theatre, were born during this decade of conflict, or at least have experienced the lingering trauma of its aftermath.

But by the 1970s it was clear that, except for a small kernel of diehards, the various practitioners in the performing arts were beginning to form a common opposition to the forces threatening them. There were many sporadic signs. In Johannesburg in 1971, to give just one example, a group called Workshop '71 was briefly formed and pioneered improvisations which would later be taken up and expanded. The first true fringe venues opened at the Space in Cape Town in 1972, where overnight it seemed that an alternative culture was not only in formation, but underway. The same confident breaks occurred at the Market Theatre in Johannesburg in 1976, and in 1977 at the Baxter in Cape Town again. All these independent arts complexes in complicated ways have evaded (or simply ignored) laws of racial exclusivity and, although they have been funded in part by municipalities and other urban bodies, have never received a cent of the government funds allocated to the furtherance of the nation's theatre. In the end their success at the box-office has had to pull them through (or has not – the Space closed in1983 and the Market is currently critically in debt). By 1977, thanks to their example, all other venues were officially opened to all racial groups.

While the state-sponsored theatre has continued to *purvey* stage-culture, often at an extremely accomplished level, the alternative centres have opted for *making* stage-culture anew. This may be baldly illustrated: in the dead Sixties only four plays of any substance were written in English within South Africa, in the Seventies a dozen. In 1974 the primarily English-language Grahamstown annual festival was founded and even that at first ignored South African plays. By 1983 their fringe had grown appreciably and the main stages began to include local work, commissioned from rising South African playwrights. (*Over the Hill* is a case in point, and was a box-office smash hit.) Today the festival's presentation of new South African scripts is not less than fifty *per year*. That suppressed alternative culture has now in fact become the South African mainstream. All the plays in this volume have come about thanks to that process. Things are as they should be on our stages, for the first time in our history.

Statistics do not tell a whole story, and a boom may easily collapse. The recession and the rise of civil violence in South Africa have almost wiped the theatre out again in the 1990s. Future funding of the arts and policy towards the stage in the post-apartheid South Africa will continue to be vital factors in the existence of its theatre.

However, there can be no doubt that during the Seventies, thanks to the perseverance and assertion of the people whose activity was focused on the Space-Market-Baxter circuit, there occurred one of those profound changes in the cultural politics of a country that are not really in view until they are complete. Resistance art had found its arena in the theatre (rather than in less communal forms) and had attracted its own ever-growing patronage. The formation of a mixed, demanding and critical audience in turn influenced developments on stage, as one successful show created the need for the next.

No one who was there for the opening of the Market in October 1976, could forget how theatre and the politics in the streets were locking into step. That was the week of the Soweto Uprising no less, resistance songs from the square outside were audible inside, the tear gas in everyone's hair, and the lights going down on Adam Small, on Pieter-Dirk Uys and on a Barney Simon version of the *Marat/Sade* that included almost every functioning performer still left in the country. Police fusillades off.

The making of plays in the 1970s and into the 1980s was expedited by the new procedures of workshopping, improvisation and other corporate and democratic means of devising shows. Fugard led the way in 1972 with his collaboration with John Kani and Winston Ntshona to create *Sizwe Bansi is Dead*, a lot of the statement of which was made even before anyone risked attending it: this was a black-white mutual effort. (Kani and Ntshona soon became the first professional black actors on the serious South African stage.) By March 1981, with *Woza Albert!* – the collaboration between Simon, Ngema and Mtwa – the life of deprivation and despair of black South Africans under apartheid had acquired an on-stage style of its own: quick-change revue sketches, body skills of song and dance and mimicry, a repartee of beguiling political commentary.

This was 'poor' theatre, necessarily eschewing large budgets and sophisticated theatrical effects, scaled down to the basics: an undefeatable presence, coping, surviving, forcing change. With nothing to lose, this school of performers took on the world. Indeed, during the 1980s there was hardly a production of this type that did not escape the restrictions of the motherland to enjoy its overseas tour. Call it the empire striking back: South African companies abroad in the Eighties would enact their messages on tour for years on end, from Aix to Belfast to Cambridge to Denver.

The courage and commitment of black performers like these filtered back into traditionally white areas as well. Play-making became pointedly multi-racial and, as a matter of opposition policy, has stayed that way. *Curl Up and Dye* and *Just Like Home* are prime examples of this. No longer merely defiant and oppositional, works like these have become fully articulate and richly varied with a life of their own. The phrase 'resistant to apartheid' seems monolithic now; that, too, has become a part of our history. A 'new' South Africa was in formation on stage, worked for by the whole Eighties generation behind the scenes and blatantly on display out front. Nor was it necessary any longer to talk of 'black' and 'white' – these were all South Africans working together in common cause.

By the mid-Eighties with its 'Second Soweto' and its successive, annually renewed States of Emergency, it was clear that the militaristic regime of P.W. Botha was no longer in control. One went to the theatre then for guidance on how to conduct one's life during the inter-regnum. In the theatre a future country had, by common consensus, been declared. The critical point had been reached where this could no longer be reversed.

The contents of this collection graphically illustrates the process described above. Sounds foreboding. But if there is one observation to be made about the plays here it is that they certainly are not dutifully tragic. Rather they are all life-giving comedies: they satirise, they sabotage, they outwit, they push through the debris for happy resolutions. No matter the despair and bleakness, the terrible mutilations of the past four decades, their programmes are positive and life-asserting. Every moment of stage-time shows why the freedom party has not yet occurred, but is on the brink of occurring. Celebration is about to break loose. These plays are written on a winning streak for humankind.

Detailed notes about each of the five plays presented here are given before each one. They appear in alphabetical order of author's surname, which fortuitously also happens to be almost exactly the order in which they first made their mark. All these scripts appear here, complete and formally published in a durable form, for the first time.

Stephen Gray
Johannesburg, 1993

ANTHONY AKERMAN was born in Durban in 1949 and went to school in Natal. In 1967 he served his country as a member of the 14th Field Regiment in Potchefstroom, rising to the rank of Lance Bombardier. At Rhodes University in Grahamstown he studied drama and then took a post-graduate director's course at the Bristol Old Vic Theatre School. He lived in exile in Amsterdam from 1975, writing short stories and publishing influential articles against apartheid in journals like *Theatre Quarterly*. In Holland he earned his living as a director, launching several South African plays – he has been responsible for the Dutch premieres of most of Athol Fugard's works, from *Statements after an Arrest under the Immorality Act* in 1976, through to *My Children! My Africa!* in 1991. Under the terms of the recent amnesty in South Africa, he has finally been able to return to live and work in the theatre.

His first play, *Somewhere on the Border*, was written in 1982 and premiered under his direction with exiled South African actors in The Hague. The first performances in South Africa were at the Grahamstown Festival in 1986, independently directed by Gerrit Schoonhoven and superbly restaged by him for PACT Drama in the Transvaal. This version proceeded with great acclaim but not without controversy: permission for the players to perform in South African Defence Force uniforms was withheld and once, at the end of a performance, even though they were in fictional costumes, members of the cast were beaten up by right-wing terrorists. In September 1990, Akerman at last obtained a visa to direct the second South African production, for the Loft Company of NAPAC, in Durban, for a sell-out season.

An Author's Note in the original programme, accompanied by a photo, reads as follows:

> Going to the army was part of growing up in white South Africa. It was the first hurdle you had to clear after leaving school. You knew it was hard and you were expected to take it like a man. No one got out of it. Most of us thought it was a waste of time. But in the back of your mind, you knew you could always be used to maintain the status quo. Now the boys are sent to the border. Now the boys are sent to Cassinga. So when I look at that photograph – with all my feelings of revulsion, compassion and shame – I am left with a single thought: there, but for the grace of God, was I.
>
> On 4 May 1978, South African forces attacked a village

260 kilometres inside Angola. The village was populated by
Namibian refugees who had fled from the South African
army occupying their country. During the attack 160 men,
295 women and 300 children were killed. The wounded
who died in the days after the attack brought the death toll
to over 1000. The village is called Cassinga. The photograph
is of a mass grave.

Characters

DAVID LEVITT
BLACK ACTOR
TREVOR MOWBRAY
BOMBARDIER KOTZE
HENNIE BADENHORST
PAUL MARAIS
DOUG CAMPBELL

The play is set in the South African Army.

Act One takes place in a training camp somewhere in South Africa.

Act Two takes place in the operational area, somewhere on the border of Namibia and Angola, and in the south of Angola.

The time is the recent past.

Somewhere on the Border was originally produced by Thekwini Theater and was first presented at Theater aan de Haven, The Hague, on 11 November 1983, directed by the author, with the following cast:

DAVID LEVITT	Joss Levine
BLACK ACTOR	Joseph Mosikili
TREVOR MOWBRAY	Richard Carter
BOMBARDIER KOTZE	Jon Cartwright
HENNIE BADENHORST	Jeroen Kranenburg
PAUL MARAIS	Ian Bruce
DOUG CAMPBELL	Allan Ivan

For Ian Bruce and Joseph Mosikili

ACT ONE

Scene One

A gate. Darkness. As the first strains of 'Jungle' by the Electric Light Orchestra are heard, a subdued, nocturnal lighting is introduced. A lone sentry on guard duty. It is LEVITT. *He wears the headphones of a walkman. As he walks across the stage, a* BLACK ACTOR *wearing civilian clothes walks along behind him, draws an imaginary six-shooter and guns him down, then crosses upstage through the gate.* LEVITT *pauses. He removes the headphones and the music stops. He looks around him.*

LEVITT. Halt! Who goes there? (*He peers into the audience.*) Is anyone there? (*He replaces the headphones and we immediately hear the music again. He begins 'composing' a letter.*) Dearest Sharon. No. Darling Sharon. My dearest, darling Sharon. Howzit? I miss you stacks. Man, I'm sorry I couldn't work a pass this weekend. Please try and understand. I only got one letter from you this week. What's going on? No. (*Pause.*) Please try and understand. Keep the letters rolling, Sharon! I'll try and write every day. I think of you all the time. Where are you tonight? Are you going to Gavin's party anyway? Did that Stan Rabinowitz ask you? Just remember Sharon, he's only after one thing and he'll have no respect for you after. Don't do it, Sharon. I need you, man. Remember I'm faithful to you, hey. I know I haven't got much choice here, but still. Fair is fair, hey. Ja, I know you get lonely, but try and see it my way. As long as I got you, Sharon, they can't break me. There's talk of us maybe going up to the border. Can you wait that long for me, Sharon? Well, spans of love. Your Dave. Holland. Hope Our Love Lives And Never Dies. (*He lights a cigarette.*) Siam. Sexual Intercourse at Midnight.

MOWBRAY *appears upstage and advances silently towards* LEVITT. *He plucks the cigarette from his lips.*

MOWBRAY. What's this, hey?

LEVITT. Hi there, Trev.

MOWBRAY. What's this, I'm asking.

LEVITT. What's the problem?

MOWBRAY. This! To my face you say you got no skyfs and then behind my back you come here to zoll on your ace.

MOWBRAY *takes a drag and blows smoke in* LEVITT*'s face.*

LEVITT. I only had one left, man.

MOWBRAY. Is it?

LEVITT. As a matter of fact, ja.

MOWBRAY. You act like I'm your china and then you come sideways at me like a crab.

LEVITT. You want to see the packet?

MOWBRAY. Ag, fuck off to Israel.

LEVITT. Take my oath.

MOWBRAY. You lie like your feet stink, Levitt.

LEVITT. Give me my smoke back.

As LEVITT *reaches for the cigarette,* MOWBRAY *makes stabbing gestures towards him with the glowing end.*

MOWBRAY. I burn you.

LEVITT. Pull out, man.

MOWBRAY. You sukkel with me, I kill you dead.

LEVITT. Don't be pathetic.

MOWBRAY. Cunt-eyed schmo of a typical Jewboy.

LEVITT. Look, cut it out.

MOWBRAY. Make me.

LEVITT. Just grow up.

MOWBRAY. Voetsek!

MOWBRAY *gives* LEVITT *a push. Upstage we can discern the figure of* KOTZE.

I don't like you. It's not personal. I just hate Jews.

LEVITT. Take that back.

MOWBRAY. Here, I'll thump you, Levitt.

LEVITT. Take it back!

MOWBRAY. You sailing for a nailing, Jewboy.

LEVITT. You making me lose my temper.

MOWBRAY. I gob in your face.

MOWBRAY *shows* LEVITT a *ball of spit on the end of his tongue.*

I land this greenie right on your Jewboy nose.

LEVITT. You forcing me to.

MOWBRAY *spits in* LEVITT*'s face.* LEVITT *lashes out at him. They end up on the ground with* LEVITT *on top of* MOWBRAY.

You asked for it.

KOTZE *moves towards them.*

KOTZE. Aandag!

MOWBRAY *and* LEVITT *scramble to their feet and stand to attention.*

I come here to inspect the guard and I find you behaving like a pair of moffies. Come here!

KOTZE *takes them each by an earlobe and knocks their heads together.*

Look out there. What you see? You see South Africa. What else? Blackness. Die Swart Gevaar. You here to watch that, not to play silly buggers. Watch it! It's black and dangerous.

Blackout.

Scene Two

The bungalow. Rows of iron beds on either side of a central walkway. Early morning. MARAIS *and* BADENHORST *are still in their sleeping bags on top of beds already made up for inspection.* BADENHORST *stirs, looks into the sleeping bag and addresses his member.*

BADENHORST. Hey, behave yourself!

MARAIS *wakes up with a shout.*

What's your case?

MARAIS. Klein Klaas, you know, he was running down there by the cement dam. He's the boy on the farm. And, no, ja, wait, I was under the bluegums. You know, just sitting.

BADENHORST. Give your mouth a chance, Paul.

MARAIS. He was running there with his knees bent carrying two buckets and they almost touched the dirt. Then he came there on the wall of the dam. It was Klein Klaas. Suddenly he klaps up into the air and falls slowly over into the water. Like a film. Then I heard this shot, Hennie. I got such a skrik I jumped, man. I tried to run there, but my legs went all slap and I fell down. Oubaas Venter said, Leave it, Paul. He was going to poison the water. I could smell the oil from his rifle. Klein Klaas was floating and there was all blood. I was then on the wall and he says, Why do you shoot me, Baas Paul? And I can't say nothing. I'm all sticky from blood. I try to catch him with my hands, but he's got no hands. Just stumps that slip. And he's saying, Why? Why? Why?

BADENHORST. Cause Y's a crooked letter and you can't make it straight.

MARAIS. How late is it?

BADENHORST. Too late, she cried.

KOTZE (off). Move, you dumb cunt!

CAMPBELL, *wearing civilian clothing and laden down with army kit, enters. He is followed on by* KOTZE.

MARAIS. Aandag!

MARAIS *and* BADENHORST *jump to attention.*

KOTZE. Here God, wat die fok gaan hier aan? You cunts is asking for shit, nè? This place looks like a whore's handbag. I try and treat you like white men and look what happens. Slaan die dek!

MARAIS *and* BADENHORST *get down and start doing press-ups.* KOTZE *turns to* CAMPBELL.

Moenie vir my loer nie, ek is nie 'n hoer nie. Weet jy wat jy is, Engelsman? Jy's 'n urk. Weet jy wat 'n urk is? 'n Urk is 'n dinges wat in jou gat in kruip en gedurende die nag sluip hy na buite en blaf vir jou ballas. Verstaan jy?

CAMPBELL. Could you repeat that in English please, Bombardier?

KOTZE. Jou ma se moer. You see how these men are shitting off, Kammel? You know why, Kammel? It's because you are full of shit, Kammel.

CAMPBELL. My name's Campbell, Bombardier.

KOTZE. Is that so?

CAMPBELL. Yes, Bombardier.

KOTZE. Wrong, Kammel! I tell you what is your name.

CAMPBELL. My name's Campbell, Bombardier.

KOTZE. Listen, my man, I'm going to tell you something. (*To the others.*) You sound like a bunch of women on the job. On your feet! Now look at this rubbish here. This is called a troublemaker. He's no trouble to me, but he's going to make trouble for you. I'm going to tell you something, Kammel, so you better listen good. You perhaps think you a big deal. But take it from me, I'm not impressed. I can eat ten of your kind before breakfast, Kammel. I'm a hard man. I take my holidays on the Caprivi Strip. I've broken men twice your size. I've heard them cry out for their mothers, Kammel. So if you coming here thinking the sun shine out your arse, you got two chances: no chance and fuck-all chance. That's not a joke, Kammel! I don't make jokes. I straighten people out. And if you don't get into line, I'll pull a cow's cunt over your head and let a bull fuck some sense into it. You understand what I'm talking, Kammel?

CAMPBELL. Yes, Bombardier.

KOTZE. You say something, Kammel?

CAMPBELL. Yes, Bombardier.

KOTZE. What was that?

CAMPBELL. Yes, Bombardier!!!

KOTZE. I hope you not pulling my legs. Right! You lot thought you had a free Saturday. That's what comes from thinking. Full-kit inspection at 1700 hours. I want to see how our troublemaker settles in. And this place better shine. Right?

ALL. Yes, Bombardier.

KOTZE. What?

ALL. Yes, Bombardier!!!

KOTZE. Who's got a driving licence around here?

BADENHORST. Me, Bombardier!

KOTZE. Put on some clothes, get up to the NCO mess on the double and wash my car.

BADENHORST *groans and starts getting dressed.*

Get your things packed out, Kammel. And get rid of those moffie clothes. You'll probably never wear civvies again. Is jy al daar, Badenhorst?

KOTZE *marches off briskly, followed by* BADENHORST. MARAIS *crosses to* CAMPBELL.

MARAIS. I'm Paul Marais.

CAMPBELL. Oh.

MARAIS *shakes his hand.*

Ja, Campbell. Doug.

MARAIS. Doug?

CAMPBELL. Campbell.

MARAIS. So. How goes it?

CAMPBELL. Does the lahnie always lay on the heavy vibes?

MARAIS. Excuse me?

CAMPBELL. The Bombardier.

MARAIS. Kotze?

CAMPBELL. Does he always go apeshit?

MARAIS. No, on the moment he seems a bit omgekrap.

CAMPBELL. Truly.

MARAIS. But if we pull together, then he's white.

CAMPBELL. Hey, well.

MARAIS. Have you been in some trouble?

CAMPBELL. Can you lend us some goeters to clean this shit?

MARAIS. No fine.

> MARAIS *gives* CAMPBELL *a cleaning kit.*

From what camp do you come?

CAMPBELL. Pretoria.

MARAIS. You weren't in the D. B. there?

CAMPBELL. Naught.

MARAIS. I just thought.

CAMPBELL. For sure.

> *An awkward pause.*

MARAIS. I think I'll perhaps go help Hennie with the car.

CAMPBELL. Safe.

MARAIS. Excuse me?

CAMPBELL. No, I'll sight you then.

MARAIS. No fine, Doug. Just make yourself at home, hey.

> MARAIS *leaves.* CAMPBELL *takes in his new surroundings.*
> *Blackout.*

We hear the following from a radio request programme for national servicemen:

And here's a card now and it goes to Corporal Brian Adams, somewhere on the border. We're praying and thinking of him daily and we pray the time will pass speedily and we pray for his safe return. And we're also thinking of all the fellows with him in C Company. And it comes from Mum, Dad, Sean and sister Desiré. That's to Corporal Brian Adams, somewhere on the border. I do hope, Brian, that you heard the message . . .

Scene Three

Lights up as CAMPBELL *lights a cigarette. The same.* LEVITT *lays out* CAMPBELL*'s kit for inspection. He walks on taxis. The sound now comes from* LEVITT*'s radio. The message is followed by commercial jingles.* CAMPBELL *turns it off. He pays no attention to* LEVITT.

LEVITT. Then you just square off your bed with your dixies so. Here the towel at the bottom and on that you put the moving parts of your rifle, your Bible, your razor and other stuff, like that see? Hey, are you watching?

CAMPBELL. What?

LEVITT. I'm not catching a thrill here.

CAMPBELL. What's cutting you?

LEVITT. Next time you'll have to do it yourself.

CAMPBELL. For sure.

LEVITT. Look, if you're still in civvies at inspection, we'll all shit off.

CAMPBELL *holds up a pair of trousers and a shirt.*

CAMPBELL. There's it now.

LEVITT. Ja. Browns, pairs one, wearing for the use of. In two sizes: too big and too small.

CAMPBELL. Hey, but true, ek sê.

LEVITT. How come they sent you to our regiment so late?

CAMPBELL. I been here and there.

LEVITT. You weren't R.T.U.-ed from the parabats or something?

CAMPBELL. Are you serious?

LEVITT. No, it's just that this other ou, Mowbray, he was.

CAMPBELL. Truly.

LEVITT. Where you been then?

CAMPBELL. That's another story again. Like I wasn't really into making choices, but come my call up I put in a no-show.

LEVITT. I wasn't stoked about doing my army either, but what can a ou do?

CAMPBELL. For sure.

LEVITT. They got us by the short and curlies.

CAMPBELL. Well, like the trick is: don't let yourself get taken within yourself. You know what I mean like?

LEVITT. Sort of.

CAMPBELL. Some Russian cat once said: To live is to burn. And me, I was into burning. I flashed on this idea: I'm going to see the country. I needed space, so I hit out.

CAMPBELL *puts the cigarette out on the floor. He starts changing into his army uniform.* LEVITT *picks up the cigarette end.*

It was a radical buzz. I had no bread, didn't graft, just lived off the land. Hey, I could really dig the beauty of the country. I tell you what, the energy out there is unreal. Some of the most amazing cats I met were black. Like I could really get into their philosophy of life. Hey, this one cat, Amos! We'd just bust a bottleneck together. The sun was like setting and we were taking hits, and then I got this full-on rush. This is Africa! Like we were so close and digging each other's company, the future could have started then. I found peace, ek sê.

By this time he has changed. He regards himself.

And now I'm doing my army. Will that pass inspection?

LEVITT. Search me. Kotze's a mad bastard and with him, you know, you never know.

CAMPBELL. Has like anything been said to you cats about going to the border?

LEVITT. Rumours. But you never know what to believe.

CAMPBELL. Hey, well.

LEVITT. If they post us up on border duty, ja, I don't know. Already I miss my cherry a stack. And you can't really, you know, expect them to be faithful, but still.

CAMPBELL. For sure.

LEVITT. Do you want to see a picture of her?

He immediately produces a photograph from his wallet.

That's Sharon.

CAMPBELL. Hey, then.

LEVITT. I really smaak her a stack. Sometimes I think it would drive me mad if she, you know.

CAMPBELL. Hey, ek sê, don't tune that.

LEVITT. Anyway.

CAMPBELL. Find the power within yourself.

LEVITT. Ja, vasbyt, I suppose.

CAMPBELL. You know then.

CAMPBELL *sits on his bed in the lotus position and closes his eyes.*

LEVITT. Not on the bed! I've just made the creases.

BADENHORST *and* MARAIS *enter.*

BADENHORST. Are the Jews and the communists getting together? Take a joke, Davy my maat.

He stops in front of CAMPBELL's *bed.*

Well I'll be buggered. What's his story?

LEVITT. I think he's meditating.

BADENHORST. Paul, come and look at this, man.

MARAIS. What's that?

LEVITT. Thinking to yourself.

BADENHORST. If he drops us in shit at inspection, I'll give him something to think about.

MARAIS. He seems like a good ou.

BADENHORST. How do you know?

MARAIS. We had a talk this morning.

BADENHORST. Well, if the Bombardier comes past and he's sitting there on his bed like a coolie, we'll all shit through the eye of a needle.

They all start laying out their kit in silence. BADENHORST *keeps looking in* CAMPBELL's *direction.*

This is now working on my nerves. Engelsman! The kaffirs are coming!

He starts bouncing CAMPBELL*'s bed.*

Stand up and fight for your country!

CAMPBELL. Don't give me that.

BADENHORST. Don't you want to fight for your country?

CAMPBELL. Go and swing in a tree.

BADENHORST. Are you a pacifist or a patriot?

MOWBRAY *enters.*

CAMPBELL. Get lost, apeman.

MOWBRAY. You talking to me?

BADENHORST. We got a troublemaker here.

MOWBRAY. You going to kill him dead?

MARAIS. Los him out, Hennie.

LEVITT. Get ready for inspection, man.

MOWBRAY. Don't give me a thousand words, Jewboy.

MARAIS. No, he's right.

All, except MOWBRAY *and* CAMPBELL, *apply themselves to their kit.*

MOWBRAY. I don't gotta stand no bladdy inspection.

BADENHORST. Do something to your bed, Mowbray, it looks like a used poeslap.

MOWBRAY. Don't tune me grief.

MARAIS. Ag, Trevor, just pull together, man.

MOWBRAY. Don't give me uphill.

BADENHORST. Jy sal jou gat sien.

MOWBRAY. Fuck you. It's a free country.

He crosses to CAMPBELL.

Howzit now, china?

CAMPBELL. Sweet. Yourself?

MOWBRAY. Crazy like a daisy. Could you see your way clear to borrowing me the lend of a smoke?

CAMPBELL. Safe.

CAMPBELL *hands* MOWBRAY *a packet of cigarettes. He takes one.*

MOWBRAY. Send it! Hennie, could I talk you into a coffin nail?

He throws the packet to BADENHORST.

BADENHORST. You could twist my arm.

BADENHORST takes a cigarette, crushes it in his hand and lets the remains fall to the floor.

CAMPBELL. That's really intelligent.

BADENHORST. Trevor, I can't interest you in a cigarette?

He throws the packet back to MOWBRAY, who puts a few more cigarettes between his lips. CAMPBELL moves towards MOWBRAY.

CAMPBELL. Hey china, we've all had a laugh now.

MOWBRAY. Is it?

MOWBRAY throws the cigarettes to BADENHORST. CAMPBELL lunges in that direction, but is not fast enough. The packet is thrown back and forth with CAMPBELL in pursuit.

Moet ek bid vir 'n weerligstraal?

CAMPBELL blocks the trajectory between BADENHORST and MOWBRAY. BADENHORST throws the cigarettes to MARAIS, who gives them to CAMPBELL.

CAMPBELL. Thank you.

MOWBRAY, with his back to the doorway, lights a match and holds it aloft.

MOWBRAY. Brand, bliksem, brand! Die enigste hoop in donker Afrika!

As he lights up, KOTZE appears in the doorway.

MARAIS. Aandag!

The men dash for their beds and come to attention. MOWBRAY conceals the cigarette in a cupped hand.

KOTZE. Septic.

He regards them in silence.

Staan stil! You at the end there with a face. You smoking?

MOWBRAY. No, Bombardier.

KOTZE. You calling me a liar?

MOWBRAY. No, Bombardier.

KOTZE. Hold out your hand. The other one, bokdrol! Now make a fist. And open it.

MOWBRAY *follows these instructions. The crushed and extinguished cigarette falls to the floor.* KOTZE *paces down the walkway leaving a trail of muddy footprints behind him.*

For crying out loud, just look at that floor. You think you can take chances with me. But you wrong. I was in uniform when you was in liquid form.

KOTZE *puts on a white glove and begins the inspection. First* MARAIS*'s kit, which seems spotless. He runs a finger under the bed frame. He shows* MARAIS *the dirt on his glove. He moves to* BADENHORST*'s bed and retrieves the remains of* CAMPBELL*'s crushed cigarette from the floor.*

This is not a kafferhok, Badenhorst. What would your mother say to this?

BADENHORST. I don't know, Bombardier.

KOTZE. Well I do, poephol. Nothing! She would just weep from pity.

KOTZE *looks long and hard at* MOWBRAY*'s bed. He turns away. As he does so, he swings around and knocks* MOWBRAY *sprawling. He stands in front of* CAMPBELL *making eye-to-eye contact.*

Did you see me hit this man, Badenhorst?

BADENHORST. No, Bombardier.

KOTZE. What happened, Badenhorst?

BADENHORST. He fell over, Bombardier.

KOTZE. On your feet, vuilgat.

MOWBRAY *gets to his feet.* KOTZE *moves to* LEVITT*'s kit.*

For crying in a bucket. You try hard, Levitt, I'll give you that. But most of all you try your luck. You call this clean? Where's the love, man? What happened to your manly pride?

He scatters LEVITT*'s kit about, then goes on to* CAMPBELL*. He takes some cotton wool from his pocket and rubs it against* CAMPBELL*'s cheek, leaving wisps clinging to his face.*

Trying to grow a beard, Kammel?

CAMPBELL. No, Bombardier.

KOTZE. Then what's this? Kammel, there's a war on the go. People is laying down their life for your freedom and you don't take the effort to shave. You letting down the whole side. Don't you care, man?

CAMPBELL. Not really, Bombardier.

KOTZE. What you say? You want these cunts to shit blood? Vat julle gewere!

The others take their R1 rifles, hold them horizontally with outstretched arms and start turning.

You lower than shark shit, Kammel. So don't try and put yourself on my level.

CAMPBELL. I won't, Bombardier.

KOTZE. You think you different. But it's us against them, Kammel, and you on our side if you like it or not.

CAMPBELL. That's not what I believe, Bombardier.

KOTZE takes a fold of loose skin on CAMPBELL's hand between his thumb and forefinger and starts twisting.

KOTZE. What colour is this, Kammel?

CAMPBELL falls to his knees.

What colour, you cunt? What colour?

CAMPBELL. Aaargh, white. White!

KOTZE. And don't you forget it.

CAMPBELL (*very softly*). Fuck you.

KOTZE. What you say?

CAMPBELL. Nothing.

KOTZE brings his face close to CAMPBELL's. He taps his chin with his index finger.

KOTZE. You want to try me, Kammel? Here, you want to hit me?

Pause.

I tell you something, Kammel. I fuck your mother. Her cunt's so big I have to push my fist in. But that's still not enough, so I push my head in. And what do I see? Roy Rogers! Hey Roy, I say, what you doing here? No man, he says, I'm just looking for my horse. But if you think I'm talking about a big cunt, you better find a mirror and take a look at yourself.

To the others.

Put down those rifles. I told you a troublemaker would only make trouble for you. All weekend passes is cancelled. You know who to thank for that? You know who?

ALL. Campbell.

KOTZE. Who?

ALL. Kammel!

KOTZE. Who?

ALL. Kammel!!!

> KOTZE *marches off briskly. As* CAMPBELL *makes a move to get up, the others put down their rifles and start moving towards him.*

BADENHORST. Get the bugger.

MOWBRAY. He'll pay for this.

> MOWBRAY, MARAIS *and* BADENHORST *grab* CAMPBELL. *He struggles, but is powerless against these odds. They strip off his trousers and spreadeagle him across a steel trunk in the middle of the walkway.*

BADENHORST. Levitt, give us some polish.

> LEVITT *remains seated.* BADENHORST *goes to his bed and gets a tin of shoepolish and a rag.*

CAMPBELL. Bloody fascists!

> BADENHORST *stands over* CAMPBELL*'s face.*

BADENHORST. Shut up or I fart in your face.

> BADENHORST *smears polish on* CAMPBELL*'s balls. When the job is done, they release him and stand back.* CAMPBELL *stands and pulls up his trousers.*
>
> *Blackout.*

Scene Four

The same. CAMPBELL *is on his bed in the lotus position. There is a timid knock at the door. The* BLACK ACTOR, *wearing overalls, stands in the doorway. He knocks a second time before* CAMPBELL *notices him.*

BLACK ACTOR. Baas?

CAMPBELL. Yes?

BLACK ACTOR. Sorry, Baas.

CAMPBELL. What?

BLACK ACTOR. I'm bring that drinks, Baas.

> *He produces a bottle wrapped in brown paper.*

CAMPBELL. For me?

BLACK ACTOR. No, Baas. I must bring it for the other baas.

CAMPBELL. Hey well.

BLACK ACTOR. Where he is, the other baas?

CAMPBELL *shrugs*.

What I must do?

CAMPBELL. Wait for him.

CAMPBELL *crosses to the* BLACK ACTOR.

Sit down and wait.

BLACK ACTOR. I'm better to stand.

CAMPBELL. What's the big deal? Sit down, man.

The BLACK ACTOR *sits reluctantly*.

Want a smoke?

The BLACK ACTOR *gets up again and crosses to* CAMPBELL.

BLACK ACTOR. Thank you very much, Baas.

CAMPBELL. Hey man, I'm not a baas. My name's Doug.

BLACK ACTOR. Yes, Baas Doug.

CAMPBELL *offers him a light, but the* BLACK ACTOR *has already put the cigarette in his pocket*.

CAMPBELL. Do you work for the army?

BLACK ACTOR. Yes. I'm work some garden jobs. Yes.

CAMPBELL. Do you like the army?

BLACK ACTOR. Yes.

CAMPBELL. You're joking.

BLACK ACTOR. Yes.

CAMPBELL. The army's up to shit.

BLACK ACTOR. Yes.

BADENHORST *and* MOWBRAY *enter*. MOWBRAY *carries a family-size Coke*.

MOWBRAY. Hey houtkop, what you fucken doing inside? This is not a bladdy kafferhok this.

BLACK ACTOR. I'm bring that drinks, Baas.

MOWBRAY *takes the* BLACK ACTOR*'s hat off and throws it on the floor*. CAMPBELL *retrieves it*.

BADENHORST. Come here, John. Why you take so bloody long,

you lazy bastard?

BLACK ACTOR. I'm run there and back, Baas.

BADENHORST. I know you people.

BLACK ACTOR. I'm wait there long, long time by the Off Sales.

BADENHORST. You mean you were having a bheba in the bushes with one of your kaffir girls.

BLACK ACTOR. No, Baas. The baas, he was close the Off Sales for one hour. He is telling me to wait.

BADENHORST. You people always got a excuse. Come on, give here. Where's the change? Hurry up, chop, chop. What's this? Why's this short? Twenty rands take away fifteen rands sixty nine is . . . .

BLACK ACTOR. Four rands thirty one.

BADENHORST. You give me back three eighty one.

BLACK ACTOR. The baas by the shop, he's give me that.

BADENHORST. You people can't be trusted.

BLACK ACTOR. No, Baas, I'm telling you. He's give me that.

BADENHORST. And here, from the goodness of my heart, I was thinking of giving you a tip.

BLACK ACTOR. Baas Bitzer, he's give me short.

BADENHORST. I tell you what. Go back and ask him that money. That's your tip.

BLACK ACTOR. He's never give me.

BADENHORST. That's your problem.

BLACK ACTOR. He's say I'm lie.

BADENHORST. That's your indaba.

BLACK ACTOR. My children, they hungry.

BADENHORST. I've heard that sob story before.

BLACK ACTOR. My wife, she is sick.

BADENHORST. Look, just don't come here crying to me.

BLACK ACTOR. How I must buy food?

BADENHORST. Sis, man, you smell. When did you wash? You mustn't come here smelling like that. Go wash. Come back and ask nicely. Then you see this fifty cent? You can have it.

CAMPBELL *grabs the coin from* BADENHORST *and gives it to the* BLACK ACTOR.

CAMPBELL. Here friend, it's yours.

BADENHORST. Fucking hell! Give here, John.

CAMPBELL. Don't listen to him. It's yours.

BADENHORST. Give here or I'll kick your bloody arse.

BLACK ACTOR. What I must do?

BADENHORST *moves towards the* BLACK ACTOR. CAMPBELL *steps between them.*

BADENHORST. You cheeky bastard.

CAMPBELL. Go! Get out of here.

BADENHORST. I'm warning you, John. For the last time.

BADENHORST *holds out his hand. The* BLACK ACTOR *is about to hand over the money.*

CAMPBELL. Don't be stupid!

CAMPBELL *pushes him out of the door.*

Take it! Get the hell out of here.

BADENHORST. What you trying to prove?

CAMPBELL. What's it to you?

MOWBRAY. He's a kaffir-lover.

MOWBRAY *sets up the drinks in enamel mugs on a steel trunk.*

BADENHORST. He doesn't know what you talking about, Trevor.

MOWBRAY. Is it?

BADENHORST. No, when he's around you must say 'black person'.

MOWBRAY. Well, I could of sworn it was a kaffir.

MARAIS *and* LEVITT *enter.*

BADENHORST. Hey, you ous, come and steek 'n dop.

MOWBRAY. Cane for the pain!

MARAIS. I'm sorry, Doug. I just went blank.

CAMPBELL. Leave it.

BADENHORST. Bring your arse to anchor, Paul.

BADENHORST *and* MOWBRAY *have embarked on some serious*

drinking. LEVITT *and* MARAIS *join them.*

MOWBRAY. Hey, black-person lover, you want to drink with the main manne?

CAMPBELL *doesn't respond.*

What's his case?

BADENHORST. He's having his period.

MARAIS. Los him out, Hennie.

BADENHORST. That reminds me. And I'm not pulling your leg, hey Kammel. There was this ou; wife, kids, steady job, the lot. Anyway he wakes up one morning, looks under the sheets and what does he see?

MARAIS. What?

BADENHORST. His balls has turned brown. No, joking apart and present company accepted, hey Kammel. You can imagine, he gets a moerava fright. So he phones this doctor and goes around to see him quick sticks. Well he's in there, rods round his ankles, and the doc's checking out his balls.

MOWBRAY. Fucken homo.

BADENHORST. No serious. But the doctor's stumped. He doesn't know where it comes from. So he says, no listen, I can't put my finger on it right now, but here's some pills what might help. So this ou drinks some pills and nothing happens. Days go by. He drinks all the pills, but still his balls stay brown. Now he's really down in the dumps and he's getting helluva frustrated. Anyway he goes home one day and there he slips over some toys on the lounge floor and that finally strips his moer. So he starts shouting the wife out. I'm out working my fingers to the bone to make our living and you let the place here go to rack and ruin, toys laying around, the works. But the wife's also been having a hard time, so she starts howling and says, Ja you do fuck all in the home and I've got to look after the kids and they been sick, and the pipe in the bathroom's burst, and the sink's blocked. I don't even have time to wipe my arse. I know, says the ou, that's another thing I want to talk to you about.

All, except CAMPBELL, *have a good laugh.*

CAMPBELL. You trying to say something?

MOWBRAY. Go gentry like a Bentley.

CAMPBELL. I wasn't talking to you. I was talking to the plank with the sense of humour.

BADENHORST. Go fuck spiders, party-pooper.

CAMPBELL. You shouldn't drink if you can't handle it.

CAMPBELL *picks up the bottle of cane, takes a mouthful which he doesn't swallow, then pours the rest over the steel trunk.*

MOWBRAY. Kill him!

BADENHORST. Now you going to come short.

BADENHORST *moves towards* CAMPBELL.

LEVITT. Break it up, you ous.

MOWBRAY. Dip his lights, Hennie.

BADENHORST *delivers a roundhouse punch, which* CAMPBELL *ducks.* CAMPBELL *spits the cane in* BADENHORST*'s eyes. As his hands go to his face,* CAMPBELL *kicks* BADENHORST *in the balls.* BADENHORST *doubles up holding his balls and* CAMPBELL *knocks him to the ground.*

CAMPBELL. Okay. Okay.

BADENHORST *gets up slowly.*

MARAIS. Enough is enough.

LEVITT. Make friends now.

CAMPBELL. I don't want to fight.

BADENHORST. Now you going to suffer, little man.

CAMPBELL. Hey, let's leave it.

BADENHORST. You going to die.

MOWBRAY *throws a webbing belt to* BADENHORST.

MOWBRAY. Here, Hennie.

BADENHORST *lashes out at* CAMPBELL *with the belt.* MARAIS *jumps in and takes the belt away from him.*

MARAIS. No, that's not right.

BADENHORST. Then I take him apart with my bare hands.

LEVITT. What you trying to prove, Hennie?

BADENHORST. Just who's a man around here.

He lunges towards CAMPBELL, *who sidesteps and trips him. He lands on the floor and* CAMPBELL *kicks him in the stomach.* MARAIS *goes to* BADENHORST.

MARAIS. You all right, Hennie?

BADENHORST. No, I'm all right. I just tripped. It's the drink, man.

LEVITT. Call it quits now.

MOWBRAY. You ous fought like men. It was just like in the Bats. But now you must be friends, hey. Shake on it.

CAMPBELL and BADENHORST shake hands. They squeeze hard and only let go when MOWBRAY has finished talking.

I say one thing about the army. Just one thing. You the best fucken mates to have. Swear to God. We go through the shit together. Through thick and thin shit. And that makes us chinas for life.

BADENHORST. Okay Doug, you heard the man.

CAMPBELL. Safe.

CAMPBELL looks at his hand.

BADENHORST. What's that?

CAMPBELL. Blood.

They look at each other and start laughing.

Blackout.

Scene Five

A parade ground. Sunlight. The laughter of the previous scene is topped by the voice of the BLACK ACTOR singing a freedom song. He enters carrying a sack filled with sawdust. His singing is drowned by the sound of approaching soldiers. He takes up a position near the audience and ad libs a humorous commentary on what follows.

KOTZE (*off*). Hik-hak, hik-hak, hik-hak, yuugh; hik-hak, hik-hak, hik-hak, yuugh; hik-hak, hik-hak, hik-hak, yuugh.

The soldiers march towards the audience at an insane pace.

Markeer die pas! Hik-hak, hik-hak, hik-hak, yuugh! Levitt!! In Hitler's day we would have made soap out of you! Hik-hak, hik-hak, hik-hak, yuugh; hik-hak, hik-hak, hik-hak, yuugh; hik-hak, hik-hak, hik-hak, yuugh. Halt! Dat klink soos boontjies in 'n pispot. Julle wil nie saamwerk nie. Julle sê fok jou Bombardier. Goed, ons gaan aan. Markeer die pas! Hik-hak, hik-hak, hik-hak, yuugh. Tel daardie vuile pote op! Parallel to the ground! Hik-hak, hik-hak, hik-hak, yuugh.

He makes them mark time for a long while. The theatre is filled with the sound of boots pounding on the floor.

Halt! Mowbray!! If you ever out of time again, I'll put your cock in your arse and carry you down to the station like a suitcase. Regs om! Count the fucking time. Links om!

ALL. Een, twee-drie, een!

KOTZE. Omkeer!

ALL. Een, twee-drie, een.

    KOTZE marches them upstage and gives them rifle drill.

KOTZE. Kammel, you cunt, I'll climb down your throat and shit on your heart. Op die plek rus! Kammel, kom hier!

    CAMPBELL *falls out of the platoon and halts in front of* KOTZE.

You see that tree over there? Go fetch me a leaf. Is jy al terug?

    CAMPBELL *runs off. The* BLACK ACTOR *is laughing and doing a send-up of* KOTZE.

Kaffer! Wat soek jy?

BLACK ACTOR. Oh shit. Baas? Ekskies Baas?

KOTZE. Kom hier, dom donder.

    The BLACK ACTOR *comes to attention in front of* KOTZE *and salutes him.*

BLACK ACTOR. Ja Baas?

KOTZE. Jy moenie kak droog maak nie, kaffer.

BLACK ACTOR. Nee Baas. Maar die Grootbaas het gesê dat ek daardie dinges in die andere dinges in moes hang.

KOTZE. Watter Grootbaas?

BLACK ACTOR. Ek weet nie sy naam nie. Hulle lyk almal dieselfde.

KOTZE. Kakstorie, kaffer.

    CAMPBELL *runs on, halts in front of* KOTZE *and presents him with a leaf.*

You trying to play stupid with me, Kammel? What's this, hey?

CAMPBELL. It's a leaf, Bombardier.

KOTZE. Sê vir my kaffer, hierdie is seker nie die regte blaar nie.

BLACK ACTOR. Nee, my Baas.

KOTZE. You heard what the kaffir said, Kammel. It's the wrong leaf. Voetsek, kaffer!

The BLACK ACTOR *gives* KOTZE *the Fascist salute. As he turns,* KOTZE *kicks him in the backside.*

BLACK ACTOR (*smiling*). Dankie Baas. Umsunu kanyoko!

KOTZE *tries to kick him again, but the* BLACK ACTOR *is too nimble and makes off, cheerfully insulting* KOTZE *in Zulu.*

KOTZE. Don't just stand there with your thumb in your bum and your mind in neutral, Kammel. Fetch me the other leaf.

They stare at each other.

Don't think it, Kammel. Just go fetch me that leaf.

CAMPBELL *starts running off.*

Kammel, kom hier!

CAMPBELL *returns and halts in front of* KOTZE.

(*Quietly*) Fall in, Kammel.

CAMPBELL *joins the platoon.*

Bors uit, pens in, poephol opgeknoop! You cunts think the army's a big fucking joke and you laugh on the other side of your face. I tell you there's a war going on and you think it's not your problem. But if they send you lot to the border, you be a sitting duck for that terrorists. They may be stupid kaffirs, but they been trained in Russia. Any questions? Right, park your arses in the dirt.

They sit at KOTZE's *feet in such a way that he can play this directly to the audience.*

I find cunts like Mowbray and Levitt shaming the white race on guard duty. As of from now on I'm putting my foot down with a firm hand. Why do you think we stand guard? Anyone?

MARAIS *raises his hand.*

Badenhorst?

BADENHORST. To be vigilant and alert at all times and to defend . . .

KOTZE. Don't talk shit to a white man. Do you want your sister to marry a Russian?

BADENHORST. No, Bombardier.

KOTZE. Then read your newspapers! That terrorists is going to Russia for training and then coming back here to stir shit. There is two kinds of terrorists. Namely, dead terrorists and live terrorists. The second two of these kinds is the problem. They just want to kill and destroy. And the rest of the world is two-face. It just turn its back on South Africa. So we on our own. And remember, if that enemy get past you, he's going to rape your mother and your sister and burn your house. Any questions?

CAMPBELL. Do you really believe that, Bombardier?

KOTZE. Dear Jesus, why do you send me cunts like this? Kammel, kom hier!

CAMPBELL *gets up and goes to* KOTZE.

You just volunteered to show us how to stand guard. That's your beat. Get your arse in gear.

CAMPBELL *starts walking.* KOTZE *starts laughing.*

Ag, nee wat, Kammel, you the biggest bloody joke since one-man-one-vote. What's he forgotten, Levitt?

LEVITT. To fix his bayonet, Bombardier.

KOTZE. Pull up your sock, Kammel. Fix that bayonet and hold that rifle like a man. It's your wife.

CAMPBELL *follows these instructions, but his manner remains defiant.*

You don't believe in it, Kammel. All South Africa place its trust in you and you going to let the side down. Badenhorst, go fetch me some grass and mud.

BADENHORST *runs off.*

Now for the love of Mike, Kammel, just look and learn.

KOTZE *takes* CAMPBELL*'s rifle and demonstrates.*

Be alert, because your enemy is. Hold your rifle at the ready. Balance your weight good, toes and heels. Go through your knees a bit, ready for everything.

He suits his actions to his words.

Always keep your back covered. Never stand still. Don't make yourself a easy target.

BADENHORST *returns with a handful of mud, branches and tufts of grass. As he approaches,* KOTZE *spins around and points the rifle at him.*

Halt! Name, rank and number? Halt!

KOTZE *cocks the rifle.*

BADENHORST. Badenhorst, gunner, 65403743.

KOTZE. If that had been for real, half of you would be hanging up a tree. Kammel, vat jou geweer.

He throws the rifle back to CAMPBELL.

Give me this mud. Stuff that branches under his staaldak.

While BADENHORST *does this,* KOTZE *blackens* CAMPBELL*'s hands and face with mud.*

Now you don't look like a girl-guide, try and act like a soldier.

CAMPBELL *makes little attempt to follow these instructions.*

Septic! On your feet, you lot. Kammel wants you to run round the shithouse. Is julle al terug?

The others mutter curses as they run off. KOTZE *manhandles* CAMPBELL *during the following speech.*

You got to hate, Kammel. No other way to survive. Let's see some hate, man. Go on, you cunt, eat your liver. Hate, you bangbroek, hate! I shit on your grandmother's grave. I fuck your mother in her mouth. I hold down your sister and rape her up the bum. Hate me, you bastard. Hate me! Let me see your hate. Give me your hate, Kammel, and when the time comes I'll know where to point it. Come on. Come! Hate me. Come. Hate me! Come with your hate. Hate me, you cunt!!!

The others enter.

Form up, you cunts. Fix bayonets!

They do so. KOTZE *stands downstage near the sack.*

If I get one good bayonet charge, you can go to supper. But let one man give me short and I'll drive you till you drop. Right! The Jew first. And I want to hear you scream. This is SWAPO, Levitt. Kill him!

LEVITT *charges, screams, stabs the sack, but loses his balance and falls.*

You'd be a dead man, Levitt. Roer jou gat! Marais, this is MPLA. Kill him!

MARAIS *charges, screams and stabs the sack.*

Mowbray, this is PAC. Kill the bastard!

MOWBRAY *does the same.*

Badenhorst, this is ANC. Kill!

BADENHORST *does the same.*

Right Kammel. See this cunt here? Don't be scared of it. It

won't bite you. So have some fun. Stick it right in. Wriggle it around and give it a good twist. Then tear the fucker wide open and make it bleed. Let's see some of your hate, Kammel. This is me, Kammel.

CAMPBELL *lurches forward, utters a blood-curdling scream, stabs, twists and disembowels the sack.*

Good, Campbell. Good.,

CAMPBELL *and* KOTZE *stare at each other from either side of the bag.*

Slow fade to blackout.

Scene Six

The bungalow. Late evening. MARAIS, *wearing shorts and a rugby jersey, is alone reading his Bible. After a while* CAMPBELL *enters carrying a weekend bag.*

MARAIS. Hello, Doug.

CAMPBELL. What a luck! A straight-through ride from Durban.

MARAIS. You have a good time?

CAMPBELL. You know then.

MARAIS. I never saw the sea.

CAMPBELL. Hey well, it's something else.

MARAIS. So you back. I thought you might go AWOL.

CAMPBELL. I'm back.

MARAIS. Tell me, why did you run away?

CAMPBELL. Why do you ask?

MARAIS. Sometimes I just don't know.

CAMPBELL. What?

MARAIS. The army.

CAMPBELL. For sure.

MARAIS. Of course, it does make you a man and that, but why this war?

CAMPBELL. Truly.

Pause.

MARAIS. Are you a religious man, Doug?

CAMPBELL. Well, like within myself I suppose I am. I'm an agnostic.

MARAIS. Practising?

CAMPBELL. Not really.

MARAIS. I believe in the Bible and I been thinking. Here Jesus says: 'Maar ek sê vir julle: julle moet julle vyande liefhê; seën die wat julle vervloek, doen goed aan die wat julle haat en bid vir die wat julle beledig en julle vervolg, sodat julle kinders kan word van julle Vader wat in die hemele is.' How can you love your enemy and then kill him?

CAMPBELL. Right.

MARAIS. It doesn't fit.

CAMPBELL. For sure.

MARAIS. Why is everybody against South Africa?

CAMPBELL. Hey man, are you serious?

MARAIS (*sharply*). Don't laugh at me, Doug.

CAMPBELL. Hey well, I tune you the way I view it: if there was no apartheid, there'd be no war.

MARAIS. In my own life I've never been unkind to the black man.

CAMPBELL. Not you, Paul. Like it's the whole thing.

MARAIS. But there's less apartheid now and there's more war.

CAMPBELL. That's not it.

MARAIS. South Africa is changing. One day the black man will be as equal as the white man.

CAMPBELL. Hey, I've heard that somewhere before.

MARAIS. I'm against apartheid.

CAMPBELL. But you don't mind going up to the border?

MARAIS. You have to defend your country.

CAMPBELL. Is that what you think?

MARAIS. Don't you love South Africa?

CAMPBELL. I don't hate Angola.

MARAIS. That's where the terrorists come from.

CAMPBELL. Hey, Paul, think man. What are we doing in Namibia and Angola? We're fighting a colonial war.

MARAIS. But the SWAPO is fighting us.

CAMPBELL. Didn't you say you have to defend your country? Maybe they think like you.

MARAIS. I just don't know.

CAMPBELL. I scheme it's simple.

MARAIS. That's easy for you to say.

CAMPBELL. Hey, where are you coming from?

MARAIS. That's what you told Kotze with your first inspection.

CAMPBELL. What?

MARAIS. That you don't care.

CAMPBELL. What do you know about that? You just do everything you're told and then you come and ask me stupid questions. Like maybe I care about something else than killing people.

MARAIS. I'm not accusing you.

CAMPBELL. Then what's your scene?

MARAIS. I was just asking.

CAMPBELL. Right on! Why don't you Boere ever think? I've got my beliefs, ek sê. And I've been made to suffer for that. First by the MPs who caught me. They were raw bastards, but it was nothing compared to Pretoria. I gave it to them straight. Like I told them what I schemed on. I said I was totally opposed to the whole concept of Angola, so they sent me to One Mil Hospital. And me, I thought I was crafty. I had a rap with this psychiatrist and I tuned him this and that and blocked for Africa. Like if you had to pretend you were fucked in the head to be exempted from killing people, I could get into that.

Pause.

Hey, but it wasn't like that. The army schemed we were bent and we'd been sent there to be straightened out. They'd been feeding me on medication, these full-on downers, like to break my resistance. One day I was lying spaced out on my bed and this ouk came in. He walked in and he was crying. So I said to him, Hey what's the matter? Ek sê Paul, he had three cases of shock treatment for refusing to go to Angola and he was expecting his fourth.

MARAIS. Where did they shock him?

CAMPBELL. In the brain.

MARAIS. Did he tell you?

CAMPBELL. I couldn't really kind of communicate with him. He just put his hands to his head and said three times.

MARAIS. Did they do that to you?

CAMPBELL. Naught. When I sussed what was going on, hey like I just tuned what they wanted to hear. No one can handle those shocks.

MARAIS. Why would people do that?

CAMPBELL *shrugs. A pause.*

CAMPBELL. Hey, Paul, I'm sorry about what I said.

MARAIS. Wasn't it true?

CAMPBELL. About the Boere.

MARAIS. No, that's all right.

CAMPBELL. For sure.

MARAIS. I like you, Doug. I didn't meet so many English people before.

CAMPBELL. Hey then.

MARAIS. I just thought I'd say so.

BADENHORST *and* MOWBRAY *enter. To the tune of 'She'll be coming round the mountain' they sing:*

BADENHORST AND MOWBRAY. She'll be all wet and sticky when she comes, when she comes, etc. . . .

BADENHORST *holds his middle finger under* MARAIS*'s nose.*

BADENHORST. Smell the good times!

CAMPBELL. Howzit?

MOWBRAY. Grand like a piano.

BADENHORST. She just sucked in my balls and spat out the pips.

MOWBRAY. We only had a good time.

MARAIS. Doug here went to Durban and back.

CAMPBELL. From door to door with this cat in a Porsche.

BADENHORST. Did I ever tell you about the time I got a lift with this goose in a E-type? There was about ten ous standing at the bypass there and she just pulled up by me and said hop in. And she was a sharp bokkie, I'm telling you; fucking blonde hair with this short skirt and shit-hot legs. And you know how you sit really low in a E-type and the pedals are far away? So when she pushes in the clutch hey, and she has to stretch far forward, this bloody skirt slides up and man . . .

ALL. She's got no fucking panties on!

They all laugh at BADENHORST.

BADENHORST. I'm never going to tell you ous nothing from now on.

CAMPBELL. Hey, is that a promise?

BADENHORST. Just los me out. You ous know fuck all about women.

LEVITT *enters carrying parcels.*

LEVITT. Hi there ous.

CAMPBELL. Is it all fixed up with Sharon?

LEVITT. Yes and no. Sometimes I just don't understand women.

MARAIS. Then you better ask old Badenhorst. He's the expert around here.

BADENHORST. Go fuck your hand.

LEVITT. There you are, Paul.

BADENHORST. What's he getting?

MARAIS. But it's mooi, hey.

CAMPBELL. Hey then, the Star of David.

MARAIS. It's a sort of Jewish Saint Christopher.

BADENHORST. What the Jews will think of next.

MARAIS. No man, it brings good luck.

MOWBRAY. It didn't bring the Yids much luck.

BADENHORST. Is he the only one who gets something?

LEVITT. For you, Hennie.

LEVITT *gives* BADENHORST *a copy of* Playboy.

BADENHORST. Jislaaik hey Davy, thanks a span.

MOWBRAY. Don't get bladdy caught with that hey.

BADENHORST. Where you come by this, Davy?

LEVITT. I got my connections.

BADENHORST. Paul, look here man. Kom kyk vir hierdie slymsloot.

MARAIS. Suck eggs.

LEVITT. And here's a cake for all of us to share. The old lady forced me to take it with.

CAMPBELL. Hey, lekker!

LEVITT *places a wonderful cake on a trunk which they slide into the walkway to serve as a table.*

LEVITT. Give us your knife there, Paul. You too, Trevor.

MOWBRAY. No, well thanks ja, okay.

MARAIS. You cut, Davy.

BADENHORST. Man, I've got a family-size Fanta. Let's make it an occasion.

CAMPBELL. Truly, like a min dae feast.

BADENHORST. Baie dae, min hare.

They talk with their mouths full.

MARAIS. Your Ma bakes nicely.

CAMPBELL. For sure.

BADENHORST. It's bloody lekker, man.

LEVITT. She's a Jewish Mama.

BADENHORST. Well, you can say what you like about the Jews, but they know how to bake cakes.

During the above CAMPBELL *has started tapping on the trunk with his fingers. The rhythm is that of a train's wheels on the track. They all join in the game.*

CAMPBELL. Hey listen!

MARAIS. What's that?

CAMPBELL. Can you hear it?

MARAIS. Luister na die spore.

They put their ears to the trunk.

BADENHORST. It's coming this way.

LEVITT. What is it?

CAMPBELL. Louis, the min dae train!

LEVITT. Taking us home!

MOWBRAY. Send it!

They all laugh and start pounding out the rhythm. KOTZE has been standing in the doorway. He is in civilian clothing and wears a ten-gallon hat. He has beeen drinking and has a beer in his hand. MARAIS sees him.

MARAIS. Aandag!

The men spring to attention around the cake.

KOTZE. I hope I'm not disturbing. This all looks very cosy. But don't let me disturb you. Carry on.

He advances into the room.

Anyone got a smoke to spare?

A few packets of cigarettes appear. He makes for CAMPBELL.

Thank you, Campbell. Offer them round. Let's have a smoke break.

CAMPBELL holds up a match to KOTZE's cigarette. He takes CAMPBELL by the wrist.

You quite hardegat, Campbell. But you shaping up nicely. You starting to understand team spirit.

CAMPBELL pulls his hand away. KOTZE sits down on MARAIS's bed. He takes a drag. Puts the cigarette in his ear and blows smoke out through his nose. Not much of a laugh. A silence.

I been in the fucking army fifteen fucking years. The best fucking years of my fucking life. Gone. Finish and klaar. Gone. Gone.

Pause.

Gone. What you got to say about that?

A long pause.

BADENHORST. Ja, nee, that's life hey.

KOTZE. You know something about life, Badenhorst?

BADENHORST. Ag, you know.

KOTZE. We all listening.

BADENHORST. Just trying to look on the sunny side.

Pause.

And learning to take the rough with the smooth.

KOTZE. Where you get that from? Life's as rough as a pig's back. I joined up after I got my JC. I done every bloody course the army's got to offer. I did the instructor's course, machine-gun course, anti-aircraft course, anti-tank course, signals course, maintenance course, field-gunnery course, mortar-bomb course . . .

CAMPBELL. Intercourse?

KOTZE (*deadpan*). The lot. But I didn't got a matric. And I was even in Angola when the government said we wasn't there. I could write a book about Angola. Fifteen years and I still only got two stripes. So just don't talk to me about life. What would you do in my place?

Pause.

Tell me.

MOWBRAY. Why do you stay in the army then, Bombardier?

KOTZE. If you thought like a soldier you wouldn't ask me that.

Pause.

You want to know why?

MOWBRAY. Ja, Bombardier.

KOTZE. Because I hate civilians.

KOTZE *gets up and starts prowling around.*

Who of you's got a woman?

BADENHORST. I'm a married man, Bombardier.

KOTZE. And how does that feel?

BADENHORST. Ja, well, you know.

KOTZE. Next time see if it smells different. Maybe you stirring the cold porridge.

He stops in front of the cake.

What's this cake?

LEVITT. You want a piece, Bombardier?

KOTZE. Your girl make this, Levitt?

He stamps on the cake.

What you bringing this woman rubbish in here? This is a army camp. Don't dirty this bungalow up with bitch cakes.

Pause.

You been on pass, but I got a small little secret for you. You all on standby. You know what that means. You going to the border.

Pause.

That's the good news. The bad news is I signed on for another fifteen years. I'll be going with. So if that terrorists don't get you, I will. And you better remember one thing. Don't ever start talking to me about women again.

KOTZE *turns at the doorway.*

You back in the army now.

KOTZE *leaves.*

Music: 'Die Onbekende Weermagman' by Bles Bridges as the lights go down.

Scene Seven

The gate. Steel trunks, kit bags and webbing. LEVITT *and* CAMPBELL *sit on trunks facing the audience. The music now comes from* LEVITT*'s radio.* CAMPBELL *turns it off.*

LEVITT. Sharon said she'd wait for me.

CAMPBELL. Well, there you go.

LEVITT. She won't.

CAMPBELL. Hey well.

LEVITT. I wish I had a broken leg, a dislocated hip, a hunchback, one eye . . .

CAMPBELL. Hey, man!

LEVITT. No, anything to get out of it.

CAMPBELL. Whew, heavy.

MOWBRAY *enters, carrying his rifle and drinking from a family-size bottle of Coke.*

MOWBRAY. You talking about me?

LEVITT. Don't flatter yourself.

MOWBRAY. I can't offer because it's full of backwash.

CAMPBELL. Safe.

MOWBRAY. If they hadn't kicked me out of the Bats, I'd be a border veteran by now.

LEVITT. Or in a plastic bag.

MOWBRAY. Fuck you ous, you know.

> BADENHORST *and* MARAIS *enter, carrying a steel trunk between them.*

MARAIS. Where's the Bedford?

BADENHORST. Selle ou storie, hurry up and wait.

> *They sit on their kit in silence. The* BLACK ACTOR *crosses the stage.*

MOWBRAY. Hey Sambo, kom hier!

BLACK ACTOR. Did the baas want something?

MOWBRAY. What you fucken doing here hey?

BLACK ACTOR. The baas, he is say I must fetch that things for to put in the Bedford.

MOWBRAY. Don't talk shit to a white man.

BLACK ACTOR. It's as true as God. I'm telling you.

BADENHORST. Hey, what's your name? You John?

BLACK ACTOR. No Baas, my name it's Sam.

MOWBRAY. What baas sent you?

BLACK ACTOR. I don't know what is he called. The stupid one.

MOWBRAY. Jy raak wit.

CAMPBELL. Hey friend, don't I know you?

BLACK ACTOR. No Baas. You don't know me, Baas.

CAMPBELL. Didn't you bring the drinks?

BLACK ACTOR. Aikona! Never, my Baas. I'm not do that.

CAMPBELL. Hey then, but I know you, ek sê.

BLACK ACTOR. No, Baas. Maybe that man, he was my cousin.

MOWBRAY. Hey Sambo! You know what we gonna do?
We gonna shoot those baboon cousins of yours in Angola.

BLACK ACTOR. Baas?

MOWBRAY. You better be a good boy or you get the same. See?

CAMPBELL. Cut it out, Trevor.

MOWBRAY. Before he fucks off i want to see a kaffir dance.

BADENHORST. Ag Trev, the ou's got work to do.

> MOWBRAY *points his rifle at the* BLACK ACTOR.

MOWBRAY. Let's see you do a war dance.

MARAIS. Put down that rifle.

MOWBRAY. Fuck you. It's a free country.

LEVITT. What's the ou done to you?

MOWBRAY. I want to see what you people do before you fight.

BADENHORST. Listen Sam, don't worry over him, see. I give you this packet of smokes if you dance.

MOWBRAY. That's a offer you can't refuse.

BLACK ACTOR. I'm not smoke, Baas.

MOWBRAY. He's a clever kaffir.

BADENHORST. Here's fifty cents then.

He throws the coin at the BLACK ACTOR*'s feet.*

Do a gumboot dance.

MOWBRAY. Here's some more. Give the kaffir some start, you buggers. Don't be so bladdy Jewish.

The BLACK ACTOR *does a gumboot dance. The others also throw coins at his feet. The dance becomes increasingly defiant and explosive.*

Blackout. The BLACK ACTOR *continues dancing.*

The house lights come up. The soldiers have gone. He stops dancing. He leaves the stage.

ACT TWO

Scene One

An improvised canteen, somewhere on the border. Sounds of the African night provided throughout this scene by a buzz-track. The men wear floppy bush hats and have their rifles with them at all times. The disco version of 'The Lion Sleeps Tonight' (by Tight Fit) is heard over the loudspeakers. The music switches to a portable radio on the stage as the lights snap on to reveal BADENHORST dancing on a table. His trousers are in a pool around his ankles and his genitals are tucked between his legs to create the illusion of a vagina.

CAMPBELL AND MOWBRAY (*shouting*). Take it off! Take it off! Take it off! Take it off!

> BADENHORST *removes his bush hat, performs a lewd ritual with it and throws it to* MARAIS.

Show us some more! Show us some more!

> BADENHORST *twists around, bends over and exposes his backside and genitals.*

CAMPBELL. Hey then, she's an imposter.

MOWBRAY. Don't strangle your dangle.

> BADENHORST *takes his rifle in one hand and his genitals in the other.*

BADENHORST (*chanting*). This is my rifle. This is my gun. This is for shooting. This is for fun!

> LEVITT *enters during the above. He turns the radio off.*

LEVITT. The batteries.

> *An awkward silence.* BADENHORST *pulls up his trousers.*

MARAIS. Dave, come pull up a chair, man.

BADENHORST. Back to the States tomorrow, Davy.

CAMPBELL. Don't count on it.

> LEVITT *sits. He is withdrawn and edgy.*

BADENHORST. Okay, beach bum, pay up.

CAMPBELL. I had my fingers crossed.

BADENHORST. Twenty five rand.

CAMPBELL. You gyppoed.

BADENHORST. Twenty five rand!

CAMPBELL. I said to the end of the song.

BADENHORST. Ja, but he . . . (*indicating* LEVITT). No, listen, my man.

CAMPBELL. You blew it.

BADENHORST. You sailing for a nailing.

CAMPBELL. Like listen. If you do it again, but properly, you'll get your bread.

BADENHORST. I know you, Campbell. You full of shit. One day you'll come short.

CAMPBELL. Give us a kiss.

BADENHORST. Watch it!

MARAIS. Never mind, Hennie. I thought you was good in the dancing.

BADENHORST. Go jump at a lake.

Silence, boredom and restlessness.

Five months without a poke.

LEVITT. What?

BADENHORST. Must be my record, man.

MARAIS. Moenie worry nie. Alles sal regkom.

BADENHORST. Suid-Wes? Tuis Bes!

CAMPBELL. I don't scheme we're splitting tomorrow.

MOWBRAY. Maybe we get a chance to waste some kaffirs first.

MARAIS. Tomorrow we go home.

CAMPBELL. Roll on tomorrow.

MOWBRAY. If you don't want your beer, Levitt, I'll buy it off you.

LEVITT. What?

A silence. LEVITT*'s mood is making them uncomfortable.*

BADENHORST. You ous heard this one about Van der Merwe?

CAMPBELL. A hundred times.

BADENHORST. No man, Van der Merwe . . .

CAMPBELL. . . . is sitting in this bar in New York. Suddenly this black dude walks in, goes up to the barman and says, I'm a millionaire and I only fuck white women. Give me a whisky. He knocks back the whisky and splits. When he's gone the barman walks over to Van and says, What did you think about that? Surely you Boere don't approve of that sort of thing. No well, says Van der Merwe, I don't really blame the ouk. If I was a millionaire I'd also only fuck white women.

MOWBRAY. That's a bladdy sick joke.

BADENHORST. Someone explain it to Paul.

MOWBRAY. Hey Levitt, can I buy that beer off you?

LEVITT. No, I want it.

MOWBRAY. All of a sudden he wants it. Typical Jewboy!

MARAIS. Leave him. It's his beer.

A strained silence.

BADENHORST. Hey, you know what I'll do when I get home? First thing, I'll get the wife to run me a bath. Nice and full of hot water. I'll get in there with a six-pack of Carling Black Labels. And while she's in the kitchen making my favourite food, I'll sommer just lay there farting and biting the bubbles. Then on comes the graze. I'll sit down to roast mutton, potatoes, rice, carrots, peas and beans, sweet potatoes, pumpkin and all that covered with a lekker, dik gravy. And when I've finished eating, the wife will slip off to the bedroom. A soft bed, crispy white sheets and her just laying there in this thin nightie. Five months I've been waiting for this! Hell of a slowly she pulls off the nightie. She's laying there against the pillows. She opens her knees slightly and you hear this soft sucking sound as the lips pull apart.

He looks at the others, who have all been listening intently.

You find this interesting? You want to hear more? Sorry, but it's my wife we're talking about.

CAMPBELL. It's enough to put anyone off sex.

BADENHORST. I'll slap you down, my man.

MOWBRAY. She sounds like a good fuck.

BADENHORST (*sharply*). Watch it!

LEVITT. I wonder what it's like to die.

A gentle shockwave.

They say you never hear the one that kills you.

MARAIS. Who can ever tell us that?

LEVITT. It must burn.

BADENHORST. Change the subject.

LEVITT. I won't cross that river again.

MARAIS. That's so. Tomorrow we go back the other side of the line.

LEVITT. I don't care what they do, I won't cross that border again.

CAMPBELL. Cool it, Dave. If you're feeling stretched, go to the Sick Bay and ask for something.

LEVITT. You think I can't take it?

CAMPBELL. Hey no.

MARAIS. Think of it, Dave. Home sweet home.

LEVITT. I'm not going into Angola again.

MOWBRAY (*chicken imitation*). Pukaak, puk, puk, puk!

BADENHORST. Davy, look on the sunny side, man. Our rear echelon has never taken casualties.

LEVITT. If my petrol truck took a hit, it would burn.

CAMPBELL. Hey Dave, like we're all in the same boat.

LEVITT. Are we?

CAMPBELL. For sure.

LEVITT. And what do you feel about it then?

CAMPBELL. Hey well.

LEVITT. No, I'm asking you straight. You were the big rebel. You've got the black friends. You didn't believe in this war. Have you changed your mind?

CAMPBELL. Hey Dave, don't lay this heavy trip on me.

LEVITT. I just thought you had principles.

CAMPBELL. Within myself I've got principles, ek sê. But like here we've just got to survive.

LEVITT. And your principles?

CAMPBELL. Whew, heavy.

BADENHORST. That's just only because he's got the wrong principle. My principle is still the same. Those Russians come here to make trouble with the black. They want to take over South Africa. Then I say, Over my dead body.

CAMPBELL. Go and fuck yourself, Badenhorst.

LEVITT. Is this something you're prepared to die for, Doug?

CAMPBELL. No way.

LEVITT. Then how come you're here?

CAMPBELL. Hey then, what are the options?

LEVITT. You know them.

CAMPBELL. Like Dave, I tune you straight. We've like passed the stage of scheming why we're here. We are, ek sê. That's our reality. It's like a choice between life and death. And I'm scheming on getting out of here alive.

MARAIS (*shouting*). Relax man, you ous!

Silence.

We done our bit. Think of the future. When we stand up tomorrow, we go south. In Grootfontein there's a C–130 standing on the runway. And you know man, it's waiting to take us home.

BADENHORST *breaks the mood with a chuckle.*

BADENHORST. That reminds me. Davy, did you hear the one about this ou who went to a prossie?

The others groan. BADENHORST *steams ahead.*

Anyway he's been sitting in this bar all night getting lekker cut. So he phones up this prossie and says, No man, I'm here in this bar and I'm feeling randy as a dog, so I'm coming round for a fuck just now. Well, she can't say no, but she hears on the phone he's as pissed as a fart, so she plans to play a trick on him. She's got one of these lifesize rubber dolls what you blow up, so she just stuffs it in the bed. Now when this ou comes there, and he's really cut hey, she says, Listen, I'm sorry but it's my time of the month, I got the drips badly, so if you don't mind, why don't you just poke my sister? She's a really very sexy bokkie with a sharp personality and she's just laying in the bed waiting for you. Well, meat is meat and a man must eat, so he says, Dop, doos en doringdraad, and he's into that bedroom like a pig into shit. Two minutes later he comes running kaalgat out the room. What's the matter? asks the prossie. No man, says the ou, but you got a funny sister. I climbed on top of her, bit her on the tit, then she farted and flew out the window.

All except LEVITT *laugh at the joke.*

MOWBRAY. Don't you find it funny, Levitt?

LEVITT. What?

MOWBRAY. He's in a dwaal.

MARAIS. Los him, Trevor.

The restless boredom re-establishes itself. The silence is oppressive.
MOWBRAY drains a can of beer, holds it like a hand grenade, performs
an elaborate mime of withdrawing the pin and hurls it against the wall.

MOWBRAY. Aitsaa!

LEVITT *dives to the floor.*

BADENHORST. Fuck off, you!

MOWBRAY. He's gone to ground.

MARAIS. Shut up, you bloody fool.

CAMPBELL. Hey like Dave, it was nothing.

LEVITT *is sobbing hysterically.*

BADENHORST. Give the man air.

MOWBRAY. It's just a bladdy act, man.

BADENHORST (*to* MOWBRAY). Listen here, you go see if you can
find Kotze by the Duty Officer there. I'll go to the NCO mess.
And you ous, for fuck's sake, just stay with him hey.

BADENHORST *and* MOWBRAY *leave.*

MARAIS. Put your head in your knees and breathe deep.

LEVITT. I don't give a fuck. I don't give a fuck. I don't give a fuck.

CAMPBELL. Take it easy, Dave.

LEVITT. I don't give a fuck. I'm going to tell them.

CAMPBELL. Naught, Dave. Tune them nothing.

LEVITT. I won't die for those bastards.

CAMPBELL. Dave, don't say nothing about refusing.

LEVITT. I'll tell him the truth.

CAMPBELL. Hey, pal, you out of your mind, man.

LEVITT. You think I'm mad? You're fucking mad. This whole
fucking war's fucking mad.

CAMPBELL. Hey, like I know, Dave.

LEVITT. Then why don't you say so?

CAMPBELL. Hey Dave, think man! Kotze doesn't scheme like that. He'll drop you in the shit.

LEVITT. It's the truth.

CAMPBELL. Hey, the truth won't help you. If you tell them that they'll shock your brain.

LEVITT. They can do what they like.

CAMPBELL. Dave, like I've seen what they do to ous.

LEVITT. I'll do nothing for them.

CAMPBELL. Don't give them a reason.

LEVITT. Nothing!

CAMPBELL. Why won't you listen to me?

LEVITT. What have you got to say for yourself.

Pause.

You're taken. The big rebel! They've got you just where they want you.

CAMPBELL. Don't give me that shit.

MOWBRAY *enters.*

LEVITT. Where's Kotze? Where's the little Hitler? He can stick his war up his arse. I'm finished with it. So far and no further. What are we doing here? This isn't even our country.

Suddenly he starts singing, loudly, almost to the point of shouting. The tune is 'Oh My Darlin' Clementine'.

Fuck the army, fuck the army
Fuck the army through and through
I would rather be a civvy
Than an army cunt like you.

MARAIS. Dave, listen, stay here.

LEVITT. Leave me alone!

MARAIS *slaps* LEVITT*'s face.* LEVITT *makes a dash for the door.* MARAIS *runs after him, drags him back into the room and floors him with a punch.*

MARAIS. Why do you make me do this?

MOWBRAY *gets down next to* LEVITT *like a boxing referee and starts counting.*

MOWBRAY. One . . . Two . . . Three . . .

MARAIS. Shut up!

MOWBRAY. The ouk's busy going mad.

MARAIS jumps at MOWBRAY, *knocks him off balance so he falls to the ground and stands over him.*

MARAIS. Listen to me, Mowbray, and you better listen good. You knew what was with him and still you threw that can. You playing dirty. But that's the last time. When Kotze comes, you heard nothing and you saw nothing. Understand what I'm saying?

MOWBRAY. What do you take me for?

MARAIS. One word and I'll find you.

MOWBRAY. I wasn't gonna to say nothing.

BADENHORST enters. KOTZE follows him on. He doesn't wear rank on the border.

KOTZE. What seems to be the problem?

He crosses to LEVITT.

You not dying there, are you, Levitt?

MARAIS. He was besides himself, so I was forced to restrain him.

KOTZE. It's not just a gyppo?

MARAIS. I think it's shell shock.

KOTZE. Well, a qualified doctor will find out quick enough. Come on, my boy. We'll have you fighting fit in no time. Get the man to Sick Bay.

BADENHORST. Paul, give us a hand.

BADENHORST and MARAIS lift LEVITT.

KOTZE. Wag 'n bietjie. What made him go funny?

CAMPBELL. He threw a can against the wall.

MOWBRAY. I never did it on purpose.

KOTZE (*harshly*). You a cunt, Mowbray.

MOWBRAY. I never knew.

KOTZE. What are you?

MOWBRAY. Swear to God.

KOTZE. What are you?

MOWBRAY. A cunt.

KOTZE. Well, don't just stand there. Get that man out of here.

Move, you dumb cunts.

BADENHORST *and* MARAIS *go off with* LEVITT.

Well, war sorts out the weeds from the men. Mowbray, for fuck's sake, don't sulk. Get some beers, man. It's on me.

KOTZE *picks up playing cards from the table.*

Tell me, Campbell, you think Levitt's really bosbefok?

CAMPBELL. He's stretched.

MOWBRAY. It's cause his chick's going it with a other ou.

KOTZE. Ja nee. In Israel those Jewboys neuk up the Arab good and proper, but here they a dead loss.

KOTZE *sits and lights a cigarette.*

CAMPBELL. Are we splitting to the States tomorrow, Bombardier?

KOTZE (*impishly*). That's a military secret, jong. That's a military secret.

CAMPBELL. Like it's what we heard.

KOTZE. Don't believe all the rumours of war.

KOTZE *smiles, takes a drag, puts the cigarette in his ear and exhales through his nose. A laugh from* MOWBRAY. *With the cigarette still in his ear, he starts dealing cards for a poker game.*

You men a bit homesick, hey?

CAMPBELL. We need to slack out a bit.

KOTZE. What you bid?

CAMPBELL. Five.

They put in matches.

KOTZE. And you, Mowbray?

MOWBRAY. Ag, not really. Only this is a shit country, man. Just bush and bladdy kaffirs.

KOTZE. I wasn't asking that.

MOWBRAY. Well, that's just how I feel.

KOTZE. Are you playing?

MOWBRAY. No, ja okay, fine.

KOTZE. What are the stakes?

CAMPBELL. Life and death?

KOTZE (*an ugly laugh*). You sure you can meet that challenge, Campbell? No. I'll raise you five.

CAMPBELL. I'll see that and raise you fifty.

KOTZE. Fuck me.

MOWBRAY. He's chaffing.

KOTZE. You bluffing, Campbell?

CAMPBELL. Try me.

MOWBRAY. See him!

KOTZE. I can read you like a book, Campbell.

CAMPBELL. Hey well, I didn't think you'd find it that difficult.

KOTZE. What you trying to say?

CAMPBELL. One rand a match.

MOWBRAY. I fold.

CAMPBELL. Just you and me, Bombardier.

KOTZE. That day will come, Campbell.

> *Pause.*

> Cards isn't life. My business is men. And I tell you something for nothing: I always win.

> KOTZE *throws in his hand.*

CAMPBELL. Hey, Bombardier, like you know what's going on here and all that shit. With the war and that.

KOTZE. What's your problem?

CAMPBELL. Like it's something I heard and I was trying to scheme whether it was true.

KOTZE. Campbell, jong, you know I can't divulge military secrets.

CAMPBELL. Hey, for sure. But like this is different. It's about this bombardier in Rundu. They say he gave his men a hard time.

KOTZE. Who's this?

CAMPBELL. Like I forget the name, but they say that while they were out on an Op, he was shot down by his own men.

> *Pause.*

> Like I just wondered if that actually happened.

KOTZE (*deliberately*). We South Africans don't go in for that kind of thing, Campbell.

Silence. CAMPBELL *and* KOTZE *are watching each other.*

MOWBRAY. What's going on?

A series of deafening bangs. CAMPBELL *and* MOWBRAY *dive to the floor. They grab their rifles and scramble to the dug-out section.* KOTZE *stands petrified in the middle of the floor. They all speak in stage whispers.*

CAMPBELL. Take cover, you cunt!

KOTZE. The bastards are shooting at us.

CAMPBELL. Take cover.

CAMPBELL lunges forward and pulls KOTZE to the floor. There is another series of bangs.

KOTZE. Those are Stalin Organs.

CAMPBELL. Shut up!

KOTZE. Ja, careless talk costs lives. That was a narrow shave.

CAMPBELL. Christ.

KOTZE. Thanks, hey Campbell, thanks, I won't forget you.

There is another series of bangs, then the muffled pounding of artillery fire takes over and continues to the end of the scene.

Vasbyt, manne!

MOWBRAY. Are those our boys?

KOTZE. Everything's under control now.

KOTZE gets up and dusts himself off.

Better strip down and oil those rifles. Come, come. Snap out of it, men. You be needing them just now.

BADENHORST bursts in.

BADENHORST. O God. O God.

KOTZE. What's the trouble?

BADENHORST. I shat myself.

KOTZE. What?

BADENHORST. We took some hits, but I didn't see what. I was coming across the vehicle park. I ran to a trench. Then I, man I bloody shat myself.

MARAIS enters. He is covered in grime and mud.

KOTZE. You all right, Marais?

MARAIS. They hit the bungalow. I don't know, I think ten are killed.

Pause.

I'm dreaming:

Pause.

Hands! Hands!

He hits himself in the face.

Hands! Hands!

He continues hitting himself in the face. KOTZE *grabs him by the wrists.*

KOTZE. Pull yourself together.

MARAIS (*matter of fact*). Dave is dead.

KOTZE. Who?

MARAIS. The blast hit him in the back. He was already running. He was all burnt.

KOTZE. Listen here. You a first-class bunch of men. I been meaning to tell you that. Just now we crossing the border and I could say I'm proud to have you boys riding with. As for, um, Dave . . . Well that's life. Now it's over to us. We must show he didn't die for nothing.

Pause.

I can't read minds, but to look at you I say we now all want the same thing: a communist to kill.

Blackout. The sound of hectic small-arms fire, followed by the sound of a motor, which defines itself as an excavator. As the next scene begins, this sound drops in level, but remains present until the end of the play.

Scene Two

The sound of an old shop till ringing and lights up on the shelled-out remains of a Portuguese trading store in the south of Angola. A shop counter, rubble on the floor. MOWBRAY *is on a looting spree. He finds nothing in the till, but discovers a framed photograph on the floor. He sits on a wooden crate and cleans the frame with his handkerchief. After a moment* CAMPBELL *and* MARAIS *enter. All the men are soiled and wear full battle kit.*

MARAIS. Is that the last box?

MOWBRAY. Check this, man. A fucken Portugoose.

They look at the photograph.

His wife's a fucken pig. I wouldn't rape her if you tied her down for me.

MARAIS. Where are they now?

MOWBRAY. Pushing up daisies.

MOWBRAY *breaks the glass covering the photograph. Holding up the frame.*

This is silver this. Man, this place is full of stuff the kaffirs didn't know about.

MOWBRAY *puts the frame inside his shirt.*

See if you can find any more stuff here. I'm going on a private search-and-destroy mission. Just don't hang around too bladdy long, hey. We got to stand to at last light and the bommie says, before we pull out, we putting the base to the torch.

MOWBRAY *picks up his rifle and leaves.* CAMPBELL *stumbles to a corner and vomits.* MARAIS *watches him. Then he lifts a corner of the crate.*

MARAIS. It's heavy.

CAMPBELL *takes a sip from his water bottle, rinses his mouth, spits and drinks.*

White people lived here.

Pause.

What happened to them?

CAMPBELL. What happened to us?

MARAIS. They gone.

CAMPBELL. You know, when Dave got killed . . .

MARAIS. What?

CAMPBELL. When Dave got killed the first thing I thought was, Thank God it wasn't me.

MARAIS. It's a sin.

CAMPBELL. Naught. It was a blind thing to think.

MARAIS. It's a sin.

CAMPBELL. What?

MARAIS. There was children there.

CAMPBELL. Hey, when this is over.

MARAIS. Why children?

CAMPBELL. Never again.

MARAIS. I saw it, man.

CAMPBELL. When we get home.

MARAIS. What have we done?

CAMPBELL. I'm leaving the country.

MARAIS. We'll be punished.

CAMPBELL. What are you talking about?

MARAIS. It's a crime.

CAMPBELL. Hey, man.

MARAIS. You can't just do that.

CAMPBELL. What?

MARAIS. Children.

CAMPBELL. We did nothing.

MARAIS. Did you look out your eyes?

CAMPBELL. Hey, you and me, we weren't even there.

MARAIS. Suffer little children.

CAMPBELL. Hey Paul, think man. We pulling out tonight. After this Op they'll send us home. This whole trip will be over, man. Take.

> CAMPBELL *hands him his water bottle.* MARAIS *holds it, but doesn't drink.*

MARAIS. Could you kill a defenceless . . .

CAMPBELL. For Christ's sake!

> MARAIS *notices something on his trouser leg.*

MARAIS. Sis, it's blood.

CAMPBELL. It's just dirt.

MARAIS. No man, it's blood.

> MARAIS *starts rubbing the spot.*

CAMPBELL. This is unreal.

MARAIS. It is blood.

MARAIS *wets his hat with water from the bottle and starts rubbing the spot.*

It just spreads.

CAMPBELL *picks up a corner of the crate.*

CAMPBELL. Come on.

MARAIS. It won't come out.

CAMPBELL. Let's go.

MARAIS. It smells, dammit.

MARAIS *empties the water bottle over his leg.*

CAMPBELL. Hey man, that's water.

CAMPBELL *grabs the water bottle.* MARAIS *won't let go and a tug-of-war ensues. Water splashes all over.*

MARAIS. It's on my skin.

CAMPBELL. Let go!

MARAIS. I'm dirty.

CAMPBELL. Okay Paul, just cool it, hey.

MARAIS. I got blood on me.

CAMPBELL *wrenches the bottle away from* MARAIS.

CAMPBELL. This is water, you arsehole.

MARAIS. Onse vader wat in die hemele is, laat U naam geheilig word, laat U koninkryk kom, laat U will geskied, soos in die hemel, so ook op die aarde. Gee ons vandag ons daaglikse brood en vergeef ons ons skulde. En vergeef ons ons skulde.

CAMPBELL *tips the water bottle and discovers it's empty.*

CAMPBELL. Christ.

MARAIS. Soos ons ook ons skuldenaars vergewe, en lei ons nie in versoeking nie, maar verlos ons van die Bose. Maar verlos ons van die Bose. Maar verlos ons van die Bose.

CAMPBELL. Stop it!

MARAIS. Maar verlos ons van die Bose.

CAMPBELL *takes* MARAIS *by the shoulders and shakes him.*

Maar verlos ons van die Bose.

The BLACK ACTOR *appears from behind the counter in combat clothing. The front of his shirt is soaked in blood. He points an AK-47 rifle at them.*

BLACK ACTOR. Come, come. You like to kill me? You go with me then, hey. Come on, die for your country.

Pause.

You scared, little soldiers? Scared of me? I'm the one that got away. I'm not a Cuba. I'm not a Russia. You see what I am?

MARAIS. From the SWAPO?

He laughs and turns on CAMPBELL.

BLACK ACTOR. You! Come here.

Pause.

Come here or I shoot you where you stand.

CAMPBELL *moves to him.*

The word you use for me? What I am.

CAMPBELL. Please . . .

BLACK ACTOR (*fiercely*). Say it!

He puts the barrel of his AK-47 to CAMPBELL's mouth.

You call me kaffir. Go on. Say it!

CAMPBELL (*almost inaudible*). Kaffir.

BLACK ACTOR. Look me in my eye, white boy. Give me a good reason why I must not kill you.

The BLACK ACTOR kicks CAMPBELL's feet out from under him and sends him sprawling.

(*shouting*) If I must die, why must you live?

CAMPBELL. Please, we've done nothing.

BLACK ACTOR. You want to make a deal with me?

CAMPBELL. What?

The BLACK ACTOR pulls CAMPBELL to his knees.

BLACK ACTOR. What must happen if I am your prisoner?

Pause.

What do you do to your prisoners?

CAMPBELL. Please, I . . .

BLACK ACTOR. You just shoot them!

The BLACK ACTOR kicks CAMPBELL in the face.

CAMPBELL. We didn't do anything.

BLACK ACTOR. Can you give me anything, white boy?

Pause.

Maybe I just kill you now.

A long moment in which the only sound is the digging.

What is that noise?

CAMPBELL. We just transport supplies.

BLACK ACTOR. What is that rifle?

CAMPBELL. Truly, we've done nothing.

BLACK ACTOR. What is that uniform?

CAMPBELL. I had no choice.

BLACK ACTOR. They going to come with fire just now. Like always. Maybe we burning together. Or must they come to fetch you? Then you must tell them to go away, or I shoot you first. You can choose.

Pause.

What is that noise?

CAMPBELL. You're wounded.

BLACK ACTOR. Don't worry. It's no matter if I die. You coming with bombs. But can't kill all African peoples. Tomorrow we still here.

Pause.

What is that noise?

MARAIS. They digging a hole.

BLACK ACTOR. Deep down?

MARAIS. Excuse me?

BLACK ACTOR. Something to hide?

MARAIS. The smell. It's the smell.

BLACK ACTOR. Who are you?

MARAIS. What?

BLACK ACTOR. What is your name?

MARAIS. Paul. My name is Paul.

BLACK ACTOR. It must be deep or the dogs will come and dig it up.

MARAIS. You hurting.

BLACK ACTOR. I don't feel this.

MARAIS. Why?

BLACK ACTOR. Because I know.

MARAIS. What?

BLACK ACTOR. One day you won't be coming here. I know that.

MARAIS. How?

BLACK ACTOR. Because then it will be finish.

MARAIS. When?

BLACK ACTOR. One day.

The BLACK ACTOR *tenses. He raises his rifle and points it first at* MARAIS *and then at* CAMPBELL. *Suddenly he drops the rifle and clutches his stomach with both hands.* CAMPBELL *leaps forward and retrieves the rifle.* MARAIS *goes to the* BLACK ACTOR.

MARAIS. Give me your hands.

BLACK ACTOR. Why?

CAMPBELL. Paul, we're going.

MARAIS *drags the* BLACK ACTOR *to his feet.*

MARAIS. Don't go.

BLACK ACTOR. One day.

MARAIS *staggers across the stage with the* BLACK ACTOR *in his arms: a grotesque pas de deux.*

MARAIS (*shouting*). Don't go now. What must happen? Tell me! What must I do? What must I do?

The BLACK ACTOR *becomes a dead weight and sags to the floor, dragging* MARAIS *with him.* MARAIS *screams and starts sobbing.* MOWBRAY, BADENHORST *and* KOTZE *hurtle into the room and fan out into firing positions. All rifles are pointed at the* BLACK ACTOR. *Before they are quite in position,* KOTZE *screams:*

KOTZE. Hold your fire! What the fuck's this?

CAMPBELL. It's okay now.

MOWBRAY. It's a fucken terr.

KOTZE. What's with Marais?

CAMPBELL. I don't know.

> BADENHORST *crosses to* MARAIS. CAMPBELL *hands the* BLACK ACTOR*'s AK-47 to* KOTZE.

BADENHORST. Kom boetie, we going.

> *As* BADENHORST *bends down over him,* MARAIS *lashes out.*

MARAIS. That was children.

BADENHORST. Fuck off.

> MARAIS *gets up, utters the scream from the bayonet charge and rushes at* KOTZE, *knocking him to the floor.*

MARAIS. Children! Children! Children!

KOTZE. Get him off me! Get him off me!

> BADENHORST *and* MOWBRAY *grab* MARAIS *and pull him off.*

MARAIS. One day!

KOTZE. Get him out of here!

> BADENHORST *and* MOWBRAY *drag* MARAIS *off.*

KOTZE. Another one completely bosbefok. These bloody children can't take it. So it goes.

> *Pause.*

Finish him off, Campbell.

CAMPBELL. What?

KOTZE. That enemy. You know how to use your bayonet.

CAMPBELL. He's wounded.

KOTZE. Do him a favour then. Put him out of his misery. Give him a bullet.

CAMPBELL. No. I can't.

KOTZE. Yes, you can.

> KOTZE *points the* BLACK ACTOR*'s AK-47 at him.*

It's you or him, Campbell. It always has been.

> *This tableau is held for a moment. Then* CAMPBELL *raises the rifle, points it at the* BLACK ACTOR *and fires. As the shot rings out, the theatre is plunged into darkness.*

THE HUNGRY EARTH ■ MAISHE MAPONYA

MAISHE MAPONYA, son of a painter, was born in 1951 in Alexander Township, Johannesburg. When he was eleven his family was forcibly removed and resettled in Diepkloof, Soweto. After school, while a semi-professional soccer-player and a clerk in an insurance company, he began writing poetry and was a member of the Allah Poets, a group of performance poets whose platform was Black Consciousness-raising. As an escape, he says, from the routine of black working life, he founded the Bahumutsi Drama Group in 1976. Their production of his first play, *The Cry*, was overtaken by the events of the Soweto Uprising of that year. A British Council Award in 1978 allowed him to study theatre and directing in the U.K.

Bahumutsi means 'comforters' . . . and they are concerned to present 'theatre for a purpose', as one programme notes:

> This is the living theatre which has a future for us because it is about us. It carries more weight because it is a mirror and a voice of the dispossessed. But it involves a lot of risks, both financially and in terms of personal safety. Black theatre is a theatre that will not subscribe to commercial slogans; it has to survive amidst all odds. Theatre is one of the most dynamic ways of raising the consciousness of black people in South Africa.

The Hungry Earth was originally drafted between January and March, 1979, in response to several theatrical experiences – Maponya has often cited Brecht's *The Measures Taken*, which he had just seen at the Edinburgh Festival, as one. Be that as it may, the piece has a clear didactic intention which has not been modified in its many changes of script and production. As a note to the script says:

> *The Hungry Earth* emerges from the different aspects of our ill-fated lifespan. Through my eyes I have seen the devastations and drenching of my people into the wide-open mouths of this 'hungry earth'. I have heard them cry for mercy and I have seen them die many a time before those who fail to understand. We shall continue to punch with a clenched fist until the walls fall . . .

Further plays of Maponya with Bahumutsi include *Gangsters*, an oblique reworking of Beckett's *Catastrophe*, in this case featuring the torture of a black consciousness poet named Rasechaba – this was permitted restricted performances only in South Africa. The script was included in the *Woza Afrika!* anthology after its performance during the Festival of South African Resistance Plays at the Lincoln Center Theater over September-October 1986. He currently lectures at the University of the Witwatersrand in the history and theory of African performance.

This is the first publication of the complete and final script.

The Hungry Earth was first performed with a cast of five at the Donaldson Orlando Cultural Club, Soweto, in May 1979, and then at the Box Theatre of the University of the Witwatersrand, Johannesburg. With the cast down to three – Maishe Maponya, Dijo Tjabane, Sydwell Yola – it toured Britain professionally over May-August 1981, and then Switzerland and West Germany, before returning to its first commercial engagement in South Africa in the Laager Theatre at the Market from January 1982.

As the house lights fade to blackout, the actors take position and sing:

> Wake up Mother Africa
> Wake up
> Time has run out
> And all opportunity is wasted
> Wake up Mother Africa
> Wake up
> Before the White man rapes you.
> Wake up Mother Africa.

As the song ends, the lights come up for:

The Prologue

ALL. We are about to take you on a heroic voyage of the Bahumutsi Drama Group.

ONE. It seems as though some people are without feeling.

TWO. If we could really feel, the pain would be so great that we would stand up and fight to stop all the suffering.

THREE. If we could really feel it in the bowels, the groin, in the throat and in the breast, we would go into the streets and stop the wars, stop slavery, destroy the prisons, stop detentions, stop the killings, stop selfishness – and apartheid we would end.

FOUR. Ah, we would all learn what love is.

FIVE. We would learn what sharing is.

ONE. And, of course, we would live together.

ALL (*singing*). Touched by our non-violent vibrations.

ONE. We will rise up.

ALL (*singing*). We will sing while we crawl to the mine.

TWO. We will rise up.

ALL (*singing*). Bleeding through the days of poverty.

THREE. We will fight hard.

ALL (*singing*). Pulsing in the hot dark ground.

FOUR. We will rise up.

ALL (*singing*). Dying in the stubborn hungry earth.

(*Spoken.*) We will fight hard.

(*Singing.*) We will rise up
And we will sing loud
Against the Hungry Earth.
It is our sweat and our blood
That made Egoli what it is today.

The lights fade, and the actors take up positions for:

Scene One: THE HOSTEL

A hostel room. Four men are asleep. One of them is restless. He mumbles and groans and talks incoherently. He tosses about and finally cries out wildly. One of the others wakes him. They all wake up.

MATLHOKO [SUFFERINGS]. For God's sake, I've been trying to wake you up, while you twisted and turned and yelled, 'No, No, No!' like a Salvation Army lass being dragged into a brothel. Do you always have nightmares at dawn?

USIVIKO [SHIELD]. An evil nightmare has been torturing me. My whole body shivers. I wonder if this is real.

BESHWANA [LOIN-CLOTH]. What is it, mgani [friend], tell us quickly.

USIVIKO. I dreamt I saw Umlungu [the White man].

SETHOTHO [IMBECILE]. But we see abelungu [whites] every day of our lives! Why do you behave like a child seeing a ghost when you just dream of Umlungu? Don't make dreams your master.

USIVIKO. You are right. This umlungu was far different from them all in a way. This one has divided me against myself. He has tinted my colour. I can no longer distinguish between right and wrong.

BESHWANA. What did this strange umlungu do to you? What did he want?

The lights fade, leaving only MATLHOKO lit.

MATLHOKO. When this land started giving birth to ugly days, things started going wrong from the moment of dawning and peace went into exile, to become a thing of the wilderness. Yes, we experienced the saddest days of our lives when umlungu first came to these shores called Africa, a total stranger from Europe. We received him kindly. We gave him food. We gave him shelter. We adopted his ideas and his teachings. Then he told us of a god and all Black faces were full of smiles. When he said love your neighbour we clapped and cheered for we had a natural love. Suddenly we drifted back suspiciously when he said you must always turn the other cheek when you are slapped. He continued to say love those who misuse you. We grumbled inwardly, smiled and listened hard as he was quoting from the Holy Book, little knowing we would end up as puppets on a string, unable to control our own lives. And whilst we were still smiling, he set up laws, organised an army, and started digging up the gold and diamonds; and by the time our poor forefathers opened their eyes, umlungu was no more – he had moved to Europe. He had only left his army behind to 'take care of the unruly elements that may provoke a revolution'.

USIVIKO. We will repeat the incident as told by our forefathers.

The lights come up.

MATLHOKO. Men and women of AFRIKA: umlungu has left us secretly. He has taken with him a great wealth of property, our sheep and cattle, our men and women as servants, gold and diamonds and all precious stones.

USIVIKO. Let us give chase and get back what he has taken from us. Those riches belong to us, the aborigines of this land.

BESHWANA. Umlungu deserves to die. Let us set out to catch him and when we catch him we will hang him from the nearest tree. His servants must also be killed: they betrayed us. Let us kill the whole lot.

SETHOTHO. You speak of being robbed, you bastards? How can you say such things about umlungu? Before he came you were savages swinging onto trees and eating bananas. You deserted your culture and allowed the hides and wood to rot in the fields. Umlungu taught you how to make leather and how to make furniture. Today you can even make money. You lived like wild animals; now you live like human beings. But no, you ungrateful creatures, you are not satisfied with the things you got from umlungu! Does it surprise you that he has run away?

BESHWANA. How dare you curse my people like that! We blew horns, we beat the drums and we sang the song Ngelethu Mawethu ['It is ours my people'], when this land was unknown to the White skins! Shit! We gave culture to the world, we built the pyramid. No! (*Pointing a finger at* SETHOTHO.) This man is trying to mislead us! You are obviously a great friend of umlungu. (*Clutching him.*) Well, don't worry, we will not separate you from him. You will both be hung from the same tree . . . (*They all lift him up above their heads*) and on your combined tombstone we will write:

ALL. In memory of the oppressor
   And his oppressed spy
   And to their love-hate.
   They were inseparable
   In life and death.
   Find no peace.

USIVIKO. We gave chase in thousands. And when we got hold of
   him, his army had received word that we meant to kill
   umlungu. We first wanted to tell him why we wanted to kill him.

UMLUNGU. What have I done to deserve your enmity? During the
   two hundred years I dwelt with you I taught you to live a better
   life. I brought you the wisdom and fertility of Europe. Why is it
   then that you are after my blood, that you want to kill me and
   my family?

BESHWANA. You are a stranger, a foreigner. By your labour you
   merely repaid your debt to our country, your debt to the country
   that extended its hospitality to you for two hundred years.

UMLUNGU. And why do you want to kill us today? What right have
   you to look upon yourselves as citizens and upon me as a
   foreigner?

USIVIKO. You are about to leave this country with all the wealth we
   sweated our lives for. You underpaid us and celebrated when we
   were starving. You gave us mirrors and knives in exchange for
   cattle. You never set foot on those vast tracts of land that are
   still in their virgin state. You did not want to get to them
   because you had no slaves to do the sweating for you.

*During the next speech and the song the lights fade to half light, and
the actors mime the battle of spears against guns.*

BESHWANA. We were still arguing when the army attacked from
   all sides. The spear matched the cowards' weapons from the
   West and only the crying tone of the singing warrior could be
   heard.

As the other actors chant softly, BESHWANA *speaks:*

Stand up all ye brave of Africa
Stand up and get to battle,
Where our brothers die in numbers
Africa you are bewitched,
But our Black blood will flow
To water the tree of our freedom.

Our brave stormed the bullets to protect their motherland from
the cruel umlungu. One – two – ten hundreds of our brave
never flinched, yet they knew they were heading for death.

Mother Africa wake up
And arm yourself,
Wipe the tears of your brave
Mother Africa wake up
Lest umlungu rapes you
Lest umlungu rapes you.

MATLHOKO. Those were ugly days lived by our great-grandfathers, the days of ISANDLWANA and the days of UMGUNGUNDLOVU. The days when our forefathers fought hard for what was theirs, for mother Afrika.

The lights fade to blackout. A song – children singing at work – begins, and the lights come up for:

Scene Two: THE PLANTATION

Three child-workers seated. THE VISITOR, *an investigator, has just entered the compound.*

VISITOR. I am the man who visited Doringkop, owned by Illovo. (*Wandering about, talking to himself.*) Ah! so many stables. This man must be very rich to afford so many horses. Let me just peep and see how many horses he has in each. No! This cannot be true. I see people inside. Or maybe they did not look after the cattle well and that's why he locked them inside. Let me find out. (*He knocks. There is a reply and he goes inside.*) Sanibonani.

ALL. Yebo!

VISITOR. I am looking for my son, Sizanani [Help one another].

SETHOTHO. USizanani is staying in B Compound. This is A.

VISITOR. Do you all stay in this stable? Why is it that there is no furniture?

ALL. Asazi [We do not know].

VISITOR. How old are you?

MATLHOKO. Mina? [me?]

VISITOR. Yes, wena [you].

MATLHOKO. I am twelve years old and will be thirteen next month.

VISITOR. You? How old are you?

BESHWANA. I am thirteen.

VISITOR. You?

USIVIKO. Twelve.

VISITOR. And you?

MATLHOKO. He is fourteen.

VISITOR. And you?

SETHOTHO. They lie, they are all thirteen years old, I know.

VISITOR. Do you go to school?

BESHWANA. No. We don't go to school. We work for Baas Phuzushugela the whole year.

VISITOR. What does he pay you?

SETHOTHO. He gives me 50c.

BESHWANA. He gives me 70c – I started working last year.

USIVIKO. He gives us all 50c – he is lying. Ubaas Phuzushugela a soze a ku nike i70c [Boss Sugar Drinker will never give you 70c].

VISITOR. Till when do you work?

BESHWANA. We start at 5 a.m. and knock off at three in the afternoon.

VISITOR. When is your lunch?

SETHOTHO. We don't go to lunch. Baas Phuzushugela gives us amageu [sour porridge] and bread at ten o'clock. And once a week we receive rations of mealiemeal, beans, salt and meat.

VISITOR. Do you work on Saturdays?

USIVIKO. Yes, Siphumula ngesonto nje [We rest on Sundays].

VISITOR. How far is the sugar field from here?

BESHWANA. Six miles only.

VISITOR. And how do you travel there?

SETHOTHO. We wake up very early and walk.

VISITOR. Tell me, where do you come from?

USIVIKO. We are all from Transkei.

VISITOR. Now how did you come here?

SETHOTHO. Size nge Joini. We are on contract. Will you excuse us – we want to sleep, it is already late.

VISITOR. Where do you sleep?

USIVIKO. Silala apha. [We sleep here.]

VISITOR. I immediately went out and eventually ended up in the compound where married men and their wives were staying. Some women told me they earned R1,10c a day and some men said they earned R2,00 a day after working nine hours. I slept there for a night. I went into the field and was chased because they said I was causing trouble.

The child-workers sing:

A SONG OF REJECTION OF TROUBLE-MAKERS

Here comes a man
To cause trouble in my home,
Bring that stick
And I will discipline him . . .

The lights fade down as the song ends. The actors move upstage to collect their props, except MATLHOKO *who moves downstage left. Lights up on* MATLHOKO *only for:*

Scene Three: THE TRAIN

MATLHOKO. Just how I wish I were a spectator of the scenes of the amagoduga [migrant labourers]. I would follow them about and just watch every little thing they do, and listen to our newly found lingo, Fanagalo. Unfortunately Blacks can never be spectators of White creations, but victims. (*Lights full up.*) Yes, my wish was misplaced for I was one of the Basotho who were driven by hunger and drought from the confines of their rugged mountains. In those days it seemed as though the god of the White man from over the sea had stamped his foot in anger upon this land for the first time since its creation. Obviously many of us were coming to the mines for the first time. The talk in the crammed compartments was all of the hunger that had fallen in Lesotho. The older men put the blame on the younger generation that had put their faith in the mystical gods of Europe, foolishly forgetting the old and safe ways of the nation's ancestors, and I will never forget what happened on that ugly day in the train . . .

The men, who have been waiting at the station, are now infuriated and angered by the endless waiting. Finally we see four actors occupying chairs which are placed in two parallel rows – the train.

SETHOTHO (*sniffing and looking about and eventually standing to look underneath the seat*). Hey, man! There is a dangerous odour here. (*Nobody takes notice. He sits down. Then he repeats the same movements.*) Hey man! I know we all want money but this odour is going to land us in shit!

Whilst he ponders absent-mindedly, the compartment door is flung open and a ticket examiner enters, his uniform cap pushed well back from his forehead.

EXAMINER. Kaartjies! Tickets! Come on you black bastards. Hurry up!

Standing in the doorway he surveys everybody and wrinkles his nose in disgust. He sniffs the air tentatively three or four times and quickly punches the tickets, and before leaving gives them another hard look.

SETHOTHO (*calling out*). Men of the chief, Kere ho a nkga mona [there is a smell here]. I can smell matekoane [marijuana]. The White man smelled it too. You saw his nose twitching like a jackal's.

BESHWANA (*interrupting*). O nkgella masepa' mmae fela. Mosima' e towe!

SETHOTHO. I tell you, someone had better throw the matekoane out of the window. At the next station he will inform the police. Will someone please hide the stuff very far lest the police arrest the innocent together with the guilty?

No one moves.

BESHWANA (*imitating the ticket-examiner*). Maak gou, maak gou, you Black skelms!

Laughter.

SETHOTHO (*warning them*). Hey, my father lived in the City of Gold and he told me there are so many crimes against the law of the white man of which Black people might be unwittingly guilty. You will end up in jail if you are found in the streets of the city and can't produce a pass any time and anywhere the police demand it – even in the toilet – I tell you, they sometimes hide in there. If you drink too much you may be arrested for over-indulgence in alcohol. Do you know detention without trial? Section ten? Or six? Do you know you can be arrested for being at the wrong place at the wrong time? Do you know house-arrest? Do you know Robben Island? Makana? My father knows them all! Pasop banna! (*Now warningly.*) Hlokome-lang! I don't want to repeat my father's experience. Lahlang matekoane ono! [Throw it away!]

Realising that his warning is falling on deaf ears, he collects his few belongings to search for another place somewhere in the crowded train. Seeing that he cannot find a place elsewhere, he returns amongst jeers and laughter. They are still laughing when a white sergeant bursts noisily into the compartment with the ticket examiner close at his heels. The travellers freeze in sullen silence.

EXAMINER (*eyeing them coldly*). Come! You Black bastards! Where's the dagga? (*No one answers.*) All right! Out onto the platform, you baboons!

He slaps and kicks the slow ones. Outside, he searches them thoroughly and as he finds nothing, he pushes his cap to the very back of his head and turns into the compartment to start his search again. Finally he comes out swelling like a bullfrog in anger, holding a bag in his hand. He lifts it up and asks:

Wie se sak is hierdie?

ALL. We do not know, Sir.

EXAMINER. Go! All into the police vans!

They all end up in the vans, after putting up some resistance in which one is threatened with a bullet in the head. 'Interrogation' and sentencing follow. The lights slowly fade except for the narrator's area downstage right.

USIVIKO. Most of us were 'requested' to produce passes and permits. Those who failed to produce spent two weeks in jail and were deported to their respective homes on their release. This is the inhuman and unjust procedure to endorse the unjust laws that make another a stranger in the land of his birth and rob him of his freedom to move wherever he wants. Is freedom not the law of nature. Then what?

The lights come up for:

Scene Four: THE MINE

MATLHOKO (*from the window of his room*). Hey, Mzala! [Cousin!]

BESHWANA (*responding through his window*). Kuyabanda namhlanje, Mzala? [Did you call me cousin?]

MATLHOKO. Yes Mzala! The wind . . . It is freezing today.

BESHWANA. The gods are angry.

MATLHOKO. Yes, but their anger can't go beneath this earth. It is quiet there.

A traditional gumboot dance with song. A siren sounds. The lights fade for scene underground. The mineworkers gather at the cage to begin their night shift. The cage descends. It slows to a shuddering halt, and they swarm out like ants to their various places of work. They stoop low; twist and turn to avoid the wooden props which pit their strength against the full weight of the rocky roof that presses down on their crouching heads. Jannie, a White miner, inspects a work-face and gives orders.

JANNIE. Tonight, I want holes to be drilled here . . . and here . . . and here . . . and here.

BESHWANA (*after a short while*). Sorry, master, this area may not be suitable, and besides the rock seems wet.

JANNIE. I did not ask your opinion. Do you want to argue with me when I tell you to work?

BESHWANA. I am sorry makhulubaas [big boss], I'm sorry.

They drill at the rock.

BAASBOY (*fuming*). Hei! Wena! Why tell makhulubaas and not me? Do you want to take my job?

BESHWANA (*apologetic*). I'm sorry, Baasboy.

BAASBOY. Next time you'll be fired! Pasop, jong!

JANNIE. Baasboy! Wat gaan aan daarso, jong?

BAASBOY. Makhulubaas, this one thinks he knows too much!

JANNIE. Werk, julle bliksems!

BESHWANA AND BAASBOY. Dankie, makhulubaas.

BAASBOY (*pointing a finger at* BESHWANA). Jy moet werk, jong!

Suddenly: a great explosion. The miners collapse. Smoke and coughing. Again and again the miners scream in pain and fright.

SETHOTHO. Without even considering the weight of the risk, I stood up passing the dead bodies of my brothers just to save this sole White skin.

As JANNIE *screams again and again,* SETHOTHO *comes to his rescue.*

MATLHOKO. And when the first two ambulances arrived, we limped towards them but only makhulubaas was allowed into one. The other turned back because the two ambulances were for the White people only. I looked back into the tunnel where my brothers were being eaten by this hungry earth. I cursed the White man and questioned the very existence of God for it was my sweat and bones and blood that made Egoli what it is today.

BESHWANA. This is actual fact. Two years after this horrible accident I was transferred to Carletonville where we staged a strike . . .

The actors change positions and start milling around, ignoring the siren that beckons them to work.

BESHWANA (*pointing a finger at* SETHOTHO, *the induna*). Wena, nduna, you side with the White man today, you must pack your belongings and go to stay with him in the city. We are sick of this induna business!

SETHOTHO (*reassuring them*). I'm behind you in everything!

COMPOUND MANAGER. Look at these fools! Didn't you hear the machine? (*The miners all keep quiet as he goes to them one by one.*) Hey, wena. Yini wena haikhona sebenza? [Hey man, you don't want to work?]

SETHOTHO. Haikhona baas, thina aiyazi sebenzela lo pikinini mali fana ga so! [No boss, we can't work for so little money!]

BESHWANA. Baas wena haikhona yipha thina lo insurance, manje thina haikhona sebenza! [You refuse to insure us, now we won't work!]

COMPOUND MANAGER. Wena yini ga lo sikhalo ga wena? [What is your complaint?]

MATLHOKO. Lo mali wena ga lo yipha thina, thina haikhona satisfied. Kudala lo thina sebenza lapha mine. Kodwa wena haikhona yipha lo thina increase. Lo room thina hlala, fana ga lo toilet! [We are not satisfied with the salary. We have long been working here without increase. The room we stay in is as small as a toilet!]

COMPOUND MANAGER. You! What is your complaint! What? No complaint! Now – all of you – listen to me very carefully because I'm not going to repeat myself! The first thing: you get free lodging. The second thing: you get free food. (*A sudden murmur of discontent.*) The third thing: you get free overalls, free gumboots . . .

A wave of angry protest: he pushes them forward to work, they push him back.

COMPOUND MANAGER. Madoda! Skathi nina haikhona hamba sebenza, mina biza lo maphoisa. [Men! If you refuse to go to work I'll go and call the police.]

ALL (*threatening him with their hats*). Hamba! Hamba! [Go! Go!]

The MANAGER can be heard from his office talking to police.

COMPOUND MANAGER. Yes sir, anything may happen – they are

about to destroy everything – they are wild – come quickly!

ALL. The police won, but not without declaring themselves enemies of the people!

COMPOUND MANAGER. We shall not be intimidated.

There is the sound of a machine-gun and as some miners fall down, some raise their hands, surrendering to go down into the mine. MATLHOKO *continues relating what happened.*

MATLHOKO. Yes, we were forced to go down in Carletonville though we knew that this earth was hungry. Who would listen to our cries? Yes, never will I forget that bloody Sharpeville for I was there in 1960 when an anti-pass campaign was opened.

They produce passes and interact with each other as they express their anger and disgust of the pass system. BESHWANA *throws his pass away, but is advised not to do so.*

USIVIKO. Hei Beshwana, not here! At the police station. Come, everybody, let us go to the police station.

BESHWANA. Let us throw stones then. We must put up a fight.

They stop him from throwing stones.

USIVIKO. You are giving them a wrong impression of us. We are not violent people. And this is a peaceful demonstration. Come everybody . . .

A procession and the burning of passbooks, with a song.

> Senze ntoni na?
> Senze ntoni na?
> Nkosi mthetheleli
> Si bhekisa kuwe
> Yini na? Ukuba sibenjena?
> Sikhulule kuwo lamatyatanga
> Sikhulule kuwo lamatyatanga
> Senze ntoni na?
> Senze ntoni na?

> What have we done?
> God our spokesperson
> We put all our faith in you
> Why have we to live this way?
> Release us from these shackles.

As they put their passes on the fire, the lights fade until only the fire remains. The song continues.

USIVIKO. The police panicked at the sight of the massed though unarmed innocent Black faces . . .

ALL. We were all of the same frame of mind . . .

USIVIKO. And they opened fire! (*Mimes firing at the protesters as they fall to the ground.*) I went to the funeral and was shocked to see how hungry this earth is, for it had opened to swallow the Black man. Those who survived were arrested and charged with incitement to violence under the Public Safety Act . . . someone somewhere did not understand 'peaceful' and 'violent' . . . Anyhow, let's forget about that because some very rich White women and some elite Black women have formed 'Women for Peace' and I hope they will forget their elitism and their socialising process and be equally dedicated to peace in Africa. (*Saluting with a clenched fist, he stretches and flexes his body like a person who's just woken up from a sleep.*)

Scene Five: THE COMPOUND

Sunday morning activity, inside a compound room.

BESHWANA (*waking up from a sleep and calling out to* USIVIKO). We mngani wami. Come here . . . I went to the biggest shebeen in the township yesterday.

USIVIKO. Kuphi lapho? [Where's that?]

BESHWANA. At Rose's place.

USIVIKO. Rose's shebeen?

BESHWANA. Ngathen'u gologo mngani wami . . . ngathi laca . . . laca . . . laca . . . [I bought liquor and had so much to drink].

USIVIKO. You must have been drunk.

BESHWANA. Yebo mngani wami . . . ngase ngi lala la – here on the floor.

USIVIKO. So you slept here, hey! That's not good for your health. You must stop drinking . . . And who was burning papers on the floor?

BESHWANA. Where?

USIVIKO. Behind you.

BESHWANA. I don't know.

USIVIKO. You will know when this place goes up in flames . . . ga!

BESHWANA (*angered*). I said I don't know . . .

USIVIKO. Okay! You don't have to shout at me!

BESHWANA. Fuck off!

USIVIKO. You must count your words when you talk to me. Ga!

BESHWANA (*emphasising every single word*). Go to hell!

USIVIKO (*as he removes the ash, frustrated*). Okay! I will meet you there!

There is tension between the two. Silence.

BESHWANA (*a little later*). Hey, my friend! Did you hear the latest news? (*Silence.*) The manager has requested us to do the traditional dance for the tourists.

USIVIKO. When will we ever have a Sunday of our own? You're used to dancing every Sunday. Are you going to do it again today in that drunk state?

BESHWANA. No, I've grown old, Sonnyboy. I can't dance anymore . . . (*Silence.*) Hey, can you see out there?

USIVIKO. What?

BESHWANA. The bus, my friend . . . (*Looking out through the window.*) Can you see it . . . there!

USIVIKO. Look . . . S. A. R. Tours. It's the tourists. Look, they've got cameras aimed at us. They are taking a picture of us.

They pose for a picture. They are now in a happy mood as they run out of the room.

BESHWANA. There it stops, my friend. They've got taperecorders. They walk towards the dance area. Hey, another picture . . . (*They pose.*)

ALL. Hi! Hello, beautiful tourists . . . Welcome to sunny South Africa! Hello . . .

BESHWANA. Another picture. (*Pose.*) They're taking their seats. Come closer. (*Talks softer to him.*) Can you see that man over there?

USIVIKO. Which one?

BESHWANA. The one with small eyes . . . He looks like eh . . .

USIVIKO. He looks like . . . Mao Tse Tung.

BESHWANA. But I'm scared, my friend. Can you see the two men beside him? They look like the Security Branch.

USIVIKO. Oh, pity he's escorted.

BESHWANA (*sudden excitement*). My friend, my friend, look . . .

USIVIKO. I see . . .

BESHWANA. That bearded one . . . what do you think?

USIVIKO. Yeh! He looks like Karl Marx!

They seem to have fun with their explorations. They point at a lady in the arena whom they agree looks 'like Lady Diana.' Finally . . .

BESHWANA. Can you see that black man sitting alone there? He looks like . . .

USIVIKO. Shame . . . That one, simple . . .

BOTH. He is the bus-driver! Ha ha ha!

They call out to MATLHOKO, whom they've nicknamed Manikiniki.

BOTH. We Manikiniki! Manikiniki!

BESHWANA. Come out!

USIVIKO. The tourists are here!

MATLHOKO. What? Just leave me alone.

BESHWANA. Come out! Come and see for yourself. Tourists!

MATLHOKO. Terrorists?

USIVIKO. No, tourists!

MATLHOKO comes out dressed in traditional garb and finally they dance and entertain the tourists, drumming and singing and posing for pictures until they are exhausted.

Scene Six: THE COMPOUND

Everyday activity. A gramophone plays a Zulu tune; gambling, cooking, finally fighting.

BESHWANA. Heje, I read a true statement in the Bible last week; it says we shall live by the sweat of our brows.

USIVIKO. Oh, how true that is, mgani [friend] – it's amazing. (*Starts coughing.*) But it's time I go on pension. I'm old and my chest seems to be dry or maybe I have run out of blood. I'm scared.

MATLHOKO. Ja we must; you remember when we started here way back in the fifties. We were still young boys. Then you could hardly speak Sesotho, only Xhosa. Of course I did not trust you.

Yooo! who could trust a Xhosa lad anyway? (*They laugh.*) You
remember we thought we would work ourselves up, bring our
families down here and buy a 'Buick master road'. But here we
are now, still struggling and about to die, no Buick and wives
still far away.

SETHOTHO. Hey, you remind me of the houses outside the
perimeter of this compound. Hey man, the scene is pathetic . . .
there are women there!

MATLHOKO. What are you talking about?

SETHOTHO. I mean, have you not seen those rusted, corrugated
iron huts mixed with pieces of wood and petrol drums?

MATLHOKO. J-jaa, I saw them.

SETHOTHO. Did you know people stay there?

MATLHOKO. Yes I went there several times. In fact let's get down
there now, I feel thirsty.

The lights fade as they exit singing.

WOMAN. My name is Chirango. This is my only home. I came here
some five years after my husband had written to me to come
and join him in this city of gold. To my dismay, I was not
permitted to stay with him. I could not go back to Rhodesia
because I had no money. He took me into his room at night.
Later when a wall was erected around the compound it became
risky to sneak in. Once I was arrested and fined R90,00 or 90
days. He did not have the money and I went to jail. When I
came back I was told that his contract had expired and since
then I have never seen or heard of him. Today I manage to live
and feed my two fatherless children out of the beers and
indambola [liquor] I sell. And when the beers don't sell I
become every man's woman. What else can I do? I can't get
permits to work here.

THE WOMAN'S SONG

I'll never get to Malawi
I'll never get to Transkei
I'll never get to Bophuthatswana

*The lights come up as the men enter, singing. They tease her, eventually
settling down.*

MATLHOKO. Sisi, is Chirango your name or your husband's?

WOMAN. It is my husband's. Why?

SETHOTHO. Yes, I thought as much. Your name rings a bell. I
worked with a Chirango some two years ago in the Western

Transvaal gold mine near Orkney. He was tall, dark, hefty – and wore a moustache . . .

WOMAN. Where is he? He is the father of my children! He is my husband! I want him.

SETHOTHO. This is a very sorry state of affairs. I even fear to talk about it.

WOMAN (*anxious*). Tell me! Where is my husband?

SETHOTHO (*relating in a rather pathetic tone*). Your husband was among the forty-one black miners trapped underground in a raging fire who were left to die when mine authorities gave the order to seal off the passageways. I was among the 233 mine workers who were affected by the fumes and were treated in hospital.

WOMAN (*hysterical and crying*). Oh, how cruel this earth is. Our men will never stop dying to feed this hungry earth. Today I have no place to stay. Today I am a widow. Today my children are fatherless. Yet I do not know. How many more have vanished like that without the knowledge of immediate relatives? My husband has died digging endlessly for gold which would help to prop up the Apartheid system. My man is dead! My man is eaten by the hungry earth! He is dead!

The lights fade slowly. Group song.

S'THANDWA S'THANDWA
S'THANDWA SE NHLIZIYO YAM
BELOVED ONE OF MY HEART
BELOVED ONE, DRY YOUR TEARS
DAUGHTER OF AFRIKA
SOMANDLA! SOMANDLA!
UPHI NA QAMATHA?
ALMIGHTY, WHERE ART THOU?
WHEN THIS HUNGRY EARTH
SWALLOWS, SWALLOWS
THY CHILDREN
SOMANDLA! SOMANDLA!
SIKELELA INSAPHO, YE AFRIKA
NKOSI SIKELELA THINA LUSAPHOLWAYO
BLESS THE FAMILY OF AFRIKA
SIKELELA INSAPHO, YE AFRIKA
NKOSI SIKELELA THINA LUSAPHOLWAYO.

EPILOGUE SONG

WHERE HAVE ALL OUR MEN GONE
THEY HAVE ALL GONE DOWN INTO THE MINES
THEY WILL NEVER RETURN AGAIN
THEY HAVE BEEN SWALLOWED UP BY THIS HUNGRY EARTH.

Lights fade to blackout.

SUSAN PAM was born in Cape Town in 1962 and gained a
performer's diploma from the University of Cape Town in 1983. As
a freelance actress she had appeared in various fringe South
African plays when, as she noted:

> In February, 1988, I was unemployed with a blank year
> ahead of me. I had two options: I could either get a job
> answering a phone or create a new project. I opted for the
> second. Research started in mid-February and I spent
> months collecting material. The best interviews were always
> the ones where I took most risks. Joubert Park makes one
> realise the extent of the changing urban scenario in South
> Africa. A year and a half later *Curl Up and Dye* is being
> staged. An added bonus – four other actors and two crew
> have got jobs.

The script of *Curl Up and Dye* was intensely workshopped during
this period by producer Michael Hunt and his director, Lucille
Gillwald, with the five performers thoroughly developing their own
roles: Susan Pam fleshed out the lead character; Val Donald-Bell –
who was returning to the stage – took over Mrs Dubois; Lillian
Dube, the well-known casting agent, took Miriam; newcomer Debra
Watson became Charmaine, and Nandi Nyembe, in one of her first
roles, took Dudu. As in many of Gillwald's previous productions of
new South African scripts, the team displayed a commitment to
engaging social commentary that far outgrew its simple sitcom
origins. Five feisty women fighting unemployment, none of whom
had been considered prominent or influential in the theatre world
before, became one of the hit shows of the late 80s. For example,
although independently produced and launched without fanfare at
the Black Sun fringe venue, after its first run at the Market Theatre
Curl Up and Dye enjoyed no less than three return seasons there,
followed by a lengthy booking at a commercial venue. Tragically
Gillwald, who had shaped the on-stage careers of so many younger
performers like these, died before the end of this, her greatest
success, and the show continued as a homage to her.

When *Curl Up and Dye* played at the Edinburgh Festival, before
moving to the Tricycle Theatre, London, John Peter of the *Sunday
Times* wrote:

I saw a bitter, biting and funny play from South Africa by Susan Pam, who herself played the manageress of a dismal little hairdressing salon in a dreadful Johannesburg slum. Outside, police sirens blare, people get carved up; inside, you watch the toing and froing of the dreary and inevitable power games which poor blacks and poor whites have to play. This is a world where life is cheap and pride is hard to hold onto, and Pam knows that under the heel of poverty, loyalties shift like quicksand. She and her four fellow actors play with a hard and touching dedication. I cannot recommend it warmly enough.

Susan Pam now acts under her married name, Pam-Grant, and says she owes a debt of gratitude to D. J. Grant, Maralin Vanrenen and the original cast and director for their contributions to the development of this script.

Characters

ROLENE, a hairdresser – mid-twenties
MRS DUBOIS, the caretaker of Freda Mansions – late fifties
CHARMAINE, a Wellconal addict – anywhere between 19 and 30
MIRIAM, a domestic helper – late fifties
DUDU, a nursing sister – late thirties

The play is set in a hair salon in Bok Street, Joubert Park,
Johannesburg. The salon, 'Curl Up and Dye International', has
fallen behind the times.

Curl Up and Dye was first presented by Michael Hunt at the Black Sun in Orange Grove, Johannesburg, on 22 June 1989, directed by Lucille Gillwald, with the following cast :

ROLENE	Susan Pam
MRS DUBOIS	Val Donald-Bell
CHARMAINE	Debra Watson
MIRIAM	Lillian Dube
DUDU	Nandi Nyembe

For its overseas tour MRS DUBOIS was played by Hanna Botha and DUDU by Thoko Ntshinga.

ACT ONE

Upstage is the front of the salon – a large window and a door which opens out onto the street – the name, Curl Up and Dye, written backwards on the window and door. A lacy curtain covers the bottom half of the window. Just inside, still upstage left, is a sink and cupboard with all its kitchen belongings – coffee cups, coffee, cleaning rags, etc. A rusty old geyser hangs precariously above the sink. Upstage right, just in front of the window, is a half-moon shaped reception desk and high stool. A telephone, appointment book and cash till are on the desk. Next to the reception desk a cupboard with shelves displays shampoos, conditioners, treatments and a radio. Downstage right is a leatherette couch with low table and old magazines. On the opposite side a wash-basin with chair and running water for washing the customers' hair. Downstage in the centre is the main hairdressing area – a long, narrow dressing table is flush against the imaginary mirrored fourth wall – the audience. Three pink leatherette chairs, each with its own footstool, stand in a row behind the table. Moveable hairdriers, trolleys with curlers, combs, brushes, scissors and other hairdressing paraphernalia add to the clutter which gives the green and pink salon its claustrophobic atmosphere. Tufts of 'yesterday's hair' lie scattered on the green and white lino floor. The overall appearance is somewhat tacky and out of touch. ROLENE arrives at the Curl Up and Dye International hair salon. She tries the door – it's locked.

ROLENE. Ag no man, Miriam – open up. Miriam! Come on now man, open up. (*She bangs on the door.*) Miriam. (*Nobody opens – she bangs louder.*) Miriam!!! Christ – where's she now? (*She looks at her watch.*) Ten past eight – now where's she?

She looks up and down the street and gets out a cig and lights up. She starts looking in her bag for the keys. She then starts emptying all the contents of her bag on to the pavement. MRS DUBOIS is on the street – we hear her voice offstage.

MRS DUBOIS. Close the security gates, man! What do you think we put them up for? For security! You got to keep them closed!! I dunno how many times I got to tell you to do that . . . Morning Mr Patel . . . Letitia! Get your head out of those bladdy railings. Go in to your mother, man. You kids mustn't play on the edge like that, it's dangerous. Inside – toe nou! Morning, morning, morning . . .

ROLENE. You perky . . .

MRS DUBOIS. Well of course, I got to be – because today, Rolene, is my lucky day. I had this dream – and there they were: 4,1,10,7,2,5 – in that order. They flashed in and flashed out. So I knew – today Rolene, my numbers is A1 – wind and weather permitting – there's no going wrong for me. So what's the matter with you now?

ROLENE. Well what does it look like?

MRS DUBOIS. Well it looks to me like you sitting on the pavement – no man, Rolene, put that tampax back in your bag, this is not the . . .

ROLENE. Miriam hasn't pitched.

MRS DUBOIS. Ja well, that's Miriam, always taking chances. You let her get away with murder, my girl – you soft as butter. I'm telling you – you give them enough rope and they'll hang you.

ROLENE. So here I sit like a bladdy moegoe, waiting to get into my own hairdressers. And you know what, I'm even lucky to be alive – I was now nearly tramped there in the street.

MRS DUBOIS. By what?

ROLENE. One of those bladdy black taxis – I must now walk in the road cause all these blacks is sitting with their furniture and things outside Belair Mansions – taking up all the pavement space – and that road is busy hey. I mean, why must they sit in the pavement? Ag, they got no shame.

MRS DUBOIS. Ag it will still take a thousand years to still educate that bunch. Look under the mat.

ROLENE. What?

MRS DUBOIS. Under the mat! Some people leave keys in their pot plants, why can't they leave it under the mat?

ROLENE. Ag please, who leaves a key under a mat?

MRS DUBOIS. I'm sure I've seen her leave it – just look! No man not now, you got to look when nobody's looking. Okay, it's clear – look!

ROLENE (*finds the keys*). My God . . . is she mad!

MRS DUBOIS. Ja, that one – she's getting very white these days. (*Phone starts to ring.*)

ROLENE (*struggles with the door*). Shit – give me a hand here quick – hurry!

MRS DUBOIS. What must I do?

ROLENE. Just kick the door here for me. Push, man. (*They battle with the door.*)

MRS DUBOIS. I'm pushing!

The door flies open. ROLENE *dashes for the phone – it rings off.*

ROLENE. Damn it – that could have been a customer . . .

MRS DUBOIS. Hell, this place looks like a bomb's gone off – no man you must get her in here. Never mind, whoever it was will phone again.

ROLENE. Jissus Miriam – just you show that face of yours in that door and you dead, my girl!

MRS DUBOIS. Okay, my sweetheart – so will you be able to do me later then?

ROLENE. Where you going?

MRS DUBOIS. To give in my Pick Six! They say if you get your numbers in early, you got a much better chance.

ROLENE. Okay bye.

MRS DUBOIS. Wish me luck.

ROLENE. Good luck.

MRS DUBOIS. Bye lovie . . . (*She exits.*)

Meanwhile ROLENE *goes over to switch the lights on. She feels something furry on her foot.*

ROLENE. Aaagh!! (*She runs to the lightswitch.*) Ooh, gonna, if that's a rat I'm going to, I'm going to . . . faint. (*She switches on the light.*) Ag sis man, it's yesterday's hair. (*She then goes to switch on the radio and then the kettle. While doing so, she's mumbling and grumbling to herself.*) This place is a mess, looks like a bladdy pigsty. I'm not picking up people's dead hair, sis – I'm a hairdresser, not a bladdy sweeping girl. This is disgusting. So now who's going to do the shampooing, and what about the mix for my highlights and my lowlights – Miriam you've had it, my girl.

(*She stands in front of mirror and starts doing something with her hair – phone rings.*)

Curl Up and Dye International, can I help you? Yes . . . Rolene . . . Ja of course it's me . . . At the salon. Ag Denzil, don't be such a doos, what number did you just dial? . . . When . . . what about five minutes ago? . . . I was trying to get in . . . Yes I am . . . About what? . . . Then talk . . . Listen Denzil, don't you bokkie me . . . Sorry se voet! Every time afterwards you come and say you sorry you sorry . . . So, are you going to get the TV back then? . . . Today Denzil! . . . But didn't I just say I'm here by myself. Well if you don't believe me, come down here and check . . . Ag nobody's whistling at me, Denzil man – shit it's the bladdy kettle.

ROLENE *slams down the phone and continues with her hair and starts to touch up her make-up. A few minutes later the phone rings again.*

Curl Up and Dye International can I help you? . . . Jissus Denzil, now what. You can't keep phoning me man – this is a business line, now hurry up, what you want? . . . Jissus Denzil sometimes you act like a real doos – the toilet paper is in the toilet and if it's not in the toilet it's at the Spar! There's five rand in my panty drawer. And don't send the child!

He puts the phone down on her. She replaces the receiver, goes to switch off the kettle and returns to the mirror – adjusts her make-up. She is totally absorbed in herself and doesn't hear or see CHARMAINE. CHARMAINE *enters.*

ROLENE. Jees Charmaine, you gave me a skrik!

CHARMAINE. Ey Rolene, score us a smoke.

ROLENE. Don't you say hello anymore?

CHARMAINE. Don't tune me nothing Rolene, just score us a smoke, ek sê.

ROLENE. Okay, all right, here take – but this will be the last time you bum a cigarette off me if you carry on like this hey. What's wrong with you man? Your pimp or whatever his name is klap you? And now you got to take it out on me!

CHARMAINE. Make a light.

ROLENE. What?

CHARMAINE. A match man.

ROLENE. Oh . . . there in my bag.

CHARMAINE. Where's Miriam?

ROLENE. Never mind where's Miriam, where were you?

CHARMAINE. When?

ROLENE. Last night Charmaine – I was in trouble, I was in the shit!

CHARMAINE. What's his pluck this time?

ROLENE. All I said was, 'Ja, you got enough money to buy a hi-fi and all that, but now they come and take our TV away because you got nothing left to pay for it.' So he moers me a left-hander like I never seen before . . .

CHARMAINE. Sss . . . that ouen . . .

ROLENE. . . . . right off my feet – I knocked my head so bladdy hard on the divider, I think I was out unconscious. Now is that fair – I mean what am I going to do every night – sit and watch a hi-fi?

CHARMAINE. That's ous for you, ek sê.

ROLENE. And it's not nice for the kid to see it hey. So I sent her next door to you – your lights was on.

CHARMAINE. I know.

ROLENE. So why didn't you answer – were you busy?

CHARMAINE. Ag kak man – I wasn't there.

ROLENE. So where was you? (CHARMAINE *turns away*.) And it was late I think, after three.

CHARMAINE. Quintus is dying.

ROLENE. What?

CHARMAINE. In hospital . . . It's radical, he's not in such a kif state.

ROLENE. I'll make you some coffee. Charmaine, are you all right?

CHARMAINE. Actually I'm not so cool. (*She grabs hold of the door and screams out.*) Jakkals you teef! You scheme you so safe on the corner there, but you way off track, goffel – that was a fucken blind move you pulled, ek sê – I scheme you going to be very fucken sorry, very fucken sorry. Fucken sorry!

ROLENE. So is Quintus going to make it?

CHARMAINE. The nurse and that don't scheme he will. He's on a drip and all that.

ROLENE. A drip! Charmaine, what happened? – here's your coffee.

CHARMAINE. Yiss . . . and he didn't want to get into a rawl, man. I was there jus watching – but I couldn't do nothing.

ROLENE. Where – there by the corner there?

CHARMAINE. Quintus didn't have the knife in his hand.

ROLENE. Come, Charmaine, drink your coffee. I'm sure he's going to be all right.

CHARMAINE. We had jus slukked a card of pinks – so we were going like a Boeing. Then this one coloured tunes me,

'Charmaine let's go for a trip under the skin.' So I chaff him, 'Ey but, can't you check I got my own guy here?' And the General tunes, 'Ey what did the coloured say?' So Quintus tunes, 'It's none of your business . . .'

ROLENE. To the General! Is he mad?

CHARMAINE. Quintus turns round, Jakkals klaps him from behind, I scream, 'Quintus, he's got a knife – duck!' Too late – he shluks open his cheek and stabs him here . . . the blood kept spilling from his chest . . . I wanted to cry . . . but I couldn't . . . and the knife, I dunno, it went in funny, it went into his heart . . .

ROLENE. Did you call the police?

CHARMAINE. The General jus laughs . . . I got to make a phone call. Rolene can I use the phone?

ROLENE. What – to the hospital?

CHARMAINE. Ey please my china – just one call.

ROLENE. All right, but just this time. And keep it short hey – this is a business line.

CHARMAINE *starts phoning.*

CHARMAINE. Howzit Spud . . . Can I have a line with PC . . . cool that's no saak. Is JJ there . . . I mean jaaa . . . who's parking off at this pozzy . . . Mellow, let me tune a few words with Des . . . cool.

MRS DUBOIS (*from street*). Ninety-five cents for a plum?! You mad man . . .

CHARMAINE. Howzit Des what's the move at your cabin, ek sê . . . Kif . . . when must I pull in? . . . Kwaai. Are you shpiking? . . . Cool. Ey but I got no bucks . . . nooit it's cool . . . I'll handle it . . . Ja.

MRS DUBOIS *enters.* CHARMAINE *carries on talking on the phone but she becomes inaudible.*

MRS DUBOIS. Hell, that Patel's a highway robbery shark . . . (*Noticing* CHARMAINE.) So what was her story?

ROLENE. What story?

MRS DUBOIS. Man this business of Quintus and the knife and all that. What was her version?

ROLENE. No shame, she says he got stabbed here by the corner last night but it wasn't his fault cause he didn't . . .

MRS DUBOIS. Se voet it wasn't his fault! One minute he's fine – the next minute he's there like a raving maniac.

ROLENE. What, were you there?

MRS DUBOIS. Of course, you know me Rolene, I don't miss a
thing. And they were making such a bladdy racket everyone else
was out there watching too – the whole world and his wife – and
the way they were performing and carrying on, Quintus
screaming and shouting, 'Leave my F . . . ing chick' and 'F . . .
you' – you know – it was embarrassing, man. Such filthy
language. And they started it hey, I'm telling you Rolene.

ROLENE. But Charmaine said it was Jakkals who . . .

MRS DUBOIS. Naag rubbish, she was so hoog on the takke she
wouldn't know what the hell was going on – so Quintus pulls
out a knife.

ROLENE. But you sure it was a knife?

MRS DUBOIS. As sure as my name is Hettie Coralinda Dubois. It
was Quintus and he pulled the knife – I saw it. Look Rolene, I
wasn't born with concrete above my ears hey. Would he be
standing there waving his arm around like a mad thing if it was
a cigarette? I mean really, it was a bladdy knife. So then this
other bloke, what's it – um – Jakkals ja, he then tries to stop
him – no luck – so he also draws a knife.

ROLENE. You serious.

MRS DUBOIS. Ja, so Quintus was in a spot of tight water, but he
was so high he didn't even notice and I think he ran right into
the knife!

ROLENE. I can't believe it.

MRS DUBOIS. Ja, that's what happened – he ran into the knife –
end of story.

ROLENE. But . . .

MRS DUBOIS. No buts . . . that's the truth Rolene – hot from the
horse's mouth – there you have it in a nutshell – take what you
want.

MIRIAM *arrives*.

MIRIAM. Morning, good morning . . .

MRS DUBOIS. And where were you Miriam? What's this coming in
at the time you arrive! For Pete's sake man, you must come on
time!

ROLENE. Miriam knows she's late, hey Miriam. Morning Miriam.
So put your things down Miriam and when you ready, get
going, all right.

MIRIAM. Thank you Rolene. Morning Charmaine.

CHARMAINE. Howzit Miriam.

MRS DUBOIS. Well next time you sitting on the pavement don't come and complain to me! I never have this kind of a problem with my staff. Make no bones about it. I don't beat around the bush – they bugger me around upstairs, they must go. I don't want to hear their troubles man. They must just do their job – that's all I ask.

CHARMAINE. Ag poes man! (*She slams down phone.*) So Rolene, can you borrow me some coupons? I got to get back to the hospital.

ROLENE. Well like how much do you want?

CHARMAINE. Thirty will be shwak!

MRS DUBOIS. For crying in a bucket Rolene – open your eyes man. Since when has she ever paid you back what she owes you?

CHARMAINE. Ey you.

MRS DUBOIS. Who me? Is she now talking to me?

CHARMAINE. Stay out of this, ek sê.

MRS DUBOIS. Ag I don't talk to druggies man – please . . .

CHARMAINE. You befuck, you know.

MRS DUBOIS. So Rolene I'm just telling you as a friend – don't be stupid man. You got to draw a line! You can't keep handing out money to 'this cause' your whole life. I mean, hell's bells . . .

CHARMAINE. Watch it Tannie – you making me lank the moer in.

ROLENE. Have a bit of heart, shame, can't you see she's going through a bad time.

MRS DUBOIS. Bad time huh – she's always going through bad times. No, she'll never get her life right. That one, she's good for nothing!

CHARMAINE. Ey what did you tune me – come speak up quick.

MRS DUBOIS. I said I don't talk to drugged-up rubbishes!

CHARMAINE. Come tune that here to my face – come!

MRS DUBOIS. I really don't know how you put up with her Rolene – she can't even talk properly she's so deurmekaar.

CHARMAINE. Come on, Tannie – come tune that here to my face – look in my eyes and say it – come you teef, come.

MRS DUBOIS. Watch it my girl – you skating thin on the edge of a wedge!

CHARMAINE. Check the worry in my eye . . . (CHARMAINE *starts moving in on* MRS DUBOIS. MRS DUBOIS *starts backing away.*) Ey you sig – are you sig?

MRS DUBOIS. Don't you dare touch me.

CHARMAINE. Touch you – I'll fucken moer you sat – I'll skop you mif you zic! Don't come be wise with me – I'll fucken klap you down so short you'll need a stepladder to get into your shoes – you fucken larney teef! (*She tries to swipe* MRS DUBOIS.)

MRS DUBOIS. Rolene! Stop her – do something!

ROLENE. Charmaine! Stop it man – this is a hair salon not the bladdy street.

MRS DUBOIS. Get her out Rolene – she's gone mad man, get her out!

ROLENE. Come Charmaine – I'll give you fifteen rands, it'll just have to do. (ROLENE *goes to get the money.*) Here.

CHARMAINE. Ey fully kif – thanks a span Rolene. (*She shouts out towards door and street.*) Ey Tiger – hold on! . . . Rolene, I got to make like Donald.

ROLENE. What?

CHARMAINE. Make a duck, ek sê. I'll check you later. (*She goes.*)

MIRIAM. Ow! that Charmaine, she's too naughty sometimes – coffee or tea, Mrs Dubois?

ROLENE. Yes, ag – but shame Miriam, her boyfriend just got stabbed here on the corner last night.

MIRIAM. Which one is that now?

ROLENE. Ag Quintus man – the one with the scar here – he's laying in hospital.

MIRIAM. Aw shame – she's got too much troubles that one.

MRS DUBOIS. Nonsense Miriam – she's the one that comes and causes all the trouble and Rolene still calls her a friend! Good God Rolene, I've said my say but really you got to choose your friends man. That's what . . .

ROLENE. Charmaine is my friend. She's always been good to me and my kid hey – so I'm going to treat her the way I want to treat her. It's got nothing to do with you – right? And second of all, Miriam works for me hey, not you.

MRS DUBOIS. But I was just . . .

ROLENE. No – this is my salon here –

MRS DUBOIS. It's not your salon, Rolene, you don't own it.

ROLENE. Ja . . . Okay . . . but I'm the hairdresser here. Now what must she think when you come and shout at her like that hey? I'm Miriam's boss – you don't come and step in – all right!!?

MIRIAM. Ja, thank you Rolene. Rolene you want tea or coffee?

ROLENE. I'll have coffee, thank you, Miriam sweetheart . . . .

MRS DUBOIS (*mumbles*). Excuse me for breathing . . .

ROLENE. And a half a sugar and skim milk.

MIRIAM. You sure you won't have any coffee or tea, Mrs Dubois?

MRS DUBOIS. No thank you Miriam, I won't have right now, I don't feel like drinking!

MIRIAM. Oh. (*She goes towards the kitchen.*)

MRS DUBOIS. So how are you today Miriam? Have you still got that terrible backache?

MIRIAM. It is still painful, Mrs Dubois, but I've got other big troubles.

MRS DUBOIS. Ag Miriam be a darling and bring me a stool. This wicked sore foot is playing up again – you know ever since that blooming car accident it's never got itself right. Aai . . . the throb . . .

MIRIAM (*brings stool*). Oh Mrs Dubois – this foot, it's too much!

MRS DUBOIS. Ouch and when the weather changes that's when I'd just like to just chop it off.

MIRIAM. And on the same side as the hip too – it never rains!

MRS DUBOIS. Mmm, it's probably connected – mind you it's a wonder it doesn't klap the knee first. Instead it shoots right past the knee and plunges like five daggers into the foot.

ROLENE. So why don't you take it to a specialist?

MRS DUBOIS. Which – the hip or the foot?

ROLENE. Any – whichever you love better.

MRS DUBOIS. Naag – I've given up on them – all big talk and no action – look what they did for Mervin – at nineteen and he's still got the mind of a two year old. When that child came out of his third coma he couldn't walk, he couldn't talk. . .

ROLENE. So what happened at Frankie and Roger's engagement?

MRS DUBOIS. Hey?

ROLENE. In the Colbys man! Did that arsehole . . . what's his name – man, the bloke with the voice – did he break up his affair?

MRS DUBOIS. Don't tell me you missed it.

ROLENE. Miriam, my coffee. And Sable, shame – did Zach walk out on her?

MRS DUBOIS. Yere, were you gallivanting on Wednesday or something?

ROLENE. Don't make jokes – since when do I go out?

MRS DUBOIS. Then what – were you otherwise engaged? . . .

ROLENE. No man – my TV's gone.

MRS DUBOIS. On the blank?

ROLENE. Ja – so Denzil took it for repairs.

MRS DUBOIS. He's a good bloke that, your husband.

ROLENE. No I can't complain. So did Fallon leave the mansion? Spoilt bitch!

MIRIAM. Ja, she left the mansion and then Frankie and Roger broke the engagement and Jeff didn't want to come back from overseas so then the other girl – what's her name? – the one who wanted Jeff to get the money from his mother? Well that one, she went also overseas to look for him but now he was with another girl and . . .

MRS DUBOIS. Naag rubbish Miriam – you got it all mixed up man – that's *Dynasty*!

ROLENE. Nonsense, man – it is the Colbys – they got Bop there in Soweto man – she's three serials ahead of us.

MRS DUBOIS. What?

MIRIAM. Ja – and Fallon she's going to marry . . .

ROLENE. No don't Miriam! – shush – don't – you spoiling it for · us!

MRS DUBOIS (*covering her ears and closing her eyes*). I'm blocking my ears. (*Shouts even louder.*) Have a heart man, Miriam.

The hysteria dies and they burst our laughing.

ROLENE. Ooh no I'm sorry, we can't sit on our arses all day and skinner about the Colbys – we got a business to run here. No, Fallon must sommer sort her own problems out. Miriam, sweetheart, check the appointment book . . .

MIRIAM. Nobody came.

ROLENE. What?

MIRIAM. Nobody came to say they want to come, so we can all go home.

MRS DUBOIS. Hey, hey, hey, hey – what kind of a attitude is this now Miriam?

ROLENE. You sure you looked on the right day Miriam?

MIRIAM. Dead sure Rolene – Saturday 29th.

ROLENE. Ja, well, then you better go stand outside with your board.

MIRIAM. But Rolene this board business – it doesn't work – we never once caught a customer with this board.

ROLENE. Miriam, just write the specials and get out there with that board!

MIRIAM *gets the blackboard, writes in the specials and goes to stand on the pavement with it, shouting out the styles.* ROLENE *is still busy with the crossword.*

ROLENE. Come help me choose the better word here, please.

MRS DUBOIS. Ag, you not into that rubbish again.

ROLENE. A hundred and ten thousand rands.

MRS DUBOIS. Sounds terrific but hell do you know what the hell they talking about?

ROLENE. Ja . . . it's simple. Like here number four across, 'In the movies the way the police barge or burst into a room shows they have turned the type of activity into a fine art.' Now we got to choose burst or barge?

MRS DUBOIS. Barge.

ROLENE. You see – barge – simple!

MRS DUBOIS. So you sommer put barge?! . . .

ROLENE. Right – now the next one . . .

MRS DUBOIS. But I thought barge was like a kind of ship . . .

ROLENE. Number five down . . . 'When the wise . . .'

MRS DUBOIS. Oh no, but I suppose you can barge in too . . . ja . . .

ROLENE. 'When the wise fisherman . . .'

MRS DUBOIS. But then you can burst in also . . . burst . . . well they burst in last night.

ROLENE. Who?

MRS DUBOIS. The cops! What – didn't I tell you what happened?

ROLENE. No, what?

MRS DUBOIS. You mean you haven't heard?

ROLENE. What?

MRS DUBOIS. You mean – nobody's told you yet?

ROLENE. Now what you talking – you already told me about Quintus.

MRS DUBOIS. No what! 'Her' story's got no flies on this one – this story is a story and a half my girl – a real drama!

ROLENE. Okay let me guess.

MRS DUBOIS. Never in a thousand years will you guess right.

ROLENE. Okay give me a clue.

MRS DUBOIS. All right – Harvard Mansions. But that's it hey – no more clues.

ROLENE (*with much enthusiasm*). They blew it up!

MRS DUBOIS. I wish – but you cold. No man, you never going to get it – all right I'll just tell you.

MIRIAM (*still outside with the board*). We have our own special – Hollywood – at only twenty-five rands – next month it's thirty – so please, save yourself five rands and come right now! (*She repeats in Zulu.*)

MRS DUBOIS. Well apparently the cops – you know, Special Branch, had been watching Harvard Mansions for the past three days. Of course I wasn't entirely aware of this because those blokes are very smart you know.

ROLENE. They got to be.

MRS DUBOIS. That's right, they know how to make themselves scarce.

ROLENE. And it's about time they took some action. The amount of dagga and liquor that's running around in that building – it's unreal, unreal.

MRS DUBOIS. Telling me.

ROLENE. And the people that stays there just hangs out their window all day . . . .

MRS DUBOIS. What a eyesore!

ROLENE. You know I really wish they would blow that block up – for once and for all now.

MRS DUBOIS. End of problem.

ROLENE. You know, it even won the Bad Conditions Award last month in the *Joburg Herald.*

MRS DUBOIS. Really, so who won the Best Conditions?

ROLENE. Ag, I can't remember. Now come on, get to the point – hurry up, I've got a business to run here – so what happened?

MRS DUBOIS. Don't rush me Rolene – you know I like to take my time so I can remember every little thing. So they say . . .

ROLENE. Who says?

MRS DUBOIS. Ag man Grieta, the caretaker at Harvard and her husband, they say twenty-five plainclothes but to me it looked more like thirty-five, from Hillbrow branch, surrounded the block just before 3 a.m. And there they sat, waiting.

ROLENE. For what?

MRS DUBOIS. Rolene, use your brain man! Waiting for things to hot up in there, you know what with it being a Friday night and all. So come 3 a.m. on the dot – and those boys are punctual hey – all thirty-five of them burst in, or barged in, whatever you want, from every direction. Caught them in the act – all red-handed.

ROLENE. That will teach them – I mean if they want to live in a white people's area, then they must behave like a white people – not so?

MRS DUBOIS. And did they do a thorough job. Mind you they made one helluva racket and a half – kicking doors down, smashing windows out, people screaming, guns shooting – honest to God, I thought a bomb had gone off.

ROLENE. Did they shoot anyone dead?

MRS DUBOIS. No – just warning shots. But I took my courage in both my hands and went out there to have a look – still in my nightie mind you – Rolene! I could not believe my eyeballs – there they were taking away two bakkie loads of prostitutes – blacks, whites, coloureds – you name it – mixed deurmekaar – all squashed in like a tin of sardines.

ROLENE. All from inside Harvard?

MRS DUBOIS. All from inside Harvard!

ROLENE. Ooh no, sis – but that's disgusting.

MRS DUBOIS. No – it was rude – not to this very day have I ever
seen such a mix in such a small space – I'm telling you it was
tragic – really tragic!

ROLENE. I'm glad I didn't see it.

MRS DUBOIS. I must say I'm quite surprised your 'friend' didn't
land up in there too.

ROLENE. She's not like one of those.

MRS DUBOIS. Hmm – you'll be a bit surprised! But that's all I'm
saying, my lips are sealed – Ooh God Rolene. (*She jumps up.*)

ROLENE. What?

MRS DUBOIS. I think I left the iron on upstairs.

ROLENE. Ooh yere – you better go turn it off then.

MRS DUBOIS. So will you do me later then Rolene?

ROLENE. Ja – anytime . . . .

(*As* MRS DUBOIS *leaves* ROLENE *shouts.*)

ROLENE. Hey, so what do I put? Burst or barge?

MRS DUBOIS (*popping head back in*). Go for barge! (*Leaves.*) Ooh
Miriam, you still at it hey? Don't worry, it won't be long before
you catch your fish. Letitia! You'll break your bladdy neck and I
won't say I didn't warn you hey – get inside you brat!

MIRIAM *still shouts to passersby outside.* ROLENE *gets up to call her.*

ROLENE. Okay, Miriam come. Now tell me – why were you late
this morning?

MIRIAM (*coming back inside*). Oh Rolene – I've got problems.

ROLENE. Listen Miriam – it's always another excuse hey?

MIRIAM. I know Rolene but . . .

ROLENE. No buts Miriam – you know I like you here at 8 sharp –
what you think this is – a free for all?

MIRIAM. I'm sorry Rolene, but we got troubles there in the
township. My little one – she must enrol at the school. Now I
haven't got the money to pay school fees and already she is
more than a month behind – so my sister-in-law she borrowed
me a little bit – to lay down as a deposit. Now this morning I

had to take the child myself so I can explain to the principal.

ROLENE. No well then that's it hey – you not to come late again – you hear?

MIRIAM. Shame and that child must learn – she wants to learn.

ROLENE. Ja, well then she better stick by that school and not start with that rubbish nonsense of strikings and what and what . . .

MIRIAM. But then they must take the soldiers out of the schools.

ROLENE. Ag Miriam you got to understand man – the soldiers is only there to keep their eyes in control. I mean can you imagine what it would be like if they wasn't there?

MIRIAM. Hallelujah!

ROLENE. Ja well anyway that's enough talk. Plus Miriam, and I haven't forgotten hey, you left here yesterday without even sweeping up that last customer.

MIRIAM. But Rolene I told you why I had . . .

ROLENE. No Miriam I'm sorry, I think you taking a bit of a advantage here with me – I give you a hand and you grab my whole bladdy foot! Just remember who's boss around here.

MIRIAM. Yes Madame – does Madame want some coffee?

ROLENE. No! All right yes. But first I want all this hair swept up and Miriam – God be with you if I then find one single strand of hair hey. And I only want half a sugar and skim milk.

MIRIAM *goes off to get her broom and starts sweeping up the hair. It doesn't take long and then she makes* ROLENE *her coffee.* ROLENE *goes back to doing her crossword puzzle. Maybe a song on the radio comes on that both* MIRIAM *and* ROLENE *sing along with.*

ROLENE (*reading the question from the newspaper*). Right, number eight down, 'Anyone who sees a school performance of *Hamlet* will feel virtuous that he can claim that he (sat or saw) it without wishing he was somewhere else' . . . My God . . . so it's sat or saw . . .

MIRIAM. Here's your coffee, Rolene.

ROLENE. Thanks Miriam. Ag sweetheart, you want to come and help me here quick?

MIRIAM. Rolene, you know I always like to learn new 'high class' words.

ROLENE. Okay – you listening?

MIRIAM. With all my ears!

ROLENE. All right – it's number eight down – this is it, 'Anyone who sees a school performance of *Hamlet* will feel . . .'

MIRIAM. *Hamlet?*

ROLENE. Miriam, first let me finish up with the sentence, then I'll explain. Now I'm just carrying straight on – '. . . a school performance of *Hamlet* will feel virtuous that he can claim he sat or saw it without wishing he were somewhere else.' Now we got to choose the right word – you know, the word that sounds better.

MIRIAM. But there so many words.

ROLENE. Miriam just choose one – is it sat or is it saw?

MIRIAM. But I still don't know what a hamlet is?

ROLENE. Yere Miriam – this is the last time I play with you man – you ask too many questions.

MIRIAM. But how am I supposed to learn these high class words if you don't teach me.

ROLENE. All right then, what do you think it means?

MIRIAM. A hamlet? I know a helmet.

ROLENE. Ag yere, Miriam, but sometimes you can be real stupid. A Hamlet is a . . . a small piece of ham – simple.

MIRIAM. Aah – a piglet?

ROLENE. Yes. So what do we put – sat or saw?

MIRIAM. Saw – put saw.

ROLENE. Why saw?

MIRIAM. You can see mos it's clear, Rolene. You can't sat a pig – but you can saw a pig . . .

ROLENE. No, you right there Miriam (*She writes in the word.*) S - A - W. You know Miriam I got this deep-down feeling that this time I'm going to win.

MIRIAM. Really Rolene?

ROLENE. Ja – cos you never know where your luck lies. And what's it to them anyway – a hundred and ten thousand rands. . .

MIRIAM. I could buy myself a house in Prestige Park, 118 Taylor Street, Diepkloof Extension, 2014. . .

ROLENE. And they never going to miss it – no ways – this time it's coming straight to me, written on a big cheque, 'To Mrs Rolene Venter – one hundred and ten thousand rands' – cash! (*She stands up and starts talking to an imaginary* DENZIL.) I'm so very sorry Denzil but it's in my name you see, in ink! I've won it on my own and you not going to get a cent!

MIRIAM. Haai Rolene – uh-uh. Then he will come in here and hit you too hard – then you will have a blue eye on your cheek.

ROLENE. Don't he dare try and touch me! And I'm taking the child!

MIRIAM. Ow shame.

ROLENE. I'm gonna get me a Mexican house – say in Parktown – a double storey with a yard for Liselle. . .

MIRIAM. Haw! Rolene that's where the posh madams live. . .

ROLENE. . . . and . . . and it's going to have carpets – edge to edge in a fluffy off-beige colour . . . and . . . and I'm going to get me that lounge suite from Garlicks – the one with the flower pattern in navy and gold.

MIRIAM. And Rolene you won't have to buy it on lay-by!

ROLENE. No ways! No sir no thanks. No I don't need to pay it off monthly – I'm putting down cash right here and now. And please deliver it to my house, please thanks. . .

MIRIAM. No wait Rolene – don't go before you buy you this smart kingsize bed here with the headboard and dressing table to match.

ROLENE. Oh yes, and I'll take two designer duvets please.

MIRIAM. And this hoover here for your carpet.

ROLENE. And that fridge there – the double door with freezer inclusive.

MIRIAM. And a big colour TV.

ROLENE. With the video and M-Net decoder please thanks.

MIRIAM. Washing machine?

ROLENE. Plus tumble dryer and ag shame just throw in that ninja turtle doll for the kid.

ROLENE *and* MIRIAM *grab hold of one another.* MRS DUBOIS *enters. They snap out of it and resume their habitual roles.*

MRS DUBOIS. Rolene – you will not believe what I have just heard my girl . . .

ROLENE. What?

MRS DUBOIS. In Harvard Mansions. Twelve ANC terrorists!

MIRIAM *starts laughing.*

ROLENE. Miriam, go stand outside with your board.

MIRIAM. But Rolene, this board . . .

ROLENE. All right then, go buy me cigarettes by the café, quick quick.

MRS DUBOIS. And Grieta doesn't lie hey. And there was no doubting this bunch that is for sure. Papers with lists – ammunitions – books – filing systems! Apparently it was so obvious, all of them sleeping in a row, you know dormitory style – just like in their camps.

ROLENE. But how did they know they were terrorists?

MRS DUBOIS. It's not difficult Rolene – Grieta says when you see one you know.

MIRIAM, *just leaving, laughs.*

ROLENE. No Denzil's right. He says it won't be long before we all get wiped out here. If it's not a bomb then it's the AIDS. He says they carrying it with them from the mines. But next time . . .

MRS DUBOIS. There won't be a next time!

ROLENE. Exactly! And why??

MRS DUBOIS. Because 'our boys' are getting jacked up man.

ROLENE. No – because next time their bombs will find us first.

MRS DUBOIS. That's not a very pleasant thought, Rolene . . .

ROLENE. I hate this place! . . .

MRS DUBOIS. . . . so let's not think about it too hard – all right?

ROLENE. He's right – we haven't got a hope in hell . . .

MRS DUBOIS (*gets up*). Ooh hell, this spare rib – I'm sure it's pierced my lung! So are you finished up with your crossword, Rolene?

ROLENE. No.

MRS DUBOIS. So come, let me help you finish it off – I was getting to quite like it.

ROLENE. Ag, I don't feel like doing it anymore.

MRS DUBOIS. Ag come now Rolene – snap out of this man – it's not making anything better. I tell you what – you tell me what number it is and I'll give it a bash on my own.

ROLENE. Seventeen across.

MRS DUBOIS. Got it. 'When organised hecklers march in and disrupt a political meeting, that is the kind of (farce, foray, furore) that makes political speakers despondent.' My God you've given me a blooming difficult one here.

ROLENE. I know, I already tried it.

MRS DUBOIS. Farce, foray or furore?

ROLENE. Do you know what a foray is?

MRS DUBOIS. A foray? Well I know a forel is some kind of a fish but a foray? Are you sure it's English?

ROLENE (*with great assurance*). Oh yes, F - O - R - A - Y.

MRS DUBOIS. Well at least I know farce – it's like going fast.

ROLENE. Farce – F - A - R - C - E. No man . . . it's . . . I feel farce . . . Well haven't you heard people say I feel farce?

MRS DUBOIS. What's this now – modern talk?

ROLENE. You know like – I feel naar – you know, sick. So you say I feel farce, I think I'm going to faint or . . . I think I'm gonna faint cause I feel farce, but foray I don't know.

MRS DUBOIS. I wish Koosie was here – my third husband – he'd know what to do. Anyway what the hell am I doing this for man? I've got my Pick Six. No I'm sorry Rolene. With the Pick Six you got a much better chance. All you got to do is choose six numbers – simple. Take for example the time when Mervin had his accident – you know, over there by the art gallery . . .

ROLENE. Ja . . . ja.

MRS DUBOIS. Now I had to write down the number plate you see – of the van that ran him down – hell, to this day I will never forget that number ND 417426. Two weeks later I'm busy with my Pick Six and this 417426 just pops into my head. So I closed my eyes – I prayed for Mervin and I sommer put them down – and that time I was one number out my girl – one number! That's how close I was!

ROLENE. So why aren't you on your balcony watching car plates?

MRS DUBOIS. No Rolene – lightning never strikes in the same place twice.

ROLENE. So how much is it?

MRS DUBOIS. How much is it? – What? – What? – How much am I going to win?

ROLENE. No man, how much to enter?

MRS DUBOIS. Two rand – and you can win my girl. You'll see me –
    Umhlanga there – right on the beach in a fancy flat, right on
    the top, so I can see all the way to Durban – I just hope it's not
    bad for my hip.

ROLENE. No, they say the sea salt is very good for a hip.

MRS DUBOIS. Come two o'clock and I don't budge from that TV
    my girl. I got the wireless going and the TV and I got the
    papers – just to double check. So you better have me finished
    here by one, hey.

ROLENE. Why don't I just do you now and finish – come, what you
    having?

MRS DUBOIS. Ag the usual, you know, a brush out to perk me up
    for the weekend. Why, you busy later?

ROLENE. Busy! Please, don't make me laugh. And you know what?
    I don't even blame the customers for not coming – what for?
    They come for a haircut they get their throat cut! No – uh-uh. I
    wouldn't come. I mean – would you?

MRS DUBOIS. But I do come Rolene.

ROLENE. And it's not just this business that's gone down, it's
    everything – rats in the street, even now in my flat there's
    cockaroaches and bed bugs . . .

MRS DUBOIS. Ooh no sis . . .

ROLENE. . . . which the blacks brings in – as if I haven't got enough
    worries – 'strue – I'm not lying – and I clean my house every
    night hey – plus Charmaine says she's seen one in our block.

MRS DUBOIS. What . . . a rat?

ROLENE. No man, a black! Apparently she moved in a couple of
    weeks ago.

MRS DUBOIS. Have you seen her?

ROLENE. No ways – cause the caretaker says she's got to be out of
    the block by six and she can't come back till 10.30 p.m.

MRS DUBOIS. Must be a prostitute – who else could afford the
    rent?

ROLENE. Must be – but I'm telling you – this is the beginning of
    the end hey? I know, I've been through it all already.

MRS DUBOIS. Where?

ROLENE. The reason we moved out those flats there by Smit Street was because I was the only white left on my floor.

MRS DUBOIS. Good heavens!

ROLENE. You should of seen that place when we moved in there, it was a very clean building, you know, serviced and all that. Now when this blacks and that moved in, it was already starting to like – put me off – like it wasn't my cup of tea – and my husband as well . . .

MRS DUBOIS. It's their cooking and that you know . . . like their smells are all very different . . .

ROLENE. Telling me – and you know how the girl comes to clean your floors, passages and dustbins and that. Right now that poor girl can just be finished with your floors to go to another floor and that floor is dirty again.

MRS DUBOIS. No respect!

ROLENE. Cos they don't care . . . and . . . and they come out on their balcony with just a little blanket around them, no nighties or nothing on.

MRS DUBOIS. Good God!

ROLENE. And there they stand – naked – for everyone to see . . . now is that nice? Then you got them walking up and down your corridors . . .

MRS DUBOIS. Ooh no!

ROLENE. . . . they peering into your flat . . .

MRS DUBOIS. Ooh Lord!

ROLENE. . . . and the fightings! It never stopped. You must just open your door at any given time and there, right in front of your eyes they half killing each other. And the blood is flying and you getting a klap here and a fist there and now what must you do? Must my child grow up with all this goings on around her? I'm sorry – no ways! But what I want to know is who gave them permission to move in in the first place? And the fault is on the government! You know, at least they could of given us a fair warning that this was going to happen here. But they don't come clear!

MRS DUBOIS. And who has to suffer? The man in the street!

ROLENE. Exactly, cos people have told me this is not a multiracial area.

MRS DUBOIS. It's nobody's area!

ROLENE. But now everybody says Joubert Park, Joubert Park – it's a grey area. My arse, this isn't grey, it's black!

MRS DUBOIS. Okay, let's be realistic now – Joubert Park is not the Joubert Park I used to live in. In my day people used to come to the park with their picnic baskets . . .

ROLENE. I wouldn't put my foot in that park – anyway Denzil won't let me, he says it's a death trap!

MRS DUBOIS. Ja well that's it – this place's turned into a blooming bioscope – skop, skiet and donner.

ROLENE. Ja and even now in our new place – they guaranteed us – and now look what's happening – and ever since she's moved in our rents has shot up. Let's face it there's no place for us here anymore. No, we got to get out while we can.

MRS DUBOIS. But Rolene, you must understand my lovie – it's very different for me – I can't just sommer pack up and move. My life is here. My children were born and bred here.

ROLENE. It's a bladdy miracle my child's still alive here.

MRS DUBOIS. Ja well its' easy for you – I mean hairdressers can work anywhere but how can I find a caretaking job now at my age. And I have sweated blood and tears to keep that block standing on its two feet today. No – I must just now put my pride in my pocket – like it or lump it – so what can one do?

ROLENE. So now what – do you get your flat there for free?

MRS DUBOIS. Now hang on a moment – um look . . . Okay . . . Ja I pay a small . . . Nothing's for free my girl.

ROLENE. Well I didn't say it was.

MRS DUBOIS. Ja – then hou jou bek about my little perks!

ROLENE. Well Denzil says they giving it away . . .

MIRIAM *returns with cigs.*

MIRIAM. Here's your cigarettes, Rolene.

ROLENE. Thanks sweetheart. (*She turns to talk confidentially to* MRS DUBOIS.) They giving it to 'you know who' – and now – where do we sit?

MRS DUBOIS. Listen I don't want to be rude, but we are now sitting in kak straat and I don't know which number.

MIRIAM. It's No. 11 here, 11 Bok Street, Joubert Park.

Phone rings.

ROLENE. Curl Up and Dye International, can I help you? . . . sorry

who? . . . Now what is that – a person or what. . . . You mad! I'm
not going to tell you what number this is – what number did
you want? . . . Hey? . . . What? . . . Then look in your trouser . . .
Then you got a problem. . . . Listen arsehole – I'm not your 702
Crisis Line! (*Slams down phone.*) Doos!

MRS DUBOIS. Now what was all that about?

ROLENE. Ag, some pervert lookin for his pinkie. . . . No man
Miriam, how many times have I told you, it's the red pack,
thirties special mild and look what she brings me – blue pack,
twenties, mild.

MRS DUBOIS. Yere Miriam – you must screw your head on proper
man.

CHARMAINE *dashes into the salon and hides.*

MIRIAM. How Charmaine – you must look where you are
running – suka!

CHARMAINE. Ey Miriam quick check, is he there?

MIRIAM. Who?

CHARMAINE. Jakkals – is he there by the corner there?

ROLENE. Never you mind Miriam – just go to the café and change
my cigarettes. (MIRIAM *goes.*)

CHARMAINE. Ey, Rolene, make like you not looking, ek sê – don't
let him check you looking!

MRS DUBOIS. So you'll do me later then, Rolene . . . (*Heading for
door.*)

ROLENE. Ja . . . (*Pushes* MRS DUBOIS *out and continues looking.*)

CHARMAINE. Ey that focken button kop – he's just a con man
with a con plan – teef!

ROLENE. Ooh yere – guess who's arrived?

CHARMAINE. The General?

ROLENE. No, Laubscher – in his aquamarine turbo. Jees that
turbo's a beautiful car – and Laubscher's the goodest-looking
cop from Hillbrow branch.

CHARMAINE. Is he pulling a action? – quick speak up!

ROLENE. No they just talking . . . ooh! – yiss! No! Laubscher just
skopped him up his arse – I wouldn't be surprised if his balls
came right through his throat – Jissus! Now's he's klapped him
in the face and he's pulled his jacket half off and . . . and . . .
and ja here come the handcuffs. (*She laughs.*) And Jakkals only

looks funny with his face pushed up against the wall like that . . .

CHARMAINE. Cute! Ey that will teach him to fuck around with my outie. Is he in the jammie yet?

ROLENE. Ja – well now he is – looks like he's lights out.

CHARMAINE. They waaied yet?

ROLENE. Ja – there's the wheelspin. (ROLENE *comes inside.*)

CHARMAINE. Now come and tune me how sorry you are, you fucken teef !

ROLENE. Those boys doesn't take nonsense from nobody – this isn't like America where they treat them lightly – here they got to be a bit more rough. And Laubscher, boy, he knows his business, that is for sure. (CHARMAINE *comes out from her hiding place.*) So Charmaine – you better speak up quick and tell me what is going on.

CHARMAINE. Ag los it man.

ROLENE. No Charmaine! I'm not going to los it – now talk and tell me what's going on!

CHARMAINE. They tune me I must make a statement.

ROLENE. Who?

CHARMAINE. The Boere.

ROLENE. So did you?

CHARMAINE. Nooit but Jakkals and the other ouens scheme I did, cause they spied me last night splabbing with the law – but I didn't. Okay, like I dig to – but I don't dig to –

ROLENE. Charmaine what are you trying to say?

CHARMAINE. Like I'm kakking off – cause the General he doesn't smaak it lank when you split especially to the pigs. But I feel like I almost want to split you know – tune them the truth – what really happened – so now the General tunes Des – my connection – tunes him, 'Ey Des – you tune Pinkie . . .'

ROLENE. Who's Pinkie now?

CHARMAINE. It's me – my street name.

ROLENE. Oh.

CHARMAINE. 'You tune Pinkie – if she makes the statement a 28 will come her way.'

ROLENE. What's 28 again?

CHARMAINE. Blood and kill.

ROLENE. Jussus Charmaine! You mean if you make it – they'll kill you?

CHARMAINE. One time. Ey like so what do I do cause I feel like I owe it, you know, like to Quintus, cause he can't do nothing. Ey and it's the first time I really smaaked a ou when he smaaked me. Okay, so it's only been two months but he really made me feel nice.

ROLENE. Listen Charmaine – I think it's better you stay here for a bit while things cool down out there.

CHARMAINE. Ey thanks a span Rolene, I scheme you are my only real china hey.

ROLENE. You got to look after yourself man – otherwise you going to end up in the shit. Now go make yourself a cup of coffee . . . or read a magazine – it will do you good to read, take your mind off things. So how's Quintus doing?

CHARMAINE. Same – still on the drip.

ROLENE. Shame – look just take it easy Charmaine and I'm sure everything will come right.

CHARMAINE (*walks over to the sink, knocks over all the cups*). Kak!

ROLENE (*looks at* CHARMAINE. *Turns back to mirror. She pulls her cardigan down and examines a large bruise on her arm. She speaks into the mirror, occasionally glancing at* CHARMAINE*'s reflection. While she speaks* CHARMAINE *responds to a whistle from the street and leaves without her noticing*). Denzil . . . 'Bokkie!' Jus' after we got married hey, 'Bokkie, in a year or two we'll have our own house, even if it's a small one, with a yard for the kids' . . . Ja those were his very words. And you know I believed him. And it's ever since 'they' started moving in that things have gone this way. I wish they would jus' go away. Ag, maybe I should of told him straight – I can't take it Denzil, I'm leaving . . . But a family's got to have a father. And every time – the same pattern; the same story – belt undone – the skeef look – laughing at me. And it's worse for the kid – shame – she really loves her father, and he's very nice to that child – takes her to the park, to the Rand Show and that, buys her sweets . . . Now how can she understand it when she sees her mother crying? . . . And then I got to lie to her, tell her I'm now upset cos I'm feeling sick. He's the one that's sick man. Ag, but as long as I live – I won't forget nothing . . . I'm telling you Char . . . (*She turns around to look but* CHARMAINE *is not there.* MIRIAM *enters*) and about time too – this is nonsense taking time off to do your private shopping Miriam. Where have you been?

MIRIAM. Aai, aai – Rolene there's a woman lying dead on the pavement – so I must wait in the shop for cigarettes because Mr Patel – he's also gone to look.

ROLENE. Where's this Miriam?

MIRIAM. Up there – by the park.

ROLENE. What happened – dead? Are you sure she's just dead?

MIRIAM. I don't know what happened – I'm just seeing many, many people standing and looking there.

ROLENE. Did it look bad?

MIRIAM. Ow – worse than bad. And there was just too much blood coming out and I can't stand to see so much blood – now my nerves are shot.

ROLENE. Shame Miriam, go have a glass of sugar water to calm you down. I'm going to have a look quick . . . And Miriam, just make sure everything's all right here by the shop . . . And if my husband phones, jus tell him – I'm on the loo. Thanks sweetheart, I won't be long.

ROLENE *exits.* MIRIAM *gets herself a glass of water with sugar. Lights fade to blackout.*

ACT TWO

MIRIAM *is sitting at* ROLENE*'s desk, drinking sugar water. Phone rings.*

MIRIAM. Curl up and Dye International, can I help you? . . . She's . . . she's on the loo. Yes master . . . yes master . . . Yes master Denzil. (*Puts down phone.*) Lo ufuna ikorobela! [This one needs blinkers!] (DUDU *enters.*) Sawubona sisi.

DUDU. Sawubona. [Good morning.]

MIRIAM. Yebo. Ngingakusiza. [Good morning. Can I help you?]

DUDU. I'd like to make an appointment please.

MIRIAM. When for?

DUDU. Well, if possible for now.

MIRIAM (*she opens the appointment book*). I'm sorry but I don't normally do this – most times the customers book in advance. What do you want – a perm?

DUDU. No, I've just taken off my braiding and my hair is broken.

MIRIAM. Take off your hat sisi, and let me have a look. (DUDU *takes off hat.*) When last did this hair have treatment?

DUDU. Oh God, it was quite a while back now. That's why I need a damn good treatment – the whole tutti. En ngfuna Dombolo – Tshabalala's daughter!

MIRIAM. Beautiful like Dombola with a bald head?! Never my darling! You see, let me explain to you. In order for the hair to grow it has got to be oily. When after you are finished – you must buy this treatment here and then you put in on to the head for the next fortnight every morning and every evening. It's not expensive – only seventeen rands fifty – then you come back in two weeks and you'll see. Your hair will feel so soft and shiny you won't know that it's the same hair that grows on your head!

DUDU. Mama can we get started then? When you're on night shift you haven't got time to play.

ROLENE (*rushes back into salon*). My God Miriam – what a mess! Shame you didn't tell me she was black.

MIRIAM. You didn't ask Rolene.

ROLENE. When I got there and saw all that blood I felt so farce – I thought I was gonna faint right there and then. Yere, my nerves is shot now.

MIRIAM. Here, sip some of my sugar water – it made me feel better.

ROLENE. Thanks Miriam but I'll go get my own. (*Suddenly notices* DUDU.) Miriam how many times have I told you, if you want to talk with your friends you go and talk outside.

MIRIAM. But Rolene she's . . .

ROLENE. I'm sorry you can't . . . And who told her she could sit in the customer's chair?

DUDU. I know you're very busy, but this lady . . .

ROLENE. Which lady?

MIRIAM. Me Rolene, I . . .

DUDU. Yes her.

ROLENE. Stop right there. Are you a customer?

DUDU. Yes.

ROLENE. So why didn't you say so right in the beginning?

MIRIAM. I was trying . . .

ROLENE. Okay, Miriam – the basin's still dirty, you haven't done the cups and you better fold up the towels. (*Goes over to stand behind* DUDU.) I'm terribly sorry but there has been a bit of a balls up here. Now, have you got an appointment?

DUDU. No. But she said you would be able to do me now.

ROLENE. What – right now?

DUDU. If possible yes.

ROLENE. Well I'll have to check. You know we were very busy. (*She looks in the book.*) Um . . . Ja okay – I can squash you in now.

DUDU. Thank you.

ROLENE. Miriam come take Mrs . . . ?

DUDU. Ms Dudu Dlamini.

ROLENE. Miss?

DUDU. No, Ms – M - S.

ROLENE. Oh – Miriam come take M.S. Lamene over to the consultation chair.

MIRIAM. Ngiyaxolisa ngalokhu. [I'm sorry about all this happening.]

DUDU. Ungakhathazeki akulona icala lakho. [No don't worry – it's not your fault, it's fine.]

MIRIAM. Ngicela unginike ibhantshi lakho ne bag ngiyokubekela zona. [Please give me your coat and bag, I'm going to put them away for you.]

DUDU. Ngiyabonga. (MIRIAM *takes* DUDU*'s bag and coat to hang up.*)

ROLENE (*goes behind* DUDU *to see what should be done*). Right, let's see – you can have the standard – that's shampoo set and style – but we've got lots of different variations to choose from. There's the Manhattan, California Curl, the Hollywood, highlights and lowlights, Black Like Me, and on special this month we've got thē Whitney Touch at only forty-five rands – next month it's fifty. The choice is yours.

DUDU. Look I'm not really familiar with all these fancy names – all I –

ROLENE. Whitney Houston – it's very popular with all my black customers.

DUDU. I don't think that's going to be right for me right now, I feel . . .

ROLENE. Nonsense! Now you've got a sort of a pear-shaped face – we need to change that shape – bring back the cheekbones and up. No I'm sorry, it's got to be the Whitney for you – it's guaranteed to bring out all the . . . um . . . ag you know . . . like the dimensions on your face.

DUDU. No really, I think what I really need is a very good treatment to start with and then I'll go for the relaxer.

ROLENE. Very well, suit yourself – Miriam come take Mrs Lamene – she needs the strongest treatment we've got – this hair is very badly damaged. Go with Miriam – she'll get you started.

DUDU. Hey! Madoda liyadelela leligxagxa! [This white trash is spiteful.]

MIRIAM. Vela ba frustrated! Woza ngapha. [Of course, they are frustrated. Come this way please.]

MIRIAM *takes* DUDU *over to the washbasin.*

ROLENE (*sits down at desk. In whispered tones*). Hey Miriam, so you know her?

MIRIAM. No, I don't, but shoo, did you see her handbag? Ostrich! That one, she's very expensive.

ROLENE. What – do you think she's a tickey-liner – you know – one of those ones that goes with white men?

MIRIAM. Maybe – I don't know.

ROLENE. That's where she gets her money from – I take you a bet.

MIRIAM (*goes back to* DUDU *at basin. Starts washing her hair*). Beka ikhanda lakho la umemeze uma usha. [Just put your head back and relax and shout if it gets too hot.]

DUDU. Kulungile. [Okay.]

MIRIAM. So how is town life?

DUDU. I've got a roof over my head.

MIRIAM. Why uhlala e town? Bathi kugcwele ama moffie e Hillbrow uzo cash i AIDS. [Why do you stay in town? They say there are gays in Hillbrow and you can catch AIDS.]

DUDU. I didn't choose to live in town – I couldn't get a room in Soweto.

MIRIAM. My dear, siyainyova. [We are protesting.] Where I stay we are not paying rent and even people in backrooms don't pay rent – so you can get a room. You are just too choosy.

DUDU. Anyway I don't know Soweto. Bhekela ngi phuma e Durban. [Look here, I'm from Durban.] I don't want to be raped every Saturday night.

MIRIAM. I've been living in Soweto for twenty years and I've never been raped. And not because I'm ugly my darling! You are black, you belong to Soweto and la bantu – they will never even borrow you salt.

DUDU. I don't need to borrow – I can scrape around . . . alone!

MIRIAM. Oh, so you live in town like a larney, but when you die you are not going to be buried in town.

DUDU. I came to work for my two children and they will bury me e nguthu – not in Soweto – I'm not a prostitute!

MIRIAM. So what work do you do, that makes you dress so smart?

DUDU. I'm a nurse – sister –

MIRIAM. Kuphi? [Where?]

DUDU. Park Lane Clinic.

MIRIAM. Un gangitholela umsebenzi ngizofaka amaepilets ngithi qhwayi ngishiye leli gxagxa no Mrs Dubois and her foot! [Oh, so can you get me a job as a nurse assistant, with the epaulettes? – then I leave Rolene and Mrs Dubois and the hip and the foot!] (*They both laugh.* MIRIAM *carries on washing hair.*) But sisi – you are not helping us. We are short of nurses in Soweto. How can you keep nursing la bantu – abanursewe bangabo baby! Banursewe sebe bedala – ba nursewe sebe ku old age home – [Sister, how can you keep nursing these white people who are nursed from the cradle to the grave?] Ow, suka sisi, you must come and work at Bara.

DUDU. Ow!! Uyangishisa! [You're burning me.]

MIRIAM. I'm sorry, I'll put more cold.

DUDU. Working at Bara is like milking into a bucket with holes. This Park Lane 'Hotel' of mine with its five star customers and its five star doctors – I take home five star pay!

MIRIAM. So you are only thinking of a five star salary hey, and not about your people?

DUDU. Just pass me that towel.

MIRIAM. So when you are finished learning to be white will you come and visit me in Soweto? Rolene, sengiqedile manje. [Rolene, I've finished.]

ROLENE. Huh?

MIRIAM. I'm finished.

ROLENE. Oh.

> MIRIAM *takes* DUDU *over to the 'consultation' chair at mirror. As* DUDU *sits,* ROLENE *orders* MIRIAM *to put her in the next chair.*

MIRIAM. Sisi sekuse clinic woza uzoshukula izitulo. [Sister we are at the clinic now, you must polish the chairs.]

ROLENE (*going over to* DUDU). I can't believe you haven't heard of Whitney Houston . . .

DUDU. I didn't say . . .

ROLENE. She's that famous black negro in America . . . who sings . . .

DUDU. Of course I've heard of her – I haven't heard of that particular hair. Ucabanga ukuthi ngiuini lomlungu? [Who does she think I am?]

MIRIAM. Ucabanga iDisco ngoba ngumuntu wama disco. [She just thinks in terms of disco – because that's where she belongs.]

ROLENE. Jees she's only good hey. Ooh yis, I wish I could sing like her. Hey Miriam, how does that Whitney song go that we always sing?

MIRIAM *starts singing 'The Greatest Love of All'* – ROLENE *joins in.*

ROLENE. I love singing. You know, if I hadn't become a hairdresser I would of become a singer . . .

DUDU. So how long must you train before you can be a pro hairdresser?

ROLENE. What kind of a hairdresser?

DUDU. A professional.

ROLENE. Oh – well . . . actually . . . like I haven't trained as such although you can say I have trained you know, like I always used to cut everyone in my family's hair.

DUDU. It sounds like a stimulating job.

ROLENE. Oh yes, and very creative as well. Like the textures and that can be so very different. And when it comes to styling – you got to know the techniques. I mean a black hair is a very different technique to a white hair. But it's never a problem, cause hair is hair. Miriam, treatment.

DUDU. Has it got Betnovate in it?

ROLENE. Betna what?

DUDU. Betnovate – ag, just give me the bottle.

ROLENE. Well . . . I've never had no complaints from my other black customers – have we, Miriam?

MIRIAM. Except for that one madame, Rolene – the one that came back last week Friday.

DUDU. Who? What was the complaint?

MIRIAM. Maybe it was this Betnaroot stuff that made her hair go straight.

ROLENE. You talking rubbish, Miriam.

DUDU. Please – before you use this stuff – what happened to this woman?

MIRIAM. Then what was the problem with that customer, Rolene?

ROLENE. Her problem, Miriam, wasn't in her hair – it was in her

head! That was her problem. Anyway she was jus' soeking – cos
I permed her hair on Thursday and it came out very nice – ask
Miriam.

MIRIAM. But what conditioner did you put on her, Rolene?

ROLENE. It had nothing to do with the bladdy conditioner man!
Cause that perm worked! I'm telling you, it was a very nice
perm. Then she has the bladdy cheek to walk in here Friday
and start shouting at me, in Bantu, cause that hair is gone all
straight now.

MIRIAM *enacts the scene for* DUDU – *walking in, showing the hair
and then swearing at* ROLENE. DUDU *laughs.* MIRIAM *also
laughs.*

MIRIAM. Wathi le Curl Up and Dye yenu is where people's hair die!
[This Curl Up and Dye is where the hair dies!]

ROLENE. Miriam!! Look I'm sorry to say it to you but if you saw
her, and everyone is agreeing with me – not so, Miriam? – you
can see it on her ways she's one of those tickey-line ones. So
now can I put on this conditioner?

DUDU. Yes.

Enter MRS DUBOIS – *she talks as she is coming through the door. She
hasn't seen* ROLENE *and* DUDU *yet.*

MRS DUBOIS. Right Rolene, I'm now ready for my end of my week
treat!

ROLENE. You back early, I thought . . .

MRS DUBOIS. Oh excuse me! I didn't realise you would be busy. I
thought . . . No never mind, I'll sommer brush it out myself.
(*She heads for the door and is about to leave.*)

ROLENE. No wait, Mrs Dubois, I'll do you, I'll do you. First let
Miriam start you so long and as soon as I'm finished here I'll fix
up your end bits.

MRS DUBOIS (*very sarcastically*). Well . . . I would hate to put you
out, Rolene. You know I'm quite capable of brushing it out on
my own.

ROLENE. Ag don't be stupid man. Come – come sit down here.
Okay, Miriam, you can start taking Mrs Dubois' curlers out. Is
your hair wet or do we need to dry it?

MRS DUBOIS. Dry.

ROLENE. Right Miriam, before you take the curlers out, give the
hair a bit of a spray – then stick Mrs Dubois under. You having
the usual?

MRS DUBOIS. The usual!

MIRIAM. Okay Mrs Dubois, let's get you going. (*Miriam takes off her scarf.*)

MRS DUBOIS. Mind where you put that scarf now, Miriam.

MIRIAM (*sprays* MRS DUBOIS' *head with water just before she gets the dryer*). Do you want a magazine while you under?

MRS DUBOIS. No thank you Miriam, I don't feel like reading.

ROLENE (*applying treatment to* DUDU*'s hair*). No, you won't be sorry, you'll just feel it, so soft and silky – my husband loves it – you married? (*She starts rubbing conditioner in.*)

DUDU. Uh-huh.

ROLENE. Your husband a miner?

DUDU. No, he's actually a schoolteacher.

ROLENE. Oh – what, there in Soweto?

DUDU. No, he's teaching in Natal.

ROLENE. Shame, you separated?

DUDU. Well . . . in a way . . . yes, I mean officially we are still married.

ROLENE. Oh, I'm sorry to hear it.

DUDU. It would be coming up for nineteen years now.

MIRIAM. You are lucky. I've been married to the same bladdy drunkard for forty-two years.

DUDU. Hau! Isikhathi eside kangaka! [Such a long time!] Shame mama – especially if he's living inside the bottle.

MIRIAM. Living?! He is drowning inside the bottle – Yo! – That man – drinking up every penny I earn.

ROLENE. Shame Miriam – how did you stick it out all this time?

MIRIAM. Well, that's the way it is and I suppose that's the way it'll be until I kick my bucket!

MRS DUBOIS. Quite right, Miriam – there's no end to getting married – no, I don't want another man – five times! Hell's bells – you try and you try and you try and you try and you try! But they all the same. No, I'm steering clear – that is for sure.

ROLENE. With me and my husband it's nearly six and so far so good. You know never once has a anniversary gone past when he hasn't bought me my twelve roses.

DUDU. Oh, my husband bought me roses, but when you know he's poking them into five other holes, you just want to tell him to stick that rose.

MRS DUBOIS. Rolene, you must give us your recipe, man.

ROLENE. Ag, it's simple, just tender loving care.

DUDU. In my book that one turned out a flop. Just burn that recipe.

MRS DUBOIS. Well obviously my oven wasn't hot enough.

ROLENE. Hot enough for what?

DUDU. For the cake to rise.

ROLENE (*after a short pause*). Oh ja . . . the cake to rise. (*They laugh.*)

MRS DUBOIS. Now what has cake got to do with the price of cheese?

ROLENE. Ag never mind. I need new recipes man – he says chops Monday, ministeaks Tuesday, curry Wednesday, à la King Thursday and cottage pie Friday is getting boring.

DUDU. Ag, they'll never be satisfied.

ROLENE. He should of married his mother.

DUDU. Always sniffing around like a dog. Even if he had ten wives he would still want another.

MIRIAM. King Mswati – twenty years old and half a dozen already!

ROLENE. Ja, I suppose sometimes it can be a bit of a uphill.

DUDU. And then bringing home all those diseases – jis, my worst was the goggas.

ROLENE. Ooh no yere – just let me catch one crab on my husband and I promise you I'll Doom it so bladdy hard – I'm telling you – that prick will just curl up and die! (*They laugh.*)

DUDU. Awuthunuelwa gundwane – Marriage stinks!

ROLENE. It was the happiest day of my life. No, it's true, I mean it takes a hell of a lot to make it work.

MIRIAM. Too too much.

ROLENE. Jissus sometimes I wonder what for hey!

MIRIAM. For our children, Rolene.

DUDU. You are right, mama. It is our children who give us our happiness.

MRS DUBOIS. Ja, they are my only reason for living.

MIRIAM. We are the ones to look after our children.

ROLENE. Ja I know that, but like what do we get back for it? I mean look at the kids today – I've seen it for myself. Just last week they picked up a nine year old, here, on the corner, for dealing and injecting drugs under his toenails. Can you believe!

MIRIAM. Nine years! She is too young!

MRS DUBOIS. Six! He was a six year old!

DUDU. Why wasn't that child in school, that's what I want to know.

MRS DUBOIS. Ag, come on Miriam man – turn me on!

MIRIAM. Here's your earpads and shout if it gets too hot.

> MIRIAM *switches on dryer.*

ROLENE (*to* DUDU). So what kind of a job do you do?

MRS DUBOIS (*shouts out from under dryer*). Miriam, pass that magazine there. (MIRIAM *picks up any magazine.*) No man – the one underneath the *Scope* – the *You.* (MIRIAM *gives it to her.*)

ROLENE. Sorry what did you . . .

MRS DUBOIS (*again shouting*). Rolene – for how much longer am I still going to sit underneath this thing?

ROLENE. Until you done.

MRS DUBOIS. How long?

ROLENE (*goes up and shouts to* MRS DUBOIS *under dryer*). Until you are done!

MRS DUBOIS. Oh.

ROLENE. Sorry what did you say you did again?

DUDU. I'm a nurse.

ROLENE. Oh. So did you see the twins, you know? The black ones – that came out stuck together?

DUDU. Mpho and Mphonyana.

MIRIAM. I prayed for those two darlings.

ROLENE. Shame.

DUDU. No I didn't see them, I'm not at Baragwanath. I work at the Park Lane Clinic up here in Hillbrow.

ROLENE. Hillbrow? Oh. (*A longish pause.*) There's a lot of black peoples what's living in Hillbrow now you know.

DUDU. Yes I know because there's a great shortage . . .

ROLENE. And this grey areas is good for blacks – cause you got restaurants and the shops and you can live here like civilised people. Cos in the locations and that there's all the burnings and the necklaces and the tsotsis. My husband told me, he went in there you know – you see he's with the FGs.

DUDU. What – is your husband – a cop?

ROLENE. No – Fidelity Guards. He even asked them for bulletproof vests – cause of the danger and that – but they didn't want to give it to him. No . . . you people must really appreciate grey areas.

DUDU. Well . . . it's got its advantages, I agree.

ROLENE. Exactly! You know I think the government is trying to make it better for you people – head down – but it's not a good area for whites anymore. You know Hillbrow, Joubert Park – they gone down – head back – you see – you can classify the people that's living here – doesn't matter if it's Coloured, Indian, Asian or Black – you know – you get the people that's larney – and you get the people that's rubbish! – in every nation – lift – in whites as well. Ag, you can see by the looks of a person what type of a person that person is – like you can just tell that you a decent, respectable type of a woman. If there was more people like you staying here – no problems – you know what I mean?

MRS DUBOIS (*shouts from under dryer*). Rolene come on man. Get this blooming thing off my head!

ROLENE. Are you dry?

MRS DUBOIS. Dry?! Good God I'm blooming roasted!

ROLENE. Miriam, get Mrs Dubois out.

MIRIAM *takes off dryer and puts it back into place.*

MRS DUBOIS. Thanks Miriam – phew I feel like I'm cooked right through.

ROLENE. Right Miriam, you can start taking Mrs Dubois' curlers out.

MIRIAM *starts taking out* MRS DUBOIS' *curlers.* ROLENE *carries on with* DUDU's *hair.*

ROLENE. You know a woman was murdered here today.

MRS DUBOIS. Who?

ROLENE. How must I know who – when I got there she was dead!

MRS DUBOIS. Are you now talking about that black one?

ROLENE. Ja – just two blocks up from here – what a mess!

MRS DUBOIS. No I missed that one – all I saw was the dent in the pavement.

MIRIAM. Shame . . .

MRS DUBOIS. Do you know what happened there?

ROLENE. Well apparently she and her husband . . .

MRS DUBOIS. I heard it was her boyfriend . . .

ROLENE. Whatever man! Anyway they were having one helluva fight – then I think – now wait . . . Ja, she stabbed him – so now he threw her out the window! They say it was from the fourth floor.

MRS DUBOIS. Wrong! I heard the sixth! And apparently she was very drunk too.

ROLENE. Must I carry on or do you want to finish off the story?

MRS DUBOIS. No carry on Rolene – it's your story.

MIRIAM. The people there told me she flew from the fifth.

MRS DUBOIS. What Miriam – where you also there?

MIRIAM. Mmm – but I didn't want to look.

ROLENE. Apparently she landed first with her head and then her body. And you know they didn't even arrest him. When they went up there – you know – the police – he told them she jumped – my arse! She never jumped –

MIRIAM. Cos the people there said she flew out of that window like a . . . like a rocket!

ROLENE. Like a rocket! And now we must believe she jumped?! I'm sorry – no ways. Shame and there she was laying – you know, her face completely squashed in – and you know what? – her legs was laying like this – and all she had on was a pantie!

MRS DUBOIS (*to herself*). Ooh no sis.

DUDU. Hillbrow Hospital – every Saturday night – five ODs, eighteen stabbings, ten gunshots, seven hit and runs – life is cheap here . . .

MRS DUBOIS (*to* DUDU *looking up from magazine*). Shame – he can't keep his girlfiends – MacGyver – a bachelor forever – shame . . .

ROLENE. Miriam come. (MIRIAM *and* ROLENE *swop jobs,*

MIRIAM *massaging* DUDU*'s hair and* ROLENE *taking out* MRS DUBOIS' *curlers.*)

MRS DUBOIS (*to* DUDU). You know I used to have my hair done – here in this very salon – every day of my life – not so Miriam?

MIRIAM. Monday, Tuesday, Wednesday, Thursday, Friday – every day, Mrs Dubois –

MRS DUBOIS. Ja – she can tell you about the good old days when people had to book at least a week in advance to get an appointment here – hey Miriam?

MIRIAM. And on weekends I walked out here with seven rands in bonus. Fifty cents for bringing in coffee and R1.00 if they liked my jokes – my pocket used to ching-ching!

MRS DUBOIS. Ja – she'll tell you. And this salon used to always attract a very respectable element – you know – blue collar type.

DUDU. What colour?

MRS DUBOIS. Blue!

ROLENE. You know, like the old ladies – shame – we call them the blue-rinse brigades.

MRS DUBOIS. That is not what I meant Rolene – I'm talking about blue collars – the professional man, with a education – like nurses, etc., etc.

ROLENE. Oh those . . . ja.

MRS DUBOIS. Nee well, that's something of the past as well – nice memories hey Miriam. Every morning, five past eight a.m. – I'd just come in with a turban around my head and I'd have my brushout – and every second day – then it's a dry – you know, a dry set. And then once a week – my wash and set –

MIRIAM. You never even knew what it was like to put a comb through your hair.

MRS DUBOIS. Nee well that's too something of the past – oh well – nice memories hey . . . ?

DUDU. You were spoilt!

MRS DUBOIS. Beg your pardon! It had nothing to do with being spoilt! That is the way it was! And it's very unfortunate but things here in this salon have gone a bit otherwise – if you get my meaning?

DUDU. Are you insinuating? . . .

ROLENE. Hey everybody – have you heard about this new Jik? Well I thought I'd take a chance so I did my curtains with it. The only thing you can't use it on is silk and I suppose . . . um . . . ag what's that other material that's like silk?

MRS DUBOIS. Crimplene?

ROLENE. No man – that's like silk.

MIRIAM. Satin?

ROLENE. Ja satin. But you can't use it as a pre-soaker – you got to use it with your soap powder. So I put in my two cups powder, my one cup biotex and a quarter cap of this Jik.

MRS DUBOIS. So did it work?

ROLENE. Oh ja – and that's on coloureds as well.

MIRIAM. At last – I'm sick and tired of trying to bleach out every stain from my children's T-shirts, and then the children are left all white.

MRS DUBOIS. Shame Miriam, I suppose with your family there's no end to washing.

MIRIAM. Ow it's true Mrs Dubois – I'm washing washing every weekend – for my husband . . .

ROLENE (to DUDU). Shame, and she's got no hot water there in Soweto, you see.

MIRIAM. And if it's raining it takes . . .

MRS DUBOIS. Ag toe maar Miriam – things will change for the better but hey – we must just pray to the Lord – remember now, it was only my faith that brought Mervin through – it was . . .

MIRIAM. Yes . . . What a friend we have in Jesus. (*Starts humming.*)

MRS DUBOIS. Yes Miriam our God is a good God but we don't spend enough time with Him. Now when Mervin was in his critical state I prayed to the Lord – day in and day out I prayed.

ROLENE. It would be much better for you, Miriam, if you had a washing machine hey?

MRS DUBOIS. A washing maching? Play the Pick Six man! A real miracle – that child died three times you know – but God has been so good to me – this God is a . . .

DUDU. I pray to the Lord but he doesn't wash my uniforms for me.

MRS DUBOIS. You can't expect the Lord to just give! give! give! And so what work do you do anyway?

ROLENE. She's a nurse, there by Park Lane Clinic – Hillbrow.

MRS DUBOIS. Oh . . . (*Long pause.*) So you must of seen the granny then?

ROLENE. Hey?

MRS DUBOIS. That granny man, you know the . . . the . . . what's it man . . . the subjugate granny – the one with the triplets.

ROLENE. Oh ja the test-tube babies?

DUDU. Aah – you mean surrogate.

ROLENE. Did you see her?

MRS DUBOIS. At her age, a miracle!

DUDU. No I didn't see the granny but I had a little peep at the triplets.

MIRIAM. Oh – I prayed for those three darlings.

DUDU. Three months prem – they looked just like little frogs.

ROLENE. Frogs?! I'm sure those kids have got coloured blood.

MIRIAM. No Rolene, they Portuguese – I read it in the paper – the mother was Portuguese.

ROLENE. Ja but you don't know who the father was hey, it comes from a test-tube.

DUDU. No, it was their own father. What I mean is, the woman's husband was the father, it was his sperm.

ROLENE. Really? Well anyway – it's a real miracle what they can do these days.

MRS DUBOIS (*to* DUDU). Then you must know about this mercy flight where they take you by plane to London for that fog – well my son invented that fog here – with the drip.

DUDU. They use it to treat patients with throat and lung cancer.

MRS DUBOIS. Ja – that's it – well he was the first one they used it on here – 73 – they say he made medical history, you know.

DUDU. Really?

MRS DUBOIS. Oh ja. Cos they used him as a guinea pig. Cos when he came round from being in a coma – for a year, his face was all done up in plastic – you see he didn't have a palate – so they made him a little windpipe here.

DUDU. Was it cancer of the oesophagus?

MRS DUBOIS. No – a van ran him over – when he was only two years old . . .

ROLENE. Shame – it sommer went straight through the robot.

DUDU. Oh . . . I'm sorry.

MRS DUBOIS. Now they say – you know the doctors – he's going to die again – this time cancer – cause his stomach inside is full of car acid.

ROLENE. He swallowed the headlights.

MRS DUBOIS. But what's even worse now is the doctors, they've put him on all these drugs and I'm telling you it's the drugs that's killing him quicker. All I can do now is just pray.

CHARMAINE *floats in and heads for the bench, greeting everyone as she floats past.*

CHARMAINE. Howzit . . . howzit . . . howzit . . .

MRS DUBOIS. And still you call this your friend, Rolene!

MIRIAM. You think she is sick, Mrs Dubois?

MRS DUBOIS. Huh! Sick, my eye! Don't make me laugh, Miriam.

MIRIAM. But she looks funny . . .

ROLENE. Ag leave her man, just let her do what she wants to do.

MRS DUBOIS. Well it's quite obvious what she's just been doing, but what those blokes see in her, I really don't know . . .

ROLENE. Miriam, go make Charmaine a cup of coffee quick.

MRS DUBOIS. And they don't choose hey – just pick them up right across the board . . .

CHARMAINE (*staring at the plant*). Ey, like those flowers – they not real, ek sê.

MRS DUBOIS. And rich! Sierras, BMWs, Mercs 230 SLCs – sis!

ROLENE. Make it three spoons of sugar, heaped, Miriam.

MRS DUBOIS. There's no apartheid on that corner! Inter-drinking, inter-drugging . . .

ROLENE. Are you drunk, Charmaine?

MRS DUBOIS. Inter-blooming everything!

MIRIAM. Here's a cup of coffee, my darling . . .

MRS DUBOIS. No – society's not normal . . .

CHARMAINE. You got funny eyes . . . ow it's hot . . .

ROLENE. Just drink, Charmaine, please man.

CHARMAINE. I'm cool man . . . stop checking me out skeef . . . stop fucking checking at me.

ROLENE. No, I dunno what's gone wrong with her.

CHARMAINE. I'm jus' checking their faces – all squashed up on the lid, but I can't hear nothing cause I'm laying in a glass coffin . . .

ROLENE. Charmaine?

CHARMAINE. Neat . . . five hairs in one hair . . .

MRS DUBOIS. And still you don't want to see nothing, Rolene.

CHARMAINE. Split . . .

MRS DUBOIS. For how much longer is she going to pull the wool over your ears?

CHARMAINE. Rolene, cut my hair. (*She passes out.*)

ROLENE. Charmaine! Charmaine are you all right? There's something funny happening here to Charmaine. (*She shakes her and slaps her face.*) Charmaine wake up man – just wake up – are you sick Charmaine? – talk to me – it's Rolene – talk! Are you sick? Lift her up, Miriam.

MIRIAM. Sisi masibize iambulance. [We must call the ambulance.]

DUDU. Leave her – I've seen enough of these cases to know when to start to worry.

MRS DUBOIS (*shouting from her seat*). That's right – tell her!

DUDU. Is she shooting Wellconal?

ROLENE. What you mean shooting?

DUDU. What drugs is she taking?

MIRIAM. I've seen her swallow those little pink tablets.

MRS DUBOIS. Pinks! I've seen her buying them – here – on the corner.

DUDU. I thought as much.

MRS DUBOIS. Twenty-five rand a tab can you believe and two hundred and forty a card.

MIRIAM. How! Where does she get all this money?

MRS DUBOIS. HBT – that's where – housebreak and theft!

ROLENE. Miriam, my cigarettes . . .

MRS DUBOIS (*to DUDU*). You know this hair of mine is black, I mean my natural colour. Now Raymondé began lifting it when the grey hairs started – he lifted me and he lifted me and he lifted me – I was here one day – eight hours for Raymondé to lift it – and hell, did he make quite a fantastic job – but then it was more platinum you know – like yellow. Although it looked terrific, I myself felt that for my complexion I needed it to be a tinge more copper – you know – like a reddy beige.

DUDU. Mm it does suit you – this colour.

MRS DUBOIS. Oh thank you . . . No I'm very pleased with it now.

CHARMAINE *comes round.*

CHARMAINE. I want to puke . . .

ROLENE *rushes over to* CHARMAINE.

ROLENE. Charmaine you stupid! . . . you bladdy . . . you gave me such a skrik man . . . If you ever try this again on me, I swear I'm gonna kill you – are you all right? It's unfair, man!

CHARMAINE. Ey nooit . . . my head . . . score me a Chestie.

ROLENE. No you always drag too hard – my smoke gets hot and I hate it. (*She gives* CHARMAINE *a full cigarette.*) Here, smoke your own.

CHARMAINE. You know what it's like without wheels hey. (*She looks at her feet.*) These are my wheels.

MRS DUBOIS. Come on Rolene – just finish me off here –

ROLENE. Miriam – let Mrs Lamene go under now.

CHARMAINE. It's so unfair – jus' cause of a small argument . . .

ROLENE. Do you want a facepack while you under, Mrs Lamene?

DUDU. Yes I will – thanks.

ROLENE. And a facepack, Miriam hey.

MIRIAM *puts the dryer on* DUDU *and does the facepack.*

ROLENE. Right – let us get you sorted out, hey?

MRS DUBOIS. I would appreciate that, Rolene.

ROLENE. It's got quite long here at the back. You want we should give you a little trim?

MRS DUBOIS. No, rather we give it another week.

ROLENE. But your ends are dead.

MRS DUBOIS. You mean split?

ROLENE. Very bad.

CHARMAINE. When I phoned the hospital – they tune me it's all over . . .

ROLENE. Charmaine . . .

MRS DUBOIS. All right, then cut them.

ROLENE. Miriam, pass me the scissor.

CHARMAINE. So like what must I do – I can't now split back to Durban. That smell . . . sis . . . the stink of the docks – I could vomit. Ten years with ship guys makes you sat, sat. 84 I'm here – Joeys – Joubert Park – as long as you do it – it's cool . . .

MRS DUBOIS. Not too short now hey Rolene.

ROLENE. I'm not, I'm just giving it a bit of shape . . .

CHARMAINE. . . . for five years I've survived now, and I'm still in one piece – you can't be scared . . . A car pulls up, 'Hello my sweetheart – how much?' Eighty bucks and I use my own flat. When I was in chookie once – I asked the welfare if they could help me like stop my drugs – but they didn't want to know – so why should I care . . .

MRS DUBOIS. Rolene – I want the sides here – like you did the last time hey – brushed back and up.

CHARMAINE. Ag I can't explain it – like why I like it . . .

ROLENE. Sort of like this?

CHARMAINE. . . . the rush . . .

MRS DUBOIS. Ja – and then curled back under – behind the ear.

CHARMAINE. . . . it helps me to get on a pluck so I can do what I have to do. Ey but I hang for my fix – like 29 . . .

ROLENE. But you can't take it all back – otherwise it's going to give you too much of the hard look – you see?

CHARMAINE. . . . scrubbing – I'm always scrubbing . . .

ROLENE. You got to have something here by your face – to soften it up a bit.

CHARMAINE. I can't now work in a straight job – it's shit . . . it's the pigs, always fixing traps – and you never know whether they come for a bust or a blowjob!

MRS DUBOIS. Ja, but not too puffed out, man – I don't want to walk out here looking like a poodle.

CHARMAINE. I'm sat with paying 200, 200.

ROLENE. But it's got to have a bit of body.

CHARMAINE. I'd rather walk up and down . . .

MRS DUBOIS. Body and bounce is fine – but no puff!

CHARMAINE. So like okay . . . I am scared and all that. But I'll never let a ou sus it. One day I'm going to use my knife.

MRS DUBOIS. No, I'm really happy with this colour now Rolene – at long last we got it right hey?

CHARMAINE. . . . but once you got your regulars it's – cool – one pays the rent – your other the food . . . ey and I don't like ask them what they do and they don't ask me . . . and that's the way I like it . . .

ROLENE. That's nice.

CHARMAINE. . . . like it . . . like it . . . I don't like it.

ROLENE. Miriam check if Mrs Lamene is ready.

MIRIAM. Sezomile izinwele zakho sisi? [Is your hair dry sisi?] (MIRIAM *takes the dryer off.*)

ROLENE (*to* DUDU). Yes – this hair is doing very nicely – so how often do you have your hair done?

DUDU. Not as often as I'd like to – I'm writing my paediatric exam in August.

ROLENE. Yes.

DUDU. On day duty I can sleep, but on night shifts I have to sit in the park to study.

ROLENE. So how come you came into this salon? Did someone tell you about it?

DUDU. No I walk past here every day, it's near my place.

ROLENE. So what – do you live in the area?

DUDU. I do.

ROLENE. You mean here by Joubert Park?

DUDU. Ja.

ROLENE. Oh. I thought you said you was in Hillbrow?

DUDU. I used to live in Hillbrow.

ROLENE. So why did you move?

DUDU. No hot water for three months – the ceiling leaked – live wires were sticking out the walls – that flat was disgusting!

ROLENE. So why didn't you complain to the landlord?

DUDU. I did, and again the usual – 'if you don't like what you got then go back to Soweto.' And then I was evicted.

ROLENE. Evicted?

DUDU. Thrown out – furniture and all in the street. Everything sitting on the pavement. No warning – no time to pack.

ROLENE. I'm sorry . . .

MIRIAM *brings coffee.*

MIRIAM. Thina i eviction sibashaya ngama stones e Soweto. You must come and live in Soweto.

MRS DUBOIS. I agree one hundred percent with you there Miriam.

CHARMAINE. Cunt!

MRS DUBOIS. Look at the time Rolene – I'm going to miss my Pick Six.

ROLENE. Please Miriam sweetheart – just finish off Mrs Dubois – it's the final touches – just spray and mirrors.

MIRIAM. Ow – Mrs Dubois – this hairdo – Mrs P.W. Botha!

MRS DUBOIS (*laughing*). Really, ag that's sweet of you Miriam, thanks, shame.

MIRIAM (*spraying hairspray*). Close eyes.

MRS DUBOIS. So how's your little one these days Miriam? She must be getting big hey?

MIRIAM. Aai, aai, aai Mrs Dubois – she is big enough to go to the school, but I haven't got school fees.

MRS DUBOIS. Ag Miriam this is not quite right here – won't you put in a few pincurls?

MIRIAM. Oh sorry Mrs Dubois.

MRS DUBOIS. You've been working here for hell now – how many years?

MIRIAM. I'm twenty years this November.

MRS DUBOIS. Now isn't that spectacular – twenty years. My God but time flashes by. So we could now say that you in fact have been brushing me out for twenty years. You must have come in at the same time as that old geyser – incredible.

MIRIAM. And I'm still without a geyser.

MRS DUBOIS. Such is life hey Miriam – we must sommer plod on.

MIRIAM. I haven't got a geyser because I've got no money.

MRS DUBOIS. Listen Miriam – be happy you got a job – how many people are out there on the streets without a job hey?

MIRIAM. But you know Mrs Dubois – when you have been at the same job for so many years then you expect a little more.

MRS DUBOIS. Miriam now what exactly are you trying to say?

MIRIAM. Mrs Dubois – I've got a long service here – twenty years – I'm working here very hard with no increase.

MRS DUBOIS. Just hang on a minute – Miriam what is your education?

MIRIAM. Standard five.

MRS DUBOIS. Standard five hey? Ja I love this – you without even a JC – still now expects to get more money – don't make me laugh – please!

MIRIAM. It's not a JC that sweeps the floors here. It's me – I'm the one that's sweeping the floors – and for twenty years.

MRS DUBOIS. Miriam you know you people think we just roll in money. It's ridiculous man! Life is also tough on us my girl – you got to realise . . .

MIRIAM. Look at you Mrs Dubois – for twenty years you have come in here to have your hair done – every week – with all that money that you have spent just on your hair – I could have used to send all my children to the school and buy the uniforms.

MRS DUBOIS. Yere! No man – what am I listening to here today? I ask you how your child is and all I get is snot and trane . . .

MIRIAM. Ask Rolene – the wages I'm getting here it's nothing! From hand to mouth and mouth to lavatory!

MRS DUBOIS. Ag nee kak with this! No I'm sorry – Rolene! I ask her how her child is and then I got to sit here and listen to all this political nonsense! Who does she think she is – a blooming member of parliament?! – that she now expects wage increases all the time.

DUDU. Uhola malini mama? [How much you get mama?]

MRS DUBOIS. Blooming cheek!

MIRIAM. Amakhulu amabali namashimi amahlanu. [Two hundred and fifty rands.]

DUDU. Two hundred and fifty rands? After twenty years! My God! Ridiculous – for how many hours?

MIRIAM. Amahora awueight amalanga awusix ngeviki. [For eight hours and six days a week.]

MRS DUBOIS. You see, as soon as they can't get their own way, they start skinnering behind our backs in their language. It's subversive! That's what it is – subversive! Cause you don't know what the hell they talking there. (*She heads for the door.* ROLENE *stops her.*)

RÓLENE. No wait, Mrs Dubois your pincurls – come sit. Do you want some coffee?

MRS DUBOIS. All right – but in my cup hey Miriam.

ROLENE. Mrs Lamene – do you want a cup of coffee?

DUDU. No thanks.

ROLENE. Miriam, two coffee.

Tension – quite a longish pause.

MRS DUBOIS. Rolene, a flat in my block is coming vacant at the end of this month. Now keep this between me, you and the lamp-post – I'm telling you cos I would very much like you and your husband to have first option on it.

ROLENE. Ag I dunno if we can move again, you know like . . .

MRS DUBOIS. Ja but Rolene, I'm not happy with the stories you told me about the place you're in man – I mean for how much longer are you going to take it?

ROLENE. Ja but . . .

MRS DUBOIS. Listen man, my block has got none of those problems. I run it on oiled wheels. We got a excellent security – a gate with a boy – it's cheap and we are serviced my girl.

ROLENE. Ja, but like whenever I come and visit you and that . . . there's such strange people what hangs out on the stairs all the time – like I don't feel safe in your block.

MRS DUBOIS. Okay, they are not exactly your best type but then we can't exactly be picky and choosy either. My main thing is to keep the block – whi . . . um, pure – you know what I mean. The rot must stop! In my block the guarantee is me. And I stick to my guns.

DUDU. Pure? You mean white! So why don't you just say it?

MRS DUBOIS. Er, this is a private conversation.

DUDU. And cheap!

MRS DUBOIS. Now listen here.

DUDU. No! You listen here. Your flats are dirt cheap because all you can get is low class white rubbish who are too lazy to work.

MRS DUBOIS. Excuse me – but would you mind repeating what has just passed your lips.

DUDU. I said the reason your flats are dirt cheap is because they are reserved for low class scum! No decent person would ever choose to live in those flats.

MRS DUBOIS. And who the hell are you to talk about my block like that?

DUDU. I know this area and I know these people – they are my neighbours. The man in the flat above mine stands on his balcony with a gun – and whenever a black person walks past he shouts, 'Hey kaffir watch out!' – Bang! And kills himself laughing. But worse, he beats his wife. I hear it right through my ceiling, night after night, and then comes the crying. Don't you come and tell me about white and pure – please!

MRS DUBOIS. If you bladdy blacks stayed put in Soweto we wouldn't have to carry guns.

DUDU. Rubbish, you carry guns because violence is the only thing you know. I see people every night with bullet holes through their heads.

MRS DUBOIS. You bladdy black nurses don't know your bladdy stomach from your liver man!

DUDU. I didn't buy my certificate. I earned it – my epaulettes cost me six years – general, midda, psychiatry – the same as any white nurse. So what standard did you get?

MRS DUBOIS. I have worked for my living all my life!

DUDU. Hayi suka! You don't know what work is – all you know is just to sit here and have your hair done.

MRS DUBOIS. Who the hell are you to come and say that to me – who the hell do you think you are? Go back to your tribe man!

ROLENE. No, please – Mrs Dubois . . . she's a customer.

MRS DUBOIS. I couldn't give a damn – they mustn't come here with their groot bekke – they must stay where they belong, up on the hills in a kraal with their animals. The further away the better!

DUDU. I don't need to go to a kraal to live with animals. I'm surrounded by them right here and now!

MRS DUBOIS. You shouldn't even be here in the first place.

DUDU. I've got every right to be here – I pay for my hair – and I pay for my flat – and double the amount that you people pay. People like you should be locked up in bladdy Boksburg! (*She gets up animatedly and goes over to* MRS DUBOIS.)

MRS DUBOIS. Just you touch me and I'll get you arrested!

DUDU. Touch you! I wouldn't even waste my spit on you.

MIRIAM. No, no, no, no. Sisi please – come sit down. (MIRIAM *takes her back to her chair.*)

MRS DUBOIS. I'm going to arrest you for verbal assault! (*Gets up and walks backwards.*)

MIRIAM. Please sisi – Mrs Dubois has been here – she is our longest customer.

MRS DUBOIS. Yes thank you Miriam.

DUDU. So you jump on her side now? You want me to come back to Soweto and as soon as they begin to shout it's yes madam, no madam – it's because of your type that we'll always be slaves!

MIRIAM. Don't you think those smart Brunno Marley shoes and that smart handbag make you a white madam. Haai suka, mind your manners! Mrs Dubois is old enough to be your mother. Don't be a cheeky!

DUDU. They rubbish man – I don't mix with people like this.

MIRIAM. Wena, you are like these women abathi they're fixing things for us kanti bazenza worse! [You are like these women who are fixing things for us, but you are making it worse.]

DUDU. Look I don't want to cause trouble with your job. Ungabi yisiduphunga. [Don't be a fool.]

MIRIAM. Kudala ngiwahlalele lamasimba – ngeke ngitshewe nguwe wena uzoya emsebenzini wakho – mina ngizabe ngiku kak straat no thank you! [I've put up with this shit – I'm not going to be told by you – you are going to go back to your job and I will be in kak straat – no thank you!]

DUDU. Ay suka uya hlanya [You are really mad.]

MIRIAM. Hei staff nurse buyela e Park Lane ngina twenty years lapha. [Hey staff nurse – go back to Park Lane – I have got twenty years in this job.]

MRS DUBOIS. Listen to them gaaning aan like screaming baboons! They can't even talk on a civilised level of conversation.

ROLENE. Miriam! Shut your bladdy mouth! What you think this salon is – a bladdy kaffir bus!!

MIRIAM. I am not a kaffir, Rolene – please!

MRS DUBOIS. Oh God, now suddenly what do we call them Rolene?

ROLENE. Ag Miriam I didn't mean it like that . . .

MIRIAM. It's always Miriam, Miriam, Miriam – you don't think of me. Now you listen to me once! I'm in troubles – my husband is dying, I got three children in school, I've got no food, I've got nothing and you don't want to give me increase! I am twenty years here and I'm working like a slave! I'm helping you here with everything – I'm cleaning – but you don't even want to say thanks – cause you don't like me, you just like my hands! Do you think I'm a stupid! I'm not a stupid! You found me here and I teach you everything you know – you didn't know nothing! I can leave this job at any time, at any moment – then you will call – 'Miriam where's this, Miriam where's that' because you can't do nothing without Miriam! This job – it's not good. Not even for a dog! So you and your Mrs Dubois and your pure white flats can all go to hell – the lot of you!

MRS DUBOIS. Good God, is this the Miriam I know – the utter filth that's . . .

MIRIAM. And as for you, Mrs Dubois – you pretend you are my friend, then when it suits you – you just shout at me. You can't even wash your own pantie – and you call me filth – ga! I don't care if I've just got a Standard Five or what. But at least I can wash my own panties! Or hide them before I can let anyone else wash them. You think I've got no blood!

ROLENE. Okay Miriam – I think you've had more than your say. Now go and get yourself a glass of sugar water to . . .

MIRIAM. I don't want a bladdy glass of sugar water. I want pay! Money – so that I can buy my own sugar!

ROLENE. Miriam – I pay you, damn it!

MIRIAM. Don't say damn it to me – I'm not your bladdy child!

ROLENE. Listen Miriam, I've given you the chance hey . . . Now any more cheek from you my girl and you are out! Take it – or leave it!

MIRIAM *walks away to the kitchen to cool off. She takes a basin of water to* DUDU *and gets a towel.* ROLENE *is obviously shaken and smokes a cigarette. Meanwhile, since a little while back* CHARMAINE *has come up to* DUDU *and has been staring at her in the mirror while everyone has been fighting behind her.*

CHARMAINE. Ey Rolene – I scheme she's the one that lives by our pozzy.

ROLENE. Huh? – what did you say Charmaine?

CHARMAINE. Do you graft as a nurse?

ROLENE. She's a sister.

CHARMAINE. So I'm spot on.

ROLENE. About what?

CHARMAINE. She's the one I tuned you about Rolene – the one that's moved in there by our pozzy.

ROLENE. Charmaine do you realise what you saying?

MRS DUBOIS. Ag please Rolene – how can you take that one seriously – look at her eyes man – they like bladdy roadmaps!

ROLENE. Do you live in Marley Mansions?

DUDU. Yes, why?

ROLENE. No, it's just that . . . that . . . well you see . . . I live in Marley Mansions and . . . and . . . it's funny because like . . . like I never seen you there before and all that . . . I just didn't realise . . .

DUDU. My heavens hey – that's incredible really – here we've been talking all this time without even . . .

ROLENE. Ja . . . so stupid hey . . .

MRS DUBOIS. Well this now finally eats the cake!

DUDU. Amazing . . . so what floor are you?

ROLENE. Ground . . . I mean not ground ground where the lifts is – you know – the one above . . . and you?

DUDU. No – I'm ground – 102.

ROLENE. Jees and I'm 202 –

DUDU. Good God –

ROLENE. I can't believe it – I mean here we've been sitting and talking nice nice and my floors is your ceilings and we didn't even know it . . . Yissus, I'm right on top of you, hey.

DUDU. That's right.

At this point realisation of the implications of the discovery hits them both as they look at each other in the mirror. ROLENE *gets to her feet in extreme nervousness.*

ROLENE. Miriam did you smoke my cigarettes?

MIRIAM. Since when do I smoke Rolene?

DUDU (*to* MIRIAM). Nkulunkulu wami Miriam lo mfazi wuye lo enigimuzwa e khala yonke imihla - eshaywa yi lanje ye ndoda. [My God Miriam, this woman is the one that I hear crying every night, being beaten up by that dog of a husband.]

MIRIAM. Shame, njalo uza nama blue eye indoda yakhe ibastard. [Shame she comes often with blue eyes all over her body. Her husband is a bastard.]

DUDU. Rolene, you must report your husband to the welfare or police. It's enough. Don't waste any more time. I just packed my things.

ROLENE. I got nowhere to go.

DUDU. Yes, but you can't let it go on for ever. For everything I've got, I fought – I had to. Is wanting a decent life so much?

MIRIAM. It's too much. So you must take it Rolene my darling – while the going is good – look, you are still young – you are a good hairdresser, and you can work.

DUDU. Get out while you can.

MRS DUBOIS. Do you think perhaps I could have a little moment to say something?

DUDU. Again.

MRS DUBOIS. Rolene may I talk?

ROLENE. Then talk.

MRS DUBOIS. I think it's about high time that you better make a choice my girl! Now are you a bladdy kaffir boetie or are you a white woman?

ROLENE. What you talking?

MRS DUBOIS. Make a choice! You take them or you take me. Am I making myself clear? Because this – what I'm seeing here today – I'm afraid I can no longer tolerate. I will send on your money by postal order and from this moment on I will only be known to you as a 'ex' customer at Curl Up and Dye. (MRS DUBOIS *leaves*.)

ROLENE. But then at least tell me what I done wrong!

DUDU. I think it was because she didn't like the way we were talking with you – you know like . . .

ROLENE. Shut up!! It's all your bladdy fault! How dare you come and tell me . . . You a witch . . . that's what you are – you a witch! My problems has got nothing to do with you. Look what you done now – she was my friend – what you? You not my

friend! You got no right to come and talk about my husband
like that. Now just get out of my shop! I'm calling the police!

DUDU (*turns to* MIRIAM). How much?

ROLENE. Fuck off out of my life man!!

DUDU. I want to pay.

ROLENE. I don't want your stinking fucken filthy money – you can
stick it up your arse!!

DUDU *puts down a R50 note on the table and walks out.*

ROLENE. Black bitch!

MIRIAM. Do you want some sugar water Rolene?

ROLENE. I don't want nothing, just leave me.

MIRIAM *picks up blackboard and goes outside, she starts shouting out
the names of the styles.* ROLENE *goes over to dressing table to look for
cigarettes. She finds half a facepack left in bowl.*

Wasting!

She sits down at mirror, trembling, starts to put on facepack.

CHARMAINE. Ey Rolene – like I scheme you a bit cheesed off, ek
sê – I checked those mense smokkeling with your brain – but
it's not worth it to get freaked out, ek sê – take it easy my china
– things will come your way. Here's a cigarette. Ey what's your
problem? It's just a job – black, grey, white – doesn't matter
what – as long as they pay you . . . (CHARMAINE *checks a
connection outside – she shouts.*) Ey rat – hold on. Rolene – I gotta
make like Donald – check you my china.

(CHARMAINE *leaves. Phone rings.*)

ROLENE. Curl Up and Dye International, can I help you? Denzil
what you want? . . . No, I'm here by myself . . . But Denzil, it's
Saturday, how can I come home, what about the customers? I'm
not lying Denzil. There is, I swear . . . no Denzil don't come
down and fetch me . . . listen man, I'll be home . . . Ja, I will . . .
Denzil? (*He hangs up.*) Bokkie? . . . Bokkie? . . .

*She places the receiver down. As lights fade to blackout we hear
MIRIAM selling in the street.*

Son of a Polish airman and a Lancastrian mother, PAUL
SLABOLEPSZY was born in Bolton in 1948. With his family he
emigrated to South Africa aged three. He grew up in a small village
near a mining town in the Northern Transvaal, matriculated in
Pietersburg, and took a B.A. degree in English and Drama at the
University of Cape Town.

In 1972 he became a founder member with Athol Fugard and
Yvonne Bryceland of the Space Theatre in Cape Town and he
earned great distinction as a performer in numerous productions
there. In 1974 he was also one of Barney Simon's first performers
at the Arena Theatre, Doornfontein, in Simon's monologue, *Men
Should Cry More Often*, which was one of the pieces that in due
course led to the locating of fringe activities in the Market Theatre
complex in Johannesburg.

As a writer-performer he has occasionally starred in
productions of his own scripts, directed by Bobby Heaney, with
whom he has a longstanding working relationship. These include
Saturday Night at the Palace (1982), one of the longest running
South African plays of the 80s, which had a season at London's Old
Vic from 11 April, 1984, and which was released as a film directed
by Robert Davies in 1987. With Heaney as director, Slabolepszy has
also done for the stage *Boo to the Moon* and *Making Like America*
(both 1986), and *Smallholding* (1989). An evening of shorter
pieces – *Travelling Shots* – was presented in 1988.

The present one-acter, *Over the Hill*, was written as the second
half of a double-bill that began with an altogether lighter piece,
Under the Oaks. This was also a three-hander using sporting
material, written for the PACT Festival in Johannesburg in
September, 1984. For the Grahamstown Festival the following July
Over the Hill was added and the three performers toured the two
matching plays to the Baxter Theatre, Cape Town, the Elizabeth
Sneddon in Durban, the Hexagon Theatre in Pietermaritzburg, the
State Theatre in Pretoria and finally the Market Theatre,
Johannesburg, where they completed a sell-out run.

As John Campbell observed in an article in the *Weekly Mail* (15
November, 1985), Slabolepszy

> has plugged into the perceptions and attitudes of a new
> generation of young South Africans, the hardened realism

and lack of sentiment that distinguishes today's anti-apartheid youth from their parents. His treatment of racism is a good example of this, making a significant and perhaps historical break from the theatre of guilt. Racism is no longer seen as the irrational expression of Afrikaner gaucheness and crudity, something to be embarrassed about (and not much more). Rather it is an attitude with historical roots and observable causes.

In *Over the Hill* Slabolepszy shows himself to be the playwright of middle South Africa, its recorder and satirist.

Over the Hill was premiered at the Grahamstown Festival, Eastern Cape, as a commissioned main event, in July, 1985, produced by Jon White-Spunner and Paul Slabolepszy, directed by Paul Slabolepszy, with the following cast:

STEVE (an outside-half)	Jonathan Rands
CHARLIE (a tight-head prop)	James Borthwick
LYNETTE (an ex-Citrus Queen)	Kate Edwards

A rugby dressing-room, Nelspruit, Eastern Transvaal. Late winter.

A rugby dressing room after a 'sport pienaar' (provincial sub-section) game.

It is like any dressing room anywhere in the world except, being Nelspruit, there are perhaps 'more orange peels on the floor than there would be if this were, say, Cardiff Arms Park.

Empty beercans, cigarette stubs and other bits of rubbish litter the floor. A low massage table stands in the centre of the room. Against the stage left wall stands a wicker kit-skip (dirty jerseys, shorts, socks hanging out). High above the skip is a long narrow window (which overlooks the carpark behind the stadium). Along the back and stage right walls is a single row of slatted benches above which are located clothes hooks – twenty odd, evenly spaced. The entrance to the dressing room (from a corridor) is located in the stage right wall, while the archway to the showers and loos (marked 'shower/stortbad') is in the back wall, stage left. A lone rugby ball is situated near the shower exit, beneath the benches.

Beneath the only hook supporting any clothing, alone and sipping at a beer, sits Steve 'Sophie' Sofianek, a twenty-four year old fly-half. His bruised face suggests the game has been a hard one and the togs he still wears positively steam with the sweat of battle.

In another part of the stadium – high, distant and quite muted, a long-winded congratulatory speech is coming to an end. The manager or coach of Steve's team is trying to speak above the din and heckle provided by the players: 'Okay, okay, I don't know what it's going to be like not having your ugly dial around anymore, but what the hell . . .' *We hear assorted boos and groans from the players as the boss continues:* 'As they say where I come from – what you lose on the roundabouts, you get back on the swings . . .' *More boos, whistling and heckling. The boss raises his voice above this:* 'Let's have the man himself.' *The 'man himself', however, is unable to start speaking because he is bombarded with broken snatches of* 'For He's a Jolly Good Fellow, Why Was He Born So Beautiful,' *etc., finally ending with the famous drinking number:* 'Here's to Charlie he's so blue, he's a drunkard through and through, he's a bastard so they say, tried to go to Heaven, but he went the other way – drink it down, two, three, four, five, six . . . etc.'

The drinking song is itself drowned by laughter, etc. and 'party music' of the Platteland kind takes over. This music – as interesting a selection as anyone would wish to hear – continues throughout the play. It should drop to a level, however, which allows the audience to become almost totally unaware of it. A distant buzz – nothing more.

Throughout the above Steve has been sitting quietly, sipping at his beer. At one point he ambles slowly to the door to the passage and gazes out and up. His face, though, shows no particular emotion. He kicks at the odd bit of rubbish. He finishes the beer at just about the same time the party music begins and tosses the empty can into a corner. He moves to where several plastic beer packets lie. Digging through them, he becomes more and more frustrated, finally slapping the empty packets with a curse. Beneath another bench, he at last finds an unopened beer.

He is busy drinking it, back at his spot beneath his clothes hook, when Charlie Theron enters. Thirty-six years old and sporting a fresh white plaster above one eye, he wears a team blazer – dark, with a distinctive gold blesbok head badge. Below the head is a blaze in gold writing with 'Blesbokke' on it. Matching tie, grey slacks and black shoes. He carries a scotch in one hand and a large, ornate 'golden' clock in the other. He is in a state of considerable agitation, shouting off down the passage.

CHARLIE. Bugger off, man . . . ja, ja – and the same to you, with brass bladdy knobs on it . . . ! Jislaaik-it . . . !

(To STEVE, *calmer.)*

How's this, hey? Oke outside here's looking for autographs – comes up to me – asks if I'm Charlie Theron. I say, who do I look like? He says Charlie Theron. I say right. I'm about to sign his bladdy book – he takes it back – he says no, he doesn't want Charlie Theron . . . Prick! *(Placing the clock on the massage table.)* How'd you like?

STEVE *does not respond.* CHARLIE *moves to the door, then back again. Still mildly agitated.*

CHARLIE. Bladdy wankers. Should do what Paul Newman does. You know what Paul Newman does? Tells them to Stuff Off. Straight. They come up to him – Stuff Off! He really lets them know where they can get off. Like that famous golfer, whatsisname? Tall bloke. Instead of signing his name, he writes 'Up Yours.' Oke comes up to him, he says sure, takes the book – *(Miming a signature.)* 'Up Yours.' Soon puts them right. Wankers. *(Indicating the clock.)* So – what d'you say?

STEVE. Hey?

CHARLIE. It's original. I'll give them that.

STEVE *sips at his beer in silence, in no mood to communicate.*

CHARLIE *(smiling wryly).* Huh. To think there are some blokes work their whole lives for one of these. My Uncle Dup in Krugersdorp. Thirty-seven years with the P.A. – clocking in, clocking out. What does he get for his troubles . . . ? A Whacking Great Clock.

They stare at the clock.

I wonder if it's gold? I mean, Gold Clock should be gold, right? (*Considers this.*) Maybe I can melt it down?

STEVE. Huh?

CHARLIE. Hey, come on – snap out of it, man. I'm asking you about this clock. You reckon it's genuine?

STEVE. Genuine?

CHARLIE. Genuine? Kosher? Halaal . . . ?

STEVE. How must I know?

CHARLIE. Soon find out.

He goes over to it and picks it up. Looks at it. Listens to it. Shakes it. Hits it. Listens again.

CHARLIE. Can you believe it? Doesn't even work.

STEVE. Would help if you wound it first.

CHARLIE (*a beat*). That's also true.

He locates the key at the back of the clock and winds it up. He checks his watch. It has stopped. He smacks it, shakes it, holds it to his ear. Looks again.

CHARLIE. Dammit. What's the time?

STEVE. Time we buggered off.

CHARLIE. Let's call it – ag, what the hell . . . (*He moves the hands to an approximate time.*) More or less . . . (*Replacing it carefully on the table.*) There. How's that? (*He steps back to admire it.*) It'll look great on my mantelpiece.

Pause.

Fourteen Years Faithful Service.

Pause.

You should've heard the Boss. The oke was really laying it on, hey. (*Dropping his voice in mock seriousness.*) 'The Blesbokke won't be the Blesbokke without ou Charlie Theron . . .'

Pause.

For that, they give me a clock.

They sit in silence, the party continuing unabated upstairs. CHARLIE looks up, listening to the distant sounds of merriment.

CHARLIE. Sounds like it's becoming quite a party up there.

STEVE. So what you doing down here?

CHARLIE. I was going to ask you the same question.

STEVE (*sharply*). If you come to look for me, you can forget it.

CHARLIE (*indicating the clock*). To tell you the truth – I was going to quietly flush this thing down the bog. (STEVE *is not amused.*) Ha-ha. That's a joke. You allowed to laugh. (STEVE *looks away.*) Hey – don't take it so serious. You win some, you lose some.

STEVE (*unconvinced*). Ja.

> CHARLIE *watches him a long time before turning to look at the clock.*

CHARLIE. You know, what they actually should've given me was one of those massive-great Cuckoo Clocks. One of those things that jump out at you in the middle of the night. You tiptoeing down a passage two o'clock in the morning – you got past the cat without standing on the damn thing and suddenly – KOE-KOEK!! – bang goes a lovely evening . . . (*Smiling at the memory.*) When I was a kid we had one in the front hall. I always used to try grab the little voëltjie – just as he popped out. Problem was, I could never crack it. The clock was a cock up. Bladdy cuckoo used to come out whenever he felt like it – and even then he only came out once – KOE-KOEK – back inside. Sometimes you sit there three hours and then all of a sudden – KOE-KOEK, gone, missed him again.

Pause.

But I got it right eventually . . . Bliksemmed the bladdy bird with a baseball bat.

Pause.

Should've seen what it did to the clock.

STEVE. Listen, Charlie – why don't you just do me a favour and Piss Off. You got something to say to me – say it – don't mess me around.

CHARLIE. You telling me to piss off?

STEVE. Just leave me alone, okay?

CHARLIE (*a beat, then angrily*). You reckon you're the only bloke who ever lost a match? Hey? You know how many matches *I* lost? I lost so many bladdy matches I get Christmas Cards from all the other Provinces. (*He allows this to sink in.*) It's history, man. You punched him so you punched him so it's finish. It's over. End of story.

Pause.

STEVE. Right in front of the bladdy poles.

CHARLIE. That's rugby. Rugby, you want to hit a bloke, you hit him so the ref can't see, otherwise you wait till the final whistle. That way you can kick him in the balls.

STEVE. And that's rugby?

CHARLIE. That's rugby.

STEVE *lifts his jersey to reveal wicked stud marks in his rib area. The flesh is torn and bleeding.*

STEVE. This rugby too?

CHARLIE (*unimpressed*). That's Bugger All.

STEVE. Oh, yes?

CHARLIE *lifts one trouser leg, revealing a long scar on his shin.*

CHARLIE. 1976. South Western Districts. Eighteen stitches.

STEVE. Big Deal.

CHARLIE. No injection.

STEVE. Big flippin' Deal.

CHARLIE. That's right, my friend. It's all part of paying your dues. And until you've done that – you'd do better to keep your mouth shut.

Pause.

Let me tell you something right now, my boy. You got one *helluva* problem. It's called Attitude.

STEVE. Attitude?

CHARLIE. Attitude.

STEVE. I'll remember that.

CHARLIE. I mean what kind of idiot comes off the pitch and tells the Boss to Get Stuffed?

STEVE. I told him to Suck Eggs.

CHARLIE. Same thing. You don't do it. Not to the Boss. (*He moves to the door, restless – peering out down the corridor.*)

STEVE. You know what he tunes me?

CHARLIE. Doesn't matter what he tunes you.

STEVE. He tunes me I should've gone blind that last scrum of the match. A two-man overlap and I should've gone blind.

CHARLIE. If the Boss says you should've gone blind, you should've gone blind.

STEVE. With a two-man overlap!?

CHARLIE. Ten-man overlap – makes no difference.

STEVE. You would've gone blind?

CHARLIE. I don't know what I would've done.

STEVE. *You* would've gone blind!?

CHARLIE. The point is – you don't argue.

STEVE. The point is – I was right!

CHARLIE. You see? Attitude.

STEVE. Stuff Attitude! I'm the one who's out there. I'm the one with his chop on the block.

CHARLIE (*looking to the door*). Shhh!

STEVE. If I had've gone blind, the stupid turd would've told me I had a two-man flippin' overlap . . . !

CHARLIE. Shhh – okay, okay – point taken – shhh!

STEVE. What you shushing?

CHARLIE. It's okay – I thought I heard something.

STEVE *kicks the bench in frustration.*

CHARLIE. I'm not trying to put you down here. I just don't want you to look like a poephol.

STEVE. I am a poephol.

CHARLIE. I'm not *saying* you a poephol.

STEVE. I'm a poephol. Say it. I'm a poephol.

Pause.

CHARLIE. You a poephol.

Pause.

CHARLIE. Look, they not going to drop a oke after his first game, so don't worry.

STEVE *looks up at him – not so sure.*

Come on, Sophie. Go shower – get dressed – we go get pissed. (*Brightly.*) Hey. You must see. They got these chicks outside here they lining them up. Looks like they hauled in every little boere-meisie from Piet Retief to Phalaborwa. (*Chuckling.*) Hey,

this is the place they pick the Orange Queen. Who knows –
maybe there's a Grapefruit Queen lurking about here as
well . . . ? A Quince Queen . . . ?

STEVE. I'm sorry, Charlie. I let the okes down.

CHARLIE *moves to* STEVE*'s kitbag and opens it.*

CHARLIE. Bull. Where's your towel?

STEVE (*angry with himself*). Just one bladdy punch, man.

He wanders into the shower area, disappearing off left. CHARLIE *goes
through his things. Tossing out spare shorts, underwear, etc.*

CHARLIE. Jeez, what's all this shit you keep in here . . . ? (*Taking
out a large pack of condoms.*) Hey, hey, hey . . . ? (*Reading.*)
'Lubricated with Sensatol.' (*Shouting off in the direction of the
showers.*) Who packs your bag . . . the wife?

STEVE *comes back out of the shower area.*

STEVE (*pointing into the showers*). How these bust windows through
here?

CHARLIE. What did you expect? Loftus bladdy Versveld? Southern
fucken Suns?

STEVE *moves to the skip, inspecting* CHARLIE*'s clock.*

CHARLIE (*taking out a bottle of aftershave*). What's this? (*Sniffing,
then reading the label.*) Macho.

STEVE (*correcting him*). Macco.

CHARLIE. Says Macho.

STEVE. It's Macco.

CHARLIE (*spelling*). M - A - C - H - O.

STEVE. That's how you say it.

CHARLIE. Says who?

STEVE. Says the oke in the shop.

CHARLIE (*a beat*). You may be Macco, baby – I'm Macho.

STEVE. You're just a bladdy Pleb.

CHARLIE *has the top off, splashing it on.*

CHARLIE. What's it like?

STEVE. Hey! Take it easy there.

He goes to grab it. CHARLIE *pulls away.*

You going to honk like a moffie, man.

CHARLIE. What – with MACHO!?

> CHARLIE *jumps up onto the benches, lifting his belt and splashing into his underpants.* STEVE *goes to grab the bottle and* CHARLIE *jumps down and runs to the massage table.*

STEVE. Stuff you, Charlie – it's sixteen bucks a bottle, man.

> CHARLIE *yanks the massage table into the centre, darting behind it.*

CHARLIE. Come on, Sophie – smile. Smile for your Uncle Charlie.

STEVE (*picking up the clock*). I'll smash this thing, strue's God.

CHARLIE. Hell, please! Do me a favour – be my guest, man.

> STEVE *places the clock on the bench and gives chase, only for* CHARLIE *to dart around the massage table, using it as a shield between himself and the youngster.*

> Brom – brom – brom, die Blesbokke kom . . . Come on, man. Who are – who are – who are we – ? Come on . . .

STEVE. Give here.

CHARLIE (*keeping him at bay*). Come on. War Cry. Who are – who are – who are we – ? Come on – we are – we are –

STEVE. Bugger Off now, Charlie – give here.

CHARLIE (*enjoying this*). You coming right now. I wanna see you smile. Now come on – War Cry –

STEVE. Don't be a moegoe, man.

> CHARLIE *continues with the mocking chant, all the while running this way and that, constantly keeping the massage table between them. He tips the bottle.*

CHARLIE. Who are – who are – who are we – ?

STEVE (*quickly, before any is spilt*). We are – we are – can't you see – ?

CHARLIE (*pointing to* STEVE). B –

STEVE. B – ?

CHARLIE. L –

STEVE. What?

CHARLIE. Come on. Come on, man . . . B –

> CHARLIE *points to* STEVE.

STEVE. B –

To himself.

CHARLIE. L –

STEVE. E –

CHARLIE. S –

STEVE. K –

CHARLIE. K . . . ? What d'you mean K? Again. B –

Pointing at STEVE.

STEVE. B –

CHARLIE. L –

STEVE. E –

CHARLIE. S –

STEVE. K –

CHARLIE. What!?

STEVE. O – ? B – ? Shit man. I dunno. What we spelling here?

CHARLIE. Jislaaik . . . !

STEVE. I don't want to play this crap.

CHARLIE. No wonder we can't win a game. Can't even spell our own bladdy name right!

STEVE. Cocks this now, man.

CHARLIE. Who are we? We bladdy Blesbokke, man. How many years you been shouting for the Blesbokke?

STEVE. Ja, Charlie.

CHARLIE. From the top.

STEVE. No, Charlie.

CHARLIE. From the top! Who are – who are – who are we – ?

CHARLIE AND STEVE. We are – we are – can't you see – ?

CHARLIE *points to* STEVE.

STEVE. B –

CHARLIE. L –

STEVE. E –

CHARLIE. S –

STEVE (*a beat*). B –

CHARLIE. O –

STEVE. K –

CHARLIE. Now it's K . . . K –

STEVE. E –

CHARLIE AND STEVE. BLESBOKKE!!

> CHARLIE *still withholds the bottle of aftershave.*

CHARLIE. You okay now?

STEVE. Ja.

CHARLIE. You fixed up now?

STEVE. Ja.

CHARLIE. Twenty press-ups.

STEVE. What?

CHARLIE. Twenty press-ups.

STEVE. Ah, no – come on, Charlie man, for . . .

CHARLIE. Nothing like a bit a' sweat to get the head right –
  (*Keeping the bottle from him.*) Down –

STEVE. I'm okay now, I swear –

CHARLIE (*shoving him down*). Down you go. One – two –

STEVE (*down but still protesting*). Charlie –

CHARLIE. *One* – two – three – four –

> STEVE *reluctantly begins doing press-ups.*

> five – six – when you pissed off, you do press-ups – gets it out of
> the system . . . eight – nine – ten – sheesh, you bladdy unfit,
> hey?

STEVE (*not stopping*). Just played a bladdy game, man.

CHARLIE. . . . twelve – thirteen – fourteen –

STEVE. Count right, man.

CHARLIE. Shaddap! This is what they call 'therapy' – faster –
  sixteen – seventeen – eighteen – nineteen – five more . . .

STEVE. Bull!

CHARLIE (*fetching* STEVE*'s half empty beer and putting down the
  aftershave*). Five more. Twenty-one – twenty-two – twenty-three –
  twenty-four – twenty-five . . .

As STEVE *reaches the final press-up,* CHARLIE *pours a stream of beer onto his head.* STEVE *leaps to his feet and* CHARLIE *escapes by running around the massage table.* CHARLIE *shakes the can all the while, working up some pressure. He lets the youngster have a jet and leaps up onto the skip.* STEVE *peppers him with empty beercans. The 'game' is stopped by* CHARLIE *spotting something through the window above the skip.*

CHARLIE. Stick around. Wait. Wait!

STEVE (*still hurling junk*). Stuff you, boy.

CHARLIE. No, give it up, man. Come check here – quick!

STEVE (*staying where he is*). Bulldust.

CHARLIE. No, swear to God – quickly, man.

STEVE *is wary, but* CHARLIE's *bubbling enthusiasm seems too sincere to be acted. He gets up onto the skip and together they crane their necks, as if trying to see something through the window in a downstage direction.*

CHARLIE. You see?

STEVE. I see.

CHARLIE. What I tell you?

STEVE. Like you said.

CHARLIE (*socked between the eyes*). Check. Check!

STEVE. I check. The one with the – ?

CHARLIE. The one with the – ja.

STEVE (*impressed*). Ja.

CHARLIE. Hey?

STEVE. Ja.

CHARLIE. On a plate, my mate.

STEVE (*taking his beer from* CHARLIE *and jumping down*). Nurses.

CHARLIE (*still ogling*). Hey?

STEVE. Nurses.

CHARLIE. What do you mean 'nurses'?

STEVE. Nurses – you know – Morning Doctor – Morning Nurse . . .

CHARLIE. What the bladdy hell's wrong with nurses?

STEVE. Nothing. You got a skyf?

CHARLIE (*shaking his head*). Poephol.

> STEVE *puts his beer down.*

STEVE. This thing's flat. You owe me one.

> CHARLIE *is looking through the window again.* STEVE *picks up his aftershave, moves to his kitbag and starts going through it.*

CHARLIE. How do you know they're nurses?

STEVE. I dunno. Maybe they a busload of Troepies in Drag.

CHARLIE (*middle-finger gesture*). This is for you.

STEVE. Save it for the nurses.

> STEVE *laughs and turns his attention to his kitbag once more. He digs around in it.*

STEVE. What you do with my soap, now?

CHARLIE (*jumping down*). Come on, stop faffing around now. Bliksem.

> *He advances on* STEVE *in mock aggression.*

STEVE. *I'm* a bliksem . . . ?

> *They grab each other and begin wrestling. A typical dressing room fight ensues. It is (to some eyes) childish, ridiculous; but it is the traditional manner in which Gladiators 'kiss and make up.'*
>
> *In the middle of it all,* LYNETTE McALLISTER *appears in the doorway. She is on the wrong side of twenty-five for an ex-beauty queen, single, and still on the make. It is her attempt to appear with it in her style of dress that immediately endears her to us – the platteland notion of high chic, made even more off-key by virtue of the fact that she is a little gone to seed. She stands watching the players roll this way and that, totally oblivious to the attentions of their silent observer. Finally they become aware of her presence and, highly embarrassed, get to their feet and dust themselves off.*

CHARLIE. Oh. Hi. Lynette. Sorry. Er . . . Steve, this is Lynette. Lynette . . . Steve.

STEVE. Hi.

LYNETTE. What happened?

CHARLIE (*misunderstanding her*). No, he punched me over here, so I just . . .

STEVE. Bullsh . . . bulldust, ou!

> *They are about to launch into their argument again when* LYNETTE *interrupts, addressing* CHARLIE.

LYNETTE. No, I mean upstairs . . . upstairs. One minute you were there – the next you were . . . I been looking for you everywhere.

CHARLIE. Oh, ja – er – (*Indicating* STEVE.) I came to look for this idiot.

LYNETTE. Are you going to take this photo now or what you want me to do?

CHARLIE. Oh, yes – picture. Dammit. Steve, where's the camera?

STEVE. What camera?

CHARLIE. Camera, man. Click-click. Thing that takes pictures.

STEVE. Cam . . . ? Er . . . (*Covering for him.*) Must be upstairs . . .

CHARLIE (*really busking now*). Must be upstairs.

LYNETTE. Someone's getting me that tape if you want to hear it.

CHARLIE. Great. Fantastic.

LYNETTE. You still want to hear it, don't you?

CHARLIE. For sure. Guaranteed. Look – er – we'll be with you in a minute. Why don't you go get us a dop in the meantime . . . Two dops. Steve . . . ? Three dops . . . we'll be right there.

She hovers in the doorway, unsure of the territory.

Swear to God. We right there.

LYNETTE. Don't be long, hey?

CHARLIE. No, we there.

She lingers briefly then makes her way down the corridor. STEVE *sniggers, on to* CHARLIE*'s game.*

STEVE. Camera . . . ? I mean, jissus . . .

CHARLIE. Shhh. Listen, do us a favour. You going to have to bail me out here.

STEVE. What d'you mean?

CHARLIE. Ag, long bladdy story, man. My own fault. Last time we played here, I told her I run this Modelling Agency in Alberton.

STEVE. You what!?

CHARLIE. Don't laugh. I had a bet with Van der Westhuizen – six bottles of J and B I scored the Orange Queen.

STEVE. She's a Orange Queen?

CHARLIE. Ex-Orange Queen.

STEVE. You obviously cracked it.

CHARLIE. Please! Where from?

STEVE. I thought it was supposed to be a piece of cake with these Platteland chicks?

CHARLIE. Ja, you smile at them – they hear Wedding Bells. Only problem is – they got to see the ring on their finger first . . .

STEVE cannot stop laughing. CHARLIE moves to the door, looking off down the passage.

Shit, I was hoping she'd bugger off. No such bladdy luck.

STEVE. What's this about a tape?

CHARLIE. Ag, she's got some tape, man. Wants to play me a tape – show me what she can do.

STEVE. Rather you than me, ou.

CHARLIE. That's why it pays to cover up your tracks, my boy. Come on. Pull finger. Let's get the hell out of here. We go grab us a coupla nurses – jol back to the hotel.

STEVE's mood abruptly changes.

STEVE. Ja, look – you go ahead.

CHARLIE (*sitting near the door*). Come on, I'll wait for you.

STEVE picks up a rugby ball and begins toying with it.

STEVE. No – look – forget it. I'm not messing around anymore.

CHARLIE. You're not messing around anymore? You . . . ! The biggest razzler in the business!?

STEVE. Ja, I'm . . . taking it easy for a while. I'm cooling it.

CHARLIE stares at him, incredulous.

CHARLIE. Hey . . . forget about the wife, you on tour now, man. (STEVE *looks away.*) She giving you grief again, or what . . . ? (*Still no response.*) Look, I've told you before – First Year of Marriage is Always the Worst.

STEVE. Ja, if it lasts that long.

This is news to CHARLIE.

CHARLIE. Bullshit.

STEVE. Swear to God. Now all of a sudden she wants to Bugger Off.

CHARLIE. Estelle? Since when?

STEVE. I'm telling you. Last week already. I come home one
night – Wednesday – Thursday – whatever. Late practice – you
know – the usual. I walk in the door – I wasn't even lousy to her.
I just said what's for supper?

CHARLIE. What's for supper?

STEVE. What's for supper? She says We Finish. Just like that.

CHARLIE. That's what she says?

STEVE. Straight. We Finish.

CHARLIE. Ei-na!

STEVE. That's what I thought.

CHARLIE. Who wouldn't.

STEVE. The way she said it. To my face. No messing about – no
nothing. We Finish. So now I'm thinking – now what's this now?
Normally she gives me uphill I just laugh, you know – grip her
arse, slap her around . . .

CHARLIE. The usual.

STEVE. That's right. Only this time I can't because she's changed –
it's not Estelle. I mean, there's this woman standing in front of
me but it's not Estelle.

CHARLIE. She's different –

STEVE. She's otherwise. These eyes – bladdy lasers.

CHARLIE. So you tune her –

STEVE. So I'm standing there. S'posed to have been at Late
Practice, but I's with, ah, shit – what's her name?

CHARLIE. Janet?

STEVE. Naah, man – the other one . . .

CHARLIE. Anyway –

STEVE. Anyway. I been at her place. So I'm standing there, hey. A
real arsehole. My dirty togs in one hand – bunch of flowers in
the other; and now I'm trying to hold them behind my back so
she can't see them . . .

CHARLIE. Women are crazy.

STEVE. Mad, man. Anyway – so it's aftershave, mint imperials, the
works, and I'm praying like hell she can't smell anything else
and all of a sudden I'm thinking, oh nice, some little groupie's
phoned her up. Or some bastard's been shooting his mouth
off –

CHARLIE. I know the type.

STEVE. Some big talker, you know. So I say is it me? Something I've done? She says no, it's not you – meaning me . . .

CHARLIE. So what do you do?

STEVE. What can I do?

CHARLIE. You give her the flowers.

STEVE. How can I give her the flowers?

CHARLIE. They not *her* flowers?

STEVE. Of course they her flowers, man. But how can I give her the bladdy flowers . . . ? She tells me she's leaving I give her this massive great bunch of carnations!

CHARLIE. Okay, okay – so what happened?

STEVE. Bugger All. She goes to her room, locks the door and that's that. Twenty minutes later she's back in the lounge and it's all okay – she's sorry, she didn't mean it.

CHARLIE. That's all?

STEVE. That's all. Except this long face ever since.

CHARLIE. Women are mad, man.

STEVE. Crazy.

CHARLIE. Temporary Insanity – hits them now and again.

STEVE. What the hell you do?

CHARLIE. You get her right, boy – but quick. You find out what's her buzz.

STEVE. She won't tell me.

CHARLIE. Where's your Balls man? You must listen to your Uncle Charlie here. I know what I'm talking about.

STEVE *stares at the older man, shocked by his directness.*

CHARLIE. Charmaine tried the same trick on me. Three weeks she doesn't talk to me. All of a sudden she's going to Pottery Classes. Pottery Classes, huh! When I ask to see her pots there's no pots because it turns out there's no classes either. We both at home – the phone rings – I pick it up, there's no one there. All that kind of crap.

STEVE. You think she was having a bit of a – ?

CHARLIE. How must I know?

STEVE. You didn't ask her?

CHARLIE (*smirking*). Stuff that! I must sink so low?

STEVE. So what you do?

CHARLIE. I kept my cool. All I did was one night I just casually brought out the gun . . . to clean it. Made sure the kid was there too. Okay, you haven't got a kid. You got a kid, it helps. She sees you, she sees the kid, she sees the gun . . . She thinks . . . She doesn't try it again.

Pause.

There's more to being the Boss than making a noise.

STEVE *simply stares at him.*

Come on. Into that shower. We going to get you arseholes tonight, boy – but totally.

He grabs STEVE's bag and tosses it to him.

He moves to the small mirror near the door to the passage and whips out a comb. STEVE watches him as he runs the comb through his thinning hair.

STEVE. You wouldn't really do it, would you?

CHARLIE (*preoccupied with his hair*). Ah, no, dammit, man . . . just look at these . . . grey hairs. Gets to the stage you stop bladdy counting them.

STEVE. Charlie . . . ?

CHARLIE. Shit, go like this –

He lifts his hair off his forehead.

STEVE. Huh?

CHARLIE (*indicating that STEVE should do it*). Go like this.

STEVE. What for?

CHARLIE. Just lift your hair, man.

STEVE *complies.*

Ja, you see . . . You too.

STEVE. Bullshit.

CHARLIE. Two-three years. You watch.

STEVE. You wouldn't *really* use it, would you?

CHARLIE. Bald as a coot in five years . . . Use what?

STEVE. The gun?

CHARLIE. You think I'm crazy or something?

STEVE. I dunno.

CHARLIE (*still into the mirror*). I might shoot a burglar – but the wife! I mean that's going too far . . . (*Suddenly horrified.*) Shit I don't believe it . . . !

STEVE. What?

CHARLIE (*holding out the comb*). More on the comb than on my bladdy head. Still. I should complain? Ou Moerdyk's getting himself a hairpiece next week. As long as he doesn't play in the damn thing. Oke gives him a high-tackle – he's left with a fur-burger in his hand . . .

He goes on combing his hair, adding the finishing touches. STEVE digs around in his bag, then unzips a side panel.

CHARLIE (*admiring the finished product*). No, I'm telling you. In this Life it all comes down to Balls, that's all. A question of Balls. Who's got the Balls.

STEVE takes his soap and a plastic miniature Donald Duck from the side panel.

STEVE. Here, Ballsey, this is for you.

CHARLIE (*catching it*). What's this?

STEVE. Donald Duck.

CHARLIE (*throwing it back*). Fuck Donald Duck. I got a Donald Duck.

STEVE. What must *I* do with it?

CHARLIE. Don't ask me!

STEVE. Thanks a lot. I graze a whole box of Corn Flakes for this.

CHARLIE. I *told* you. I *got* a Donald Duck. I got a Donald Duck, a Mickey Mouse, a Goofy and a Porky Pig. It's *Pluto*. I want a Pluto. I get a Pluto – I got the whole set.

STEVE (*about to put it back*). Oh, well – stuff you then.

CHARLIE. No, no. Give here. I'll swop it.

STEVE (*giving it to him*). Jissis – why you got to waste your time with the kid's stuff . . . ?

CHARLIE. Kid's stuff!?

STEVE. I mean how's your bladdy head with all that?

CHARLIE. Please! Woman next door won herself a flippin' Deep Freeze. Fourteen cubic foot!

STEVE (*removing his boots and socks*). All my life . . .

CHARLIE (*fired up now*). I'm telling you! How's this, hey? She comes to me two weeks ago she asks me if I got a Mickey Mouse. I say okay, I give her my spare Mickey Mouse – she already had a Pluto, the bitch. Fuck me if she doesn't win a bladdy Deep Freeze.

Pause. STEVE is inspecting his toes.

What I couldn't do with a Deep Freeze.

STEVE gets up and goes to his bag, digging around in it.

Mincer-Mixer-Shredder-Liquidiser . . .

STEVE. You got any nail clippers?

CHARLIE. I mean just the other day this bloke down the road wins one of those big outside swings . . . (STEVE *finds an emery board and begins working on a toe nail.*) One of those huge couch swing things for the garden – two-tone – blue-and-white, tassles round the side . . . Okay, it's not a Deep Freeze but who's complaining? I mean – hell. I could use a bladdy outside swing. Stick it outside. Middle of the lawn. Look fantastic the middle of my lawn.

STEVE (*filing his toes*). You haven't got a lawn.

CHARLIE. I know. But if I had a swing I'd flippin' grow one, wouldn't I?

STEVE blows at the emery board, tosses it and his boots into his kitbag.

Ag, I dunno. It's just not fair, man. Friday I buy eight packets. Eight! I get seven Porky Pigs and one Goofy. There's no bladdy justice in the world.

STEVE. Where's my soap?

CHARLIE. I didn't touch your soap.

STEVE looks down at his jersey, reluctant to take it off. CHARLIE toys with the Donald Duck.

CHARLIE. Why is it that every man must always try screw the next man? You know I'm willing to bet that for every five thousand Porky Pigs, Donald Ducks and Mickey Mouses – they only got about half a dozen Plutos . . .

STEVE. Mickey Mice.

CHARLIE. Hey?

STEVE. Mickey Mice. One mouse – two mice.

CHARLIE. You think I'm joking?

STEVE. No, I'm with you. Those okes know what they're on about. It's what they call Consumer Incentive – the Big Carrot.

CHARLIE. Carrots . . . ? What shit you talking now?

STEVE. Carrot on the Stick. Oldest trick in the book.

CHARLIE. Why don't you just stop talking shit and go shower? Before we know it, that bladdy Quince Queen's going to be down here again, man.

STEVE pulls his jersey over his head, but stops short of taking it completely off. He stands with his arms still in the sleeves, staring down at it. CHARLIE thinks he is looking at his muscles.

Boy-oh-boy, check the Tarzan here. Looks to me you need to get back on weights, my friend.

STEVE (*preoccupied*). I haven't stopped.

CHARLIE. What you pumping? Toothpicks?

In a single motion STEVE has pulled his jersey back on again. CHARLIE half suspects the young player's motives.

What the bladdy hell's your case now?

STEVE shrugs, embarrassed, unsure what to do next.

CHARLIE. Don't tell me. You want to kip in the damn thing?

STEVE. Laugh, my friend – you were probably the same.

CHARLIE. You bladdy right, yes. Okes had to tear it off my back.

Pause.

Well, come on. You can't sit here all bladdy night.

STEVE. I wonder if I should kiss the collar?

CHARLIE. What for?

STEVE. When I played Schools rugby I always kissed the collar before I took it off.

CHARLIE (*sceptical*). You reckon that did the trick?

STEVE. I never got dropped.

STEVE looks at the jersey. CHARLIE looks at STEVE.

CHARLIE. So? What you waiting for? Kiss the damn thing.

STEVE. I dunno, man.

CHARLIE. What's the problem?

STEVE. 'S different.

CHARLIE. Different?

STEVE. Different. Different team – different . . . you know . . .

CHARLIE. Christ, you're worse than the bladdy Irish.

STEVE. I'm serious.

CHARLIE. You ever been into a Irish dressing room? Got to be seen to be believed. Okes are outa their minds, man – spitting on their boots, hitting their heads against the wall . . .

STEVE. It's not funny.

CHARLIE. There was this one poephol played for Shamrocks had to walk on the ceiling before he went out onto the pitch.

Pause. STEVE *looks up.*

STEVE. How the hell he do that?

CHARLIE. Don't ask me. Okes had to stand on the table. Hold him upside down.

Pause.

STEVE. Now that's crazy.

CHARLIE. That's what I'm saying.

Pause.

So what's it going to be? Spit – ? Kiss – ? Fart – ?

STEVE (*he has the ball again*). How d'you like my dummy scissors just before half-time?

CHARLIE. What dummy scissors?

STEVE. Just before half-time, man . . . (*Demonstrating.*) Half-gap . . . held onto it . . . little grubber through . . . (*Leaping up on to the bench.*) That much further . . . *That* much further, ou Pinky would've been over.

CHARLIE. Ja.

STEVE. You didn't think I'd crack it, hey? That first time I jolled into Old Boy's – that practice – you didn't think I'd crack it . . . ?

CHARLIE. I always knew you'd crack it.

STEVE (*indicating the emblem on his chest*). North-Easterns, my mate . . . (*He wanders along the bench, squatting near the clock. He points to it.*) Been a long time for you already, hey?

CHARLIE. Bladdy sure. Fourteen years. Seems like yesterday.

STEVE. They give everybody a clock?

CHARLIE. Depends. Some okes get nothing. On the other hand three years ago they gave ou Wally Joubert a Dinner Service. Bone china. Bladdy wankers.

STEVE. You feel shit about it?

CHARLIE. About the clock?

STEVE. About retiring?

CHARLIE. Ah, what the fuck.

Pause.

STEVE. I'll never forget. First time I saw you was against those South Americans at the Pam Brink. You scored two tries and the blokes carried you off.

CHARLIE. You were there?

STEVE (*demonstrating*). I was so high.

CHARLIE. You never told me you were there.

STEVE. *That* was the game I first said to myself I'm going to be a Blesbok.

CHARLIE (*bitterly*).Two tries. And then for that Gazelle game they went and picked that bladdy poephol from South West.

STEVE. It was always going to be different. I was always going to score a couple of tries. Maybe put over a drop . . . One thing's for sure – I was never gonna lose us the game.

CHARLIE. Lesson Number One in this kind of Rugby – it means bugger all. You play like a Champion you find out afterwards they been watching somebody else.

Pause.

You mustn't take it to kop. This game can bladdy kill you.

Pause.

STEVE. How you reckon I played today?

CHARLIE (*not relishing this*). Today?

STEVE. Ja.

CHARLIE (*a beat*). Okay. You were okay.

STEVE. Sort of okay or quite okay or what?

CHARLIE. For a first game, you were bladdy okay.

STEVE. No, but I mean not counting first game. Just taking it as a game. Any old game . . .

CHARLIE. What do you want me to say, Sophie?

STEVE. I want you to say what you think.

CHARLIE. I told you what I think. I think you were great.

STEVE. You mean that?

CHARLIE. Listen, are you coming upstairs or not?

STEVE. I want to *know*, Charlie. I want to know from you – not from the other okes, or from the papers, or some arsehole in the street . . . I want to hear it from somebody who knows what I can do.

Pause. There is no avoiding it.

CHARLIE. You played like a first class prick.

Pause.

STEVE. Thanks.

CHARLIE. In fact you were worse than that.

STEVE. Okay, okay –

CHARLIE (*shrugging*). You wanted to know.

STEVE. Well, fuck you.

CHARLIE. Fuck you too.

STEVE. *You* played like an arsehole.

CHARLIE. Oh yes?

STEVE. Arsehole de luxe.

CHARLIE. Well after a hundred and thirty-four games for this province I can afford to, can't I?

STEVE. Stick your bladdy province, man!

CHARLIE. Don't get pissed off with *me* now.

STEVE. You said I was great.

CHARLIE. I said you were okay.

STEVE. And now you telling me I'm shit.

CHARLIE. You're not at school anymore, man. This isn't the first fucken fifteen.

STEVE. What's that supposed to mean?

CHARLIE. Listen, Sunshine, why they pick you for this game?

STEVE. Because I'm fucken good.

CHARLIE (*exploding*). Don't talk shit to me now, I'm being serious!

STEVE. Because de Waal's injured.

CHARLIE. Okay, de Waal's injured. But why they pick *you* – not somebody else?

STEVE. I dunno – they fucked in the head.

CHARLIE. Because you kick, poephol. You're a kicker. Everybody knows we got the worst backline in ten years, so they pick someone who's going to play the forwards – right?

STEVE. Right.

CHARLIE. A Fly-half whose going to kick – right? (STEVE *remains silent.*) Right. So what do you do? You're letting it out behind your own bladdy tryline, for fuck's sake.

STEVE. What else could I do?

CHARLIE. You play safe, poephol. You kick, and you kick, and keep on bladdy kicking.

STEVE. But the oke was on top of me.

CHARLIE (*pacing about*). Where these beers? Don't tell me you drank all these beers? Look at this mess.

STEVE. You can't bladdy kick *all* the time.

CHARLIE. Now you know why these places stink like a beerhall. Come on, let's get out of here, man. Sis!

STEVE. So you reckon that's it, hey?

CHARLIE. You know I came into a dressing room once. It was in Durban. Kings Park. There were these wankers pissing up the wall, seeing who could piss the highest.

STEVE. Charlie . . . ? You reckon I'm out?

CHARLIE. Whole bladdy team – slashing up the walls . . .

Pause.

Animals . . . Pigs . . .

STEVE. You know what Danie Craven said to me?

CHARLIE. Disgusting.

Pause.

STEVE. You know what Danie Craven said to me . . . ?

CHARLIE. I know what Danie Craven said to you.

STEVE. How can you? I've never told you.

CHARLIE. Danie Craven said a lot of things to a lot of people.

STEVE. He told me to come to Stellenbosch.

CHARLIE. Is that so? He said the same thing to me eighteen years ago.

STEVE *stares at* CHARLIE. *He has hit rock bottom.*

There's a lot of fish in this little pond, my boy . . . fucken lot of fish.

Slowly STEVE *peels off his jersey and allows it to drop to the floor. They sit in silence for a while. The party upstairs continues, unabated.*

CHARLIE. You didn't kiss the collar.

STEVE. Hey?

CHARLIE. Collar. You didn't . . . you know.

STEVE (*unconcerned*). Ja.

Suddenly CHARLIE *gets to his feet, heading for the door.*

CHARLIE. I don't know about you, but I gotta have a dop. I tell you what. I'll slip back to the hotel maybe score us some chicks. By the time you rock up I'll have them ticking, how's that? Even better you can take your pick – first choice.

STEVE (*unamused*). Always the joker, hey?

CHARLIE. Got to take your chances, boy. Chances is chances. Grab them while you can – you catch?

STEVE *looks away, hassled – preoccupied.*

Okay. You want it straight. Fine. They probably going to drop you. In fact they *are* going to drop you . . . You're out on your arse. How's that?

STEVE (*beyond it now*). Let's just los it, okay?

CHARLIE. What do you want from this Game? You want to play Rugby or you want a clock? You want a clock – you can have this one with pleasure.

STEVE. Talk crap, man.

CHARLIE. Then what is it? What's the Big Deal? I mean where the bladdy hell you come from, man? You mope around this dressing room worrying if and when you going to wear that jersey again – you're what? You're twenty-three!

STEVE. Twenty-four.

CHARLIE. You know how old I am?

STEVE. It's enough, okay?

CHARLIE. I said do you know how old I am? Tonight's supposed to be my bladdy Farewell in case you'd forgotten.

STEVE. I hadn't forgotten.

CHARLIE. Ja, well maybe I'm feeling a bit shit too. Maybe right now I'd like to be getting pissed out of my mind, trying to forget I've played my last bladdy game for the Blesbokke.

STEVE. Ja, but for you it's okay – you've had a good go of it. And even if you wanted to, you could always come back.

CHARLIE. That simple, hey?

STEVE. For sure. You got a couple more years – at least!

CHARLIE. Says who?

STEVE. Ah, come on, man . . . you're . . . I mean you're Charlie Theron.

CHARLIE. Oh, yes? You know what the Boss says to Charlie Theron half-way through the season . . . ? Hey . . . ? You really want to know . . . ?

STEVE *stares at the older man. Way out of his depth now.*

You know bugger all about this game, do you? You think it's a matter of choice. Am I going to play or am I not going to play? Choice never comes into it, Sunshine. It's Politics.

STEVE *is silent.* CHARLIE *points to the clock.*

That clock's not just a Farewell Gift. It's part of a deal. It's like a medal they give to a foot-soldier whose had his bladdy legs blown off.

There is a long silence. STEVE *knows that for* CHARLIE *there is no going back.*

CHARLIE. You think *you've* been cheated? Remind me to tell you sometime.

He heads for the door.

STEVE. Charlie.

CHARLIE. Ja.

STEVE. I'm sorry.

CHARLIE. What for?

STEVE. I didn't know it was like that, I swear.

CHARLIE. It's okay.

STEVE. I didn't really mean it just now when I said you played like an arsehole.

CHARLIE. Forget it. How *I* play doesn't matter anymore.

STEVE (*passionately*). But it does. You got to show them. You got to prove it to them.

CHARLIE. Prove what?

STEVE. That you're still the best.

CHARLIE. What for . . . ? (STEVE *stares at him, nonplussed.*) I'm sick of this Game. I've had it up to here. For years already. The busted kneecaps – the dislocated shoulders. And as for the newspapers – Christ, the crap they write about you in the newspapers!

STEVE *is the picture of utter confusion.*

STEVE. I don't understand –

CHARLIE. I know, I know – it's crazy – it's madness. I want to play and I don't want to play. But what else is there? When you're me? When rugby's the only thing you know? Half the reason I'm not going upstairs is because I'm too shit-scared to face up to it. Wondering what the bladdy hell I'm going to do. I mean where do I go from here? What happens to me now?

STEVE *has to search for this.*

STEVE. What happens to anyone?

CHARLIE (*not letting him off the hook*). No. I'm not talking about anyone. I'm talking about me. About Charlie Theron. Two-three years down the line. Sixty years old. Hanging round the Clubhouse bar till they kick me out at Closing Time.

STEVE. Like Fats Vorster.

CHARLIE. Ja . . .

STEVE. Fats is a joke, man.

CHARLIE. That's exactly what I mean. (*He suddenly smiles, remembering something.*) Huh. A coupla weeks ago I go in for this interview . . . new job . . . hopefully. This bloke asks me what experience I got. I tell him playing rugby and selling jockstraps.

STEVE. There's no crime in that.

CHARLIE. Bloke says to me Occupation? How's this, hey? He's
   filling out this form. He says to me Occupation? I say to him
   Tight Head Prop. Just as a joke. He looks at me. He's never
   heard of a Tight Head Prop. Can you believe it? A fully grown,
   so-called educated man – he's never heard of a Tight Head
   Prop!

STEVE (*quietly*). Jesus.

Pause.

CHARLIE. Ag, what the hell . . . (*He moves to the door.*) Look, if I
   spot you, I spot you, okay . . . ?

He exits. STEVE, *moved by the older man's plight, calls out after him.*

STEVE. Charlie . . . ?

CHARLIE (*stopping some distance down the passage*). Ja?

STEVE. Charlie . . . ?

   CHARLIE *ambles back to the dressing room door. He pops his head in.*

   Cha . . . ? Hey, Charlie . . . go order the dops, man. Let's get out
   of our bladdy minds.

CHARLIE (*beaming*). Now you talking, ou.

He is gone.

   CHARLIE *has barely disappeared when he comes bursting back in,
   catching* STEVE *in the process of removing his shorts and jockstrap.*

CHARLIE. Shit, I don't believe it! Get decent. Here she comes . . . !

STEVE (*pulling on his shorts*). What's up?

   CHARLIE *has whipped* STEVE*'s blazer off the clothes hook and is
   thrusting it into his hands.*

CHARLIE. Listen, you haven't seen me, okay? (*Heading for the
   shower arch.*) I'm going to get out through the window in the
   shower . . .

STEVE (*bewildered at the frenzy*). What?

CHARLIE (*pointing off*). I'm getting out the window here . . .

STEVE. Talk junk, man. Stick around . . .

CHARLIE. Just give me enough time to get my stuff upstairs and
   bugger off . . .

STEVE (*his blazer on now too*). Wait a minute. What am I going to
   tell her . . . ?

CHARLIE. Tell her anything. Just give me enough time to get away.

STEVE. Bull. This is your bladdy Stuff Up, not mine . . .

CHARLIE notices he has forgotten the clock. He darts back to fetch it.

CHARLIE. Give a guy a break, man. I'd do the same for you.

As he whips up the clock, LYNETTE, wine glass in hand, sticks her head in the door.

LYNETTE. Coo-ee . . . Hello there.

CHARLIE (*rapidly changing gear*). Hi, Lynette. I was just coming to find you. (*Replacing the clock.*)

She holds up a tatty portable taperecorder.

LYNETTE. I've got the tape.

CHARLIE. Wonderful. Let's hear it. Come inside.

LYNETTE. Thanks. It's getting a bit wild up there. I don't know why it is that rugby players must always stand on the tables.

CHARLIE. Ja, well better on top than underneath, hey?

LYNETTE. There some there too.

She has had a couple of drinks and is very slightly tipsy. CHARLIE indicates her glass.

CHARLIE. I see you're fixed up.

LYNETTE. Oh, this – ja. I should of brought a bottle down, hey?

CHARLIE. Never mind. I'll go get some.

He turns to go.

STEVE. Where you going?

CHARLIE. To get a dop.

STEVE. You coming back?

CHARLIE. Of course I'm coming back. What're you having? It's okay, I know what you're having . . . Lynette? Same again?

About to leave, he spots the clock, moving to fetch it.

STEVE. Charlie . . . ? What am I going to . . . ?

CHARLIE shrugs him off, gratefully whipping up the clock and heading off. STEVE is in a virtual state of panic.

CHARLIE. It's okay, it's okay – don't panic.

STEVE is left alone with LYNETTE. A tricky silence.

LYNETTE. God, I'm so nervous. You think he'll take me?

STEVE. Hey?

LYNETTE. Weren't you also playing today?

STEVE. How did you guess?

LYNETTE. No, I'm sorry, I didn't say anything earlier – I thought everyone who was playing was supposed to be at the party.

STEVE. When I'm allowed to have a shower, I might eventually get up there.

LYNETTE. Ag, hell – forgive me. I didn't mean to interrupt.

STEVE. It's okay. It's not serious.

Pause.

LYNETTE (*looking around, a girlish giggle*). This is my first time in a Dressing Room. I mean in a proper sort of Men's Dressing Room. I've been in a Dressing Room before, but not this kind of a Dressing Room, if you know what I mean . . . you know what I mean . . . ?

STEVE *stares at her.*

LYNETTE. Ag, I'm being stupid now. (*Touching her cheek.*) Are my cheeks red?

STEVE. Not that I can notice.

LYNETTE. Whenever I've had too much wine my cheeks go red and people think I'm blushing. Not that I'm not blushing, but it looks like I'm blushing all the time . . . which I'm not. (*Slapping her own cheek.*) Ag, shut up, Lynette – you talking rubbish now, man.

Pause.

STEVE. Charlie tells me you were the Quince Queen.

LYNETTE. The what?

STEVE. Sorry – Orange Queen.

LYNETTE (*smiling*).You mean the Citrus Queen.

STEVE. Citrus Queen.

LYNETTE. I *was* the Citrus Queen.

STEVE. What I mean, ja.

LYNETTE. Ja. Long time ago.

Pause.

How did you know?

STEVE. Charlie told me.

LYNETTE. Oh, ja . . . I thought maybe you recognised me.

STEVE. No, no . . .

LYNETTE. No. No such luck, hey?

STEVE. No.

Pause.

LYNETTE. Ja. Nineteen-eighty-two.

STEVE. 82? . . . That was a good year.

LYNETTE. People say that, ja.

STEVE. For wines too. (*Trying to crack a weak joke.*) Not to mention orange juice.

It falls flat, wasted on her at this point.

LYNETTE. I've still got my sash.

STEVE. Is it?

LYNETTE. Ja, my big orange sash with gold writing on it. I've got it hanging above my bed. My mother thinks it's vain – but like they say in that ad for the perfume – when you've got it, flaunt it.

STEVE. For sure.

STEVE *gets up and goes to the door. He looks down the passage and turns back into the room.*

LYNETTE. Weren't you playing Fullback?

STEVE. Me . . . ?

LYNETTE. Wait a minute – Wing. You were Wing . . .

STEVE. How about Lock?

LYNETTE. Was that you . . . ? *That* wasn't you.

STEVE. Says a lot for my game, hey?

LYNETTE. Ag, don't tease now, man.

STEVE. I was Fly-half.

LYNETTE. Is it . . . ? (*She knows her rugby.*) You and Naas Botha.

STEVE. Please! All my life.

LYNETTE. You know I almost nearly met him once. It's true. In Pretoria. He was opening this new Checkers in Sunnyside . . . or was it Menlo Park? Pick 'n Pay – that was it . . . ! If I put my hand out, I could of actually touched him. (*She gives another girlish giggle.*) I was still quite silly in those days.

STEVE. Listen, you haven't perhaps got a smoke, have you?

LYNETTE (*opening her handbag*). I'm afraid they're not Camel.

STEVE. What makes you think I smoke Camel?

LYNETTE. All rugby players smoke Camel.

STEVE. Is that so . . . ?

> *She produces the packet.* STEVE *changes his mind as she reveals the pack – Craven A Menthols (the long ones.)*

On second thoughts – forget it.

LYNETTE. You sure? You don't mind if I do?

STEVE. Go ahead.

> *He returns to the door, rapidly losing hope that* CHARLIE *will ever come back. She lights up a smoke.*

LYNETTE (*sipping at her wine, loosening up*). Ag, no – you know, the night I was crowned they were all there. *Sarie – Rooi Rose – Darling.* They even took some pictures of me for the *Farmer's Weekly.* Cover Story. The Girl with the Bubbly Personality. I mean – me! I nearly died. Some of my friends at the Building Society laughed because I was half-hidden by this cow, but I didn't mind. Anyway, they were just jealous. None of them ever got *into* a magazine, forget about the *cover.* And inside. Inside there was this big colour picture of me on my own in a swimming costume holding a bowl of oranges and it said 'Quo Vadis, Lynette McAllister.'

> *Pause.*

Where to now, Lynette McAllister.

STEVE. Oh.

LYNETTE. Ja. I had it all worked out. I can still remember the adjudicator – one of the judges – he was that Deputy something-something-or-other of Transport Affairs. Not the one with the moustache – the other one. He also picks the Cherry Queen in Ficksburg. Anyway. Him. He said to me I must go to Joburg. He said in Joburg a girl like me can go far. But I didn't. Like a fool I stayed here. Now what have I got to show for it . . . ? (*Reading the name tag on* STEVE*'s kitbag.*) Steve Sofi-who . . . ?

STEVE (*at the door*). Sorry?

LYNETTE (*indicating the tag*). Your name . . . ? Steve

Sofi-what . . . ?

STEVE. Sofianek.

LYNETTE. Is that Jewish?

STEVE. It's Czech.

LYNETTE. Check . . . ?

STEVE. My old man was Czech.

LYNETTE. What's that? Like Hindu or something?

STEVE. No, no – Czechoslovakia – the country.

LYNETTE. Oh, ja – you mean like Russian?

STEVE. Ja. I mean, no. I mean Russia's up there – Czechoslovakia's down here . . .

LYNETTE. Oh, I see – ja . . .

STEVE. Also the Russians are Commies . . . We Commies too, but there are Commies and Commies . . .

LYNETTE (*reading the name tag*). So-fi-a-nek.

STEVE. That's right.

Pause.

LYNETTE. No prizes for guessing what they call you for short, hey?

STEVE *smiles thinly.*

LYNETTE. Ja. My ancestors also come from overseas . . . Scotland.

Pause.

God, I'm so nervous I could die (*She indicates the tape.*) Listen, you don't mind if I just quickly go through my steps, do you? If I practise my routine? (*She fetches the recorder and takes it to the massage table.*)

STEVE. What, you want to . . . ?

LYNETTE. I just want to play the tape – quick.

STEVE (*not too happy about this*). Look, er –

She sets the machine up, re-winding it.

LYNETTE. Do you know anything about ramp?

STEVE. Ramp . . . ?

LYNETTE. Ramp-work. It's the Art Form of the Future as far as Modelling's concerned. That's what they all say, anyway. I know I've got the height and all that, but I read in a magazine somewhere the Model of Tomorrow doesn't only have to look good – she must be able to sing, dance, act – sparkle – everything. (*Chuffed with herself.*) Now that I've said bye bye to the Building Society, I must maar take it seriously.

STEVE. You what?

LYNETTE. Ja. Quite a Big Step, hey?

STEVE. You left your job?

LYNETTE. You are looking at a Full Time Model – TA-RAAAM! (*Striking a 'model' pose.*) That's if Charlie takes me. He could hardly believe his ears when I told him I took his advice.

STEVE *stares at her in disbelief.*

LYNETTE. It's true. Last time he was here he said to me if ever I decided to take up Modelling Full Time, I must come to him. So about three months ago when I finally bust up with my ex, I said to myself – come on, McAllister, what've you got to lose . . . So here I am with this tape. Marcia de Bruyn thinks it's okay, but then what does she know? She only takes the local kids for Ballet . . .

STEVE. Look, er – Lynette . . . I don't want to sort of . . . throw a spanner in the works here, but . . .

LYNETTE. Look, if you don't want to listen, you must just say so. I mean, I don't want to force you.

STEVE (*doing his best to be tactful*). No, no – it's just that between you and me, I think you might be just sort of . . . wasting your time sort of thing.

LYNETTE. You mean you don't think he'll take me . . . ?

STEVE. No, no . . . What I mean is – he's taking a long time. Maybe he's sort of . . . not coming back.

LYNETTE. You mean like right now, you mean?

STEVE. Maybe he's got sidetracked.

LYNETTE. No, he's probably looking for a camera. Prolly gone to fetch a Poly. He told me he needed a head-and-shoulders and like a fool, ol' Dizzy Dora here loses the only new pic she's got . . . (*Not giving him a chance to answer.*) Look, all I want you to do is just sort of tell me if it's sort of okay – okay . . . ?

STEVE *stares at her, helpless in the face of her blinkered enthusiasm.*

LYNETTE. Am I being a Pain? If I'm being a Pain, you must just say so, hey. (*Carrying on regardless.*) Now this is not sort of professional or anything, it's just sort of, well – let me show you and then . . .

She starts the tape. A series of odd noises issues forth before the actual music begins.

Ag, that's a lorry outside. Had to do it at home . . . (*To the tape.*) Come on, come on . . . !

A dog starts barking – harsh, incessant.

Bladdy brak next door . . . there millions of dogs in our neighbourhood – one starts – they all go off . . .

A number of dogs begin barking on the tape, while she goes on describing the format.

This isn't me singing – it's just a demo. I sort of mouth the words while . . .

The intro to the music begins, throwing her. She is forced to break off and stop the tape.

Dammit. Took me by surprise. This always happens . . .

The actual song she has recorded is TINA TURNER*'s 'Private Dancer.'* LYNETTE *has 'learnt' a dance routine which she endeavours to perform, while at the same time mouthing the words a la Sun City Extravaganza time.*

God, imagine if Charlie'd seen that? He'd of died . . .

STEVE *can take this lot no longer.*

STEVE. Look, Lynette – maybe you should just practise so long and I'll go hop in the shower.

LYNETTE. It won't take long.

He moves to his hook and grabs the remainder of his clothes, kitbag, shoes, etc. and heads for the showers.

STEVE. No, you go ahead. Carry on.

LYNETTE. I had to record it holding the microphone in front of the speaker because I didn't have one of those . . . one of those . . . what do you call those little plug things.

STEVE. Jack.

LYNETTE. Jacks – that's right.

STEVE slinks out through the shower arch. She is preoccupied with her machine.

Of course, if my boyfriend was still around he'd of fixed it in no time. He knew all about recording. He had tapes of everything – Bobby Angel, you name it . . .

She pushes the play button. The music resumes where it left off – the opening bars to 'Private Dancer'. The music underscores the following.

Ja. The first time I went to Joburg was with my ex. School holidays – Standard Nine. We came in on the Heidelberg Road and there was this Drive-In on top of a Mine Dump with the biggest Neon Sign I'd ever seen . . . I thought – My God – I've arrived . . . (*Spotting the mirror.*) It was like New York . . . (*Moving to the mirror and fiddling with her hair.*) My boyfriend hated it. He just wanted to get back home. I'm sure that's why we broke up in the end. He wanted me just to sommer settle down and be a housewife. He was so lomp . . . like everyone else in this dump . . . I was lomp before I met Charlie . . .

She becomes aware that TINA TURNER *has started on the words 'I'm Your Private Dancer' and, cross with herself, runs across to the tape, snapping it off. She shouts off to where she imagines* STEVE *to be.*

It's just as well I'm trying this out. You forget so quick if you've had couple of sips of wine . . . Do you think this music's okay? Tina Turner? Or do you think I should try something more 'show-busy' . . . ? Steve . . . ? Steve . . . !?

There is no answer from the shower area. She stands in the archway perplexed, yet unable to go in and look. She calls his name again and then goes to the door to the dressing room, looking out down the passage. Not giving it much further thought, she returns to her tape recorder and snaps it on. TINA TURNER'*s voice singing 'I'm Your Private Dancer' the second time comes through.*

LYNETTE *begins her routine. It is sad, almost pathetic. The steps she has learnt are her own – as the music swells she really gets into it. The sound of crowds cheering and whistling melt into the soundtrack, creating the sensation that she herself is appearing on stage at some concert. Isolated in a pool of purple light – the crowds still cheering and* TINA *singing full bore now – she lives out her fantasy as we fade to blackout.*

PIETER-DIRK UYS was born in Cape Town in 1945 of Afrikaner-Jewish parentage, thus he 'belongs to both chosen people.' After graduating from the University of Cape Town Drama School he attended the London Film School. On his return to South Africa in 1973 he joined the original Space Theatre in Cape Town where over a decade he became noted for his independent-minded scripts. A quick worker, Uys managed to outwit censorship controls with some two dozen works, including *Selle Ou Storie* (1974), *Karnaval* (1974) and *Die Van Aardes van Grootoor* (1977), which became one of the longest running plays in South African theatre history. Three of his scripts (in Anglicised versions) are published by Penguin as *Paradise is Closing Down and Other Plays* (1989).

Uys has alternated the production of his straight plays with writing – and usually appearing in – his own cabarets and revues. A collection of his early humour, *No One's Died Laughing*, was published by Penguin in 1986. One of these shows, *Adapt or Dye*, which played in updated versions through most of the 80s, saw the arrival and development of his drag character, Evita Bezuidenhout – the National Party ambassador to the fictitious 'homeland' of Bapetikosweti. With Evita and her family he has performed over 2500 times to people of all colours and cultures, always in 'non-racial' venues, throughout South Africa. Uys has also toured as South Africa's equivalent of Dame Edna Everage in the U.K., Canada, Australia, Holland and Germany, opening with her at the Edinburgh Festival in the same week as *Just Like Home* in 1989. Spin-offs of his satirical entertainment include feature films, videos, two documentaries for the BBC and Evita's biography, *A Part Hate, A Part Love* (1990). Many of Uys's sayings have entered the vernacular, a language which he is uniquely able to reflect and exploit.

Just Like Home was written in 1988 as a vehicle for the remarkable Cape Town actress, Shaleen Surtie-Richards, who played the role of Cathy throughout the work's run and to considerable acclaim in South Africa and abroad. The programme included this note:

> You always have a perfect picture of somewhere you thought you were once happy – and you probably were in between hours of worrying. Somewhere it's always perfect and quiet and warm, because you're not there. Maybe because it

doesn't even exist.

The play's first 'home' was the ironically named Laager theatre at the Market, redecorated for the occasion – fittingly so, as Uys's *Van Aardes* had originally opened the venue a dozen years before.

Reaction to *Just Like Home* has in general been highly favourable at home and abroad. During the King's Head run Irving Wardle's review was typical:

> Uys's play and production represent a notable triumph of common humanity over lacerating experience. He knows the political crimes that have made these people what they are. He knows the landscape of exile, where identities are propped up by reliving the past to the extent of play-acting. His theatrical achievement is to bring these rancorously self-encapsulated victims out into the fresh air, and to place their obsessive melodramas in the wider context of comedy . . .

Characters

CATHY SEPTEMBER, a Cape Coloured woman who has lived in London for twelve years.

HECTOR PRINCE, a young white South African exile who is an actor.

GUPTA, an Indian man who runs the restaurant where Cathy worked and lives in the room above.

TREVOR JURIES, a young Coloured man from Cape Town, just arrived illegally in the U.K.

The setting is Cathy's small flat in London NW1, autumn in the late 1980s.

Just Like Home opened in the Laager at the Market Theatre, Johannesburg, on 7 March, 1989, an independent production, directed by the author, with the following cast:

CATHY	Shaleen Surtie-Richards
HECTOR	Robert Finlayson
GUPTA	Royston Stoffels
TREVOR	Paul Savage

The production was presented at the Edinburgh Festival in August of that year, followed by a run at the King's Head, Islington, during October-November. A return season began at the Market in May, 1990, redirected by Lynne Maree, with Shaleen Surtie-Richards and Russell Copley (Hector), Kurt Egelhof (Gupta) and Soli Philander (Trevor).

ACT ONE

CATHY *is sitting in a chair with her back to us. She is gagged. Her hands are bound. There is a pillowcase over her head.*
HECTOR *plays the Afrikaner policeman grilling her.*

HECTOR. 'Black bastard! Four innocent people you killed! A little girl whose birthday was going to be tomorrow, won't be having candles on her cake because she's lying in the mortuary in little pieces – because of you, you terrorist animal!

CATHY *mumbles. Squirms. He whips off the pillowcase.*

Shut up when I'm talking to you! Two old ladies were out buying food for their cat and an old dog called Rambo, who will now not be fed or stroked ever again, because of you, you communist murderer!

More grunts from CATHY.

Shit man, one more attempt to escape and it will be the end of you, I promise. Okay. Okay. Okay. Then there was also the dead black man splattered in so many bits and pieces against the toothpaste adverts in the supermarket, that not even when they scraped him off that Colgate smile, will he fill an icecream cone, and that's all thanks to you. Your own people, not just us! You're not just a bastard, you're a fucking stupid bastard!

She squirms.

Ja, it was lucky for you most of the white kids who were usually playing the computer games in the Valhalla Arcade was on Sunset Beach windsurfing. It was lucky for you most of the schoolkids that are usually there buying sweets from the shop were not buying sweets at the shop because they were on school holidays. Why are you so lucky? Are you aware of your blessings? Are you grateful? I can't hear you, you ungrateful piece of black rubbish!

He 'hits' her.

Because without your incredible luck you'd be even more guilty of mass murder, not just the cold-blooded massacre of three innocent white citizens and one unemployed black! How old are you? Hey? . . .'

He falters.

Is that right?

Checks his script on the sofa.

Ja. 'How old are you? Sixteen? Do you have many friends?

He changes his tactics to smooth and intimate.

Do you have many friends? Did they help you place that bomb? Trust me. I won't even remember their names. We'll just refer to them as annonymous associates. Hey? Ja, man, we'll tell the court it was their influence on you, a child. Sixteen? Maybe fifteen? You can trust me . . .' Then you spit at me.

She struggles and grunts.

Oh . . .

He undoes her gag.

CATHY. I'm suffocating!

She spits and gasps for breath.

Sis man, that rag tastes like Brasso! God, you know, I suffer from asthma, man! Untie my hands! You're stopping the blood from getting to my heart! This is damn ridiculous . . .

He unties her hands.

HECTOR. 'You fucking little terrorist . . .'

CATHY. No, come on man, Hector man! This language is too terrible! All those f-words in a row! Who speaks like this?

HECTOR. Police.

CATHY. Not on my television.

HECTOR. This is a white security policeman torturing a black suspect.

CATHY. Well, I've never heard language like that.

She goes off to the bedroom.

HECTOR. Then you're lucky.

She returns with an armful of clothing. Sorts the clothes as she talks.

CATHY. I've been here in the U.K. for over twelve years, my boy, and I've never heard any policeman say things like that!

HECTOR. Police here are different.

CATHY. Sis, man, you call this a good part?

HECTOR. Later my character puts electrodes on the kid's you-know-what . . .

CATHY. No details, Hector, I've heard enough.

HECTOR. But the torture makes him reveal the real suspects.

CATHY. And what are these suspects suspected of doing?

HECTOR. I don't know.

CATHY. If you don't know what happens in the story, how can you play a part?

HECTOR. This is my only big scene with dialogue.

CATHY. 'S horrible.

Pause. HECTOR waits for her opinion. She packs the boxes.

HECTOR. So, what do you think?

CATHY. You sound just like a Boer.

HECTOR. Good. The director's Welsh and needs some background input from me.

CATHY. Too heavy with the Rrrrr's.

HECTOR. I agree, but the dialect coach demands heavy Rrrrr's.

CATHY. What's that?

HECTOR. He helps me with the Afrikaans accent. Here, listen, he's doing it on a cassette for me.

He puts the walkman earphones onto her head. She listens with growing distaste. She speaks loudly.

CATHY. People here make a decent living teaching actors who speak good English to do horrible South African? I should get the job.

HECTOR. It's a very competitive business.

CATHY (*loudly*). Where's this dialogue coach from?

HECTOR. Blackpool.

CATHY (*loudly*). A black man from Johannesburg?

HECTOR. No, he's British!

CATHY. Ja, that's why the Rrrr's are too heavy.

Hands him back the walkman.

But Hector love, you know the right sound.

HECTOR. I can't remember.

CATHY. You heard enough of it in the Army.

HECTOR. Only for a couple of months.

CATHY. You need this British dialect man to remind you of the horrible sounds that made you run away from home? And then he gets it wrong!

HECTOR. There are very few British actors who can do a good South African accent.

CATHY. Ja, I'm telling you, man, too heavy with the Rrrrr's.

HECTOR. It really pisses me off when they do all these TV plays and films about South Africa and they can't even get the accent right.

CATHY. At least their facts are right, Hector. No one here just wants a lesson in the South African accent.

HECTOR. And I thought you never watched TV films about South Africa?

CATHY. That's right, because I find the phony Afrikaans accent too ridiculous. Come, help me with these boxes.

HECTOR. I got a letter from a friend in Cape Town this morning. Crazy . . . all these cuttings . . . the ANC flag flying over the City Hall, marches, a new era. Says it's like the Berlin Wall coming down . . . crazy. He sent me this cassette. Listen . . . you'll crrrryyyy . . .

CATHY. I'll put all the things for you to take home to your flat in these boxes.

HECTOR. Don't you want to hear something 'rrrreally South Effrrrrrican'?

CATHY. You know I can't stand Boeremusiek!

She holds up the gag he used on her.

No sis man, Hector man, how could you put this horrible Brasso rag over my mouth? Go put it in the little broom cupboard in the kitchen where you found it!

He takes it and exits. Enters during following: She moves boxes around. Packs clothes.

The last time I watched a film about South Africa was over twelve years ago. I was still working for the Sharps. We were in Belsize Park; just moved into that flat. New carpets were down and the mess was just horrible. Then Mrs Sharp organises a dinner party for other South African exiles, my dear, and I have to suddenly make bobotie 'like you used to make back in Cape

Town, Cathy' – we never once had bobotie in all those years I worked for the Sharps in Cape Town – always some fancy French or Italian or Chinese food. But now suddenly everybody's here as a so-called refugee who nearly brought down the government back home – nearly, but not quite, you know? I never thought I'd meet so many people here who fought apartheid there. Pity they didn't stay at home and do it properly.

HECTOR *is listening to his walkman.*

HECTOR. This tape is amazing . . .

CATHY. So anyway, here they come, all these exiles looking as if they'd just come from the hairdresser in Sea Point and eating my Afrikaans bobotie, like it was manna from the promised land – and the whole flat is such a mess, still covered in little white threads from the new carpet. As true as God, that night I could've killed Barbara Sharp.

She sits on her over-full suitcase but can't close it.

Then someone switched on the TV because there was this documentary film about the Cape. God, Hector, and there was Table Mountain and us coloured people in Adderley Street selling flowers and all talking like my family and friends and hell, it made me so upset.

HECTOR (*loudly*). You really want to be homesick?

CATHY. Not homesick; just angry – me, standing in the door to the kitchen with my apron on in London England, and the Master and Madam and their fancy expat pals watching our old hometown and bitching about the good times they had making money there and then making such horrible comments about those they left behind. Superior like they were never part of it once. Hector, I'm telling you, I heard the cock crow three times!

HECTOR. A wildlife film?

CATHY. Unplug your blerrie brains and listen to me!

She pulls off his earphones.

I'm telling you, man: there it was – Langa and Soweto and the schoolkids marching in 76.

HECTOR. Before my time.

CATHY. Oh no, I know your date of birth, my boy. You can't fool me. Capricorn!

HECTOR. 1976?

CATHY. You were still at school.

HECTOR. I remember the teachers' fear – first time I saw a grown-up frightened. We heard the blacks would come and panga us to pieces in the classroom!

CATHY. How terrible for you children.

HECTOR. Listen, we planned to put a trail of 20c pieces on the ground to lead them to old Hellcat Hewitt the maths teacher, so that his throat would definitely be cut . . .

CATHY. Shame.

HECTOR. . . . he was an old bugger, Hellcat Hewitt.

CATHY. Anyway, so I made up my mind then and there: why must I sit here and be forced to watch terrible things happening there? Remember the good things, Cathy, I said to myself. So I did and I'm much healthier for it.

HECTOR. I still wish you'd stay and watch me in this! We can have bobotie and Cape wine!

CATHY. And I must sit here and eat my dinner and watch you put electrical gadgets on a boy's testicles? No sis man, Hector man, I'll just vomit.

HECTOR. But I won't be phony! Cathy, I can give it all that stuff of real life! I've been there, Cathy, I know!

CATHY. Shame Hector, did they do that to you too?

HECTOR. 'Okay you fucking black bitch – up against the wall, this is a raid!'

He pushes her against the sofa.

CATHY. Hey hey hey, listen here, for your information I'm not a black bitch! I'm a coloured person! And I'm sorry, man, I just don't like this part, really I don't . . .

A loud knocking on the door.

Now see what you've done . . .

Calls down to passage.

It's okay, Gupta, my door's open . . .

GUPTA *enters concerned.*

GUPTA. And what is going on down here?

CATHY. The boy is just acting for me . . .

She exits to bedroom. GUPTA *comes into the room.*

GUPTA. That is not the sort of language one wants to encourage in this area, Hector Prince. Black people also live here. You must choose your insults more carefully. 'Fucking black bitch against the wall' – with apologies to Cathleen – is not the sort of investment towards a peaceful weekend.

HECTOR. It's only for a TV film, Gupta!

GUPTA. Violence resides in this neighbourhood in the guise of calm. It needs only one of those words to spark the dried bush of racial war. You should know that, coming from a racist state.

HECTOR. Gupta, I will not be drawn into another pointless argument about my roots. So please don't waste your breath trying to provoke me.

He plugs in his walkman and listens.

GUPTA. Provoke? My goodness me, how you make me laugh. You call my friend and colleague here a 'fucking black bitch' – with respect, Cathleen – and you then announce that I am the one who provokes? This is typical of your race, Hector Prince. So used to being the overlord that any mild form of criticism is regarded as provocation.

CATHY *has re-entered, sorting things.*

CATHY. He can't hear with all that in his head. Stop it now, Gupta, you two always fight. Not today, please!

GUPTA. Oh yes, Cathleen . . . today is a special day.

CATHY. Good. I've found all the spices for the bobotie: the djirra, barishap and koljanna. Will you take them with you to the Taj Mahal?

She exits off to the kitchen. GUPTA *moves in on* HECTOR *who sits, pages through a stack of magazines.*

GUPTA. You might be pleased to hear, which I'm sure you can, that your racist Afrikaan dish called 'bobotie' is now legitimately on the menu of a decent Indian Eating Establishment in Northwest London. You may inform your superiors that your infiltration of our very respected cuisine has been successful.

HECTOR. It's not that Cathy is a great cook, Gupta, or that her bobotie is world-famous in North London. What really bugs you is the fact that she is an independent woman. It's a hard pill to swallow for an old chauvinist snob like yourself.

GUPTA. Your verbal sticks and stones will not silence me, my young friend. Experience is my guiding light, compassion my compass.

CATHY *enters with a small packet.*

CATHY. Stop fighting now. Here Gupta. Keep it dry. I looked all over for these ingredients and found some in Nottinghill Gate. Still, it doesn't even smell like the stuff from Rashid's little shop. Shame . . .

HECTOR. Wonderful smell . . . What's happened to Rashid?

GUPTA. Thatcher's Britain finally caught up with Rashid. A Safeway Supermarket came and ate his curry shop up. Besides, Rashid was pining too much and went back to Uganda.

HECTOR. And tomorrow there'll be another Idi Amin and Rashid will be back here knocking on our door.

GUPTA. He will not knock on your door, be assured. He will be welcome to knock on mine.

CATHY. No more fighting, you two! Gupta, you want some cooldrink? Hector brought me some fancy little farewell cakes from Harrods.

GUPTA. I am not hot, Cathleen.

CATHY. The cooldrink's not cold, man.

She exits to the kitchen.
GUPTA *sits. Glances across out of the window.*

GUPTA. This so-called Indian Summer is neither Indian nor Summer; so English, so quaint. Now why don't they call it an English Autumn, which it is – but no: Indian Summer – which it isn't.

HECTOR. Who teach you English, Gupta?

GUPTA. Who taught you English, Afrikaan!

CATHY *enters with cooldrink.*

CATHY. Gupta!

GUPTA. Yes, yes, Cathleen, I must prepare to go to the restaurant now.

HECTOR. It will be strange there without you, Cathy.

GUPTA. My goodness me, yes – we've all got so accustomed to you being there.

CATHY. Now don't gang up on me, you two. We said: today we wouldn't get depressed and tearful and damn pathetic. Life goes on and so do I. Gupta, you want Hector to help you upstairs with your box now?

GUPTA. But you've already given me your television.

CATHY. Ag, it's just a few things of mine I thought you might like. The rest is going to charity.

GUPTA. Surely, this is too much? Thank you, but I'm still trying to find space up in my room. Let me do that first.

HECTOR. You couldn't swing a cat in your room, Gupta. Rather let's give this stuff to those people living under the bridge.

CATHY. Yes, those poor homeless people, shame.

GUPTA. White people.

HECTOR. But really, you could get quite a lot for these things if you put an ad in the local paper, Cathy.

CATHY. Now don't complain: I've left you my nice kettle and my radio cassette player.

HECTOR. My walkman does it all.

GUPTA. Also makes tea?

HECTOR. They're working at it. We've got a kettle at the flat, Cathy.

CATHY. What else can I give you, love?

He looks around at her things.

HECTOR. Nothing . . . really.

CATHY. Take the kettle, man! See which one makes the best tea – mine or yours.

HECTOR. Okay, I'll take yours. I don't think those white people under the bridge have enough plugs, Gupta.

GUPTA. And then you could get a lot of money for the kettle you reject if you put an ad in the local paper.

He exits on a triumphant note.

HECTOR. I won't be provoked.

CATHY *laughs. She is busy packing a cardboard box.*

CATHY. Cardboard never changes, hey?
When me and my sister Eileen were your age, we had to put everything we owned in cardboard boxes. Cardboard boxes piled up on the pavement outside; cardboard boxes being loaded into old Beasley's wagon, still drawn by his half-dead horses, Milly and Grace. Most of the familiar places round us were already rubble. But my pa kept saying: 'I know those whites. They will never throw us out of our home.' But they did.

So out we and our boxes went into the suburbs. Unpacked the boxes. Then the Law came and ate up our new neighbourhood and back came old Beasley, this time with an old truck.

HECTOR. And Milly and Grace?

CATHY. Dogmeat by now, shame. Back went the boxes and there trekked the September family and its cardboard treasures – over the sanddunes of the Cape Flats. Then luckily someone died in Athlone: out with the cardboard coffin, in with the cardboard boxes, up with the cardboard dividers, making one room four. Yes, that's where the family still is. In a half-cardboard house with an outside brick lavatory.

HECTOR. And it's all my fault!

CATHY. Silly boy. The point I'm making is right here: cardboard boxes. Every time I move, the boxes seem to get less, but the belongings get more. Hey Hector, what do you think happens in those cardboard boxes when we switch off the lights?

She laughs with him.
A coughing fit. He slaps her on the back gently.
Pause.

HECTOR. What about my Courtroom Scene?

CATHY. No hell man, I've got things to do. Go upstairs and get Gupta to help you.

HECTOR. How can I say all those things to him?

CATHY. You can say them to me, but not to him? How come?

HECTOR. You're more understanding. He's . . . Indian.

CATHY. He was young like you back in India. He also left home because he was disgusted with the way things were going there. Ask him about his understanding.

HECTOR. Oh please, what happened in India makes South Africa look like a picnic.

He tries to close her bulging suitcase.

CATHY. You go and tell him that.

HECTOR. And then he constantly points a finger at me!

CATHY. You two are like a cat and a wild dog . . . Will you be wearing SAP uniform again?

HECTOR. Depends on when it's set.

CATHY. Khaki? Camouflage?

HECTOR. It's happening now.

CATHY. Blue.

HECTOR. Not camouflage?

CATHY. Police blue, man. Anyone who watches TV will tell you that.

HECTOR. Which, of course, you never watch.

CATHY. No, I never watch.

Pause.

They jump on you when you're not ready to run. Usually at the end of the News, just after you've seen the Princess of Wales wearing something new and gorgeous – God, I love those girls – and you're still smiling at the Queen Mother, when suddenly: Table Mountain, tin shacks and the young policemen in blue. Young. Pretty. Like you.

HECTOR. I wonder if I should dye my hair for this part . . .

CATHY. Polite young Christian cops from good homes, brought up to love God and their neighbour, but not in the same church. Fat white Boere boys. By that time I'm ice-cold all over . . .

HECTOR. Those Boere boys eat too much red meat.

CATHY. . . . can't even remember if it was the Princess of Wales . . .

HECTOR. . . . drink too much beer . . .

CATHY. . . . or the Duchess of York that made me so happy.

HECTOR. Fat arses, fat bellies.

CATHY. Not all Boere boys. Some like you, more English than the Brits.

HECTOR. I'm not fat . . .

CATHY. Boere boys beating left and right with their quirts like they're trying to put out a fire. I even once recognised the street where we eventually grew up in Athlone . . . barricades over the road . . . where our dog Phyllis used to sleep in the sun and stop the bus. The trees looked so big on TV. We never thought they'd grow in that sandy earth, what with the wind always blowing them skew. But on the TV they looked strong and full of life. Even the houses. But I couldn't make them out properly. The camera was running and wobbling along the pavement after some kids, they were throwing stones and rolling burning tyres at the police. Young young kids and young young cops.
God, that rioting must've messed up so many pretty little

gardens, with kids jumping over the walls to hide from other kids among the dahlias and the honeysuckle. And who would've thought they would grow in the sand?

But walls don't keep out violence: boots and blood there among the sweet peas and the Christmas roses. Hell, it broke my heart.

Pause.

HECTOR. You'll miss London, Cathy.

CATHY. I'll miss my friends. And my kettle.

HECTOR. I still don't understand how you can go back.

CATHY. Things are different now.

HECTOR. You reckon?

CATHY. Your cuttings say so.

HECTOR. You don't believe all that propaganda.

CATHY. Let's rather listen to that tape you got from home.

HECTOR. No, no, don't hide in the walkman! I can't imagine after twelve years here in the Real World, why you would volunteer to go back to that . . . cage!

CATHY. All right, I'll listen to your Courtroom Scene. Just don't call me names. And no more f-words!

HECTOR. You're free, Cathy! You belong here now. You're happy! You're mad!

CATHY. None of that is in this script.

HECTOR. Do you know, after three years, I still wake up in the middle of the night in a cold sweat.

CATHY. Say Johnny-Jimmy-Lancelot . . .

HECTOR. I'm back in Detention Barracks and that staff sergeant with the moustache . . .

CATHY. Handlebars Hesselton?

HECTOR. You remember? He comes for me because I refuse to use a rifle on kids. So I shoot the fucker in his eye . . .

CATHY. Ag no, shame man . . .

HECTOR. . . . but no human blood comes out, except thick spurts of red stinking . . .

CATHY. Say Johnny-Jimmy-Lancelot! Johnny-Jimmy-Lancelot!

HECTOR. . . . and I run, slipping and sliding in the slime and it's like running slow-motion over wet corpses. And I get to the airport and the plane's ready to go and I hand in my passport – but it's not a real passport.

CATHY. What then?

HECTOR. It's that little book of recipes from the Cape you gave me.

CATHY. My bobotie strikes again.

HECTOR. And I'm trapped, Cathy . . . I'm trapped by their laughter and the beatings and every time I just blink my eyes a gun goes off and another child falls crippled . . .

CATHY. A nightmare.

HECTOR. . . . . and here you are wanting to leave this and go back to that?

CATHY. Not that!

HECTOR. Giving up!

CATHY. I gave it up over twelve years ago. Now I want it back.

HECTOR. But why?

CATHY. It's my home!

HECTOR. This is your home!

CATHY. The mountains, the city, the Afrikaans language, the hatred and the hope: the whole blerrie catastrophe. Look! These British cardboard boxes didn't hold sunshine and fresh air. They're not full of the smell of apples and smoked snoek . . .

HECTOR . . . . and petrol bombs!

CATHY. These nice little British boxes are all so polite, so decent and full of fair play. Not like our Boere boxes: full of skiet, skop and donner.

HECTOR. Yes. There they kill you with guns!

CATHY. And here I'll be killed with kindness. It's a long time since I've heard the dogs barking at me. I miss that too.

HECTOR. Well, I think you're out of your cottonpickin' mind.

CATHY. Listen here, Hector Prince. You're standing in line for political asylum in Britain, because they tortured you in the South African Army. And the only parts you can get here are playing South African policemen and soldiers, who do to others like you say they did to you – and you call me out of my cottonpicking mind? Let's point no loaded fingers around here, my boy.

He has lit up a cigarette.

CATHY. And don't smoke!

HECTOR. I won't spill the ash!

CATHY. You want to smoke, you go outside. Like always. This is still a smokeless zone!

HECTOR (*in Italian accent*). Katherina September, sometimes you're a Fascist!

He exits.

CATHY. And sometimes, you're a blerrie fool!

HECTOR (*off*). I heard that!

CATHY *takes a packet of money – £10 notes – out of her airline travelbag and sorts it on the table.*

CATHY. This is for a dishwasher for my sister Eileen. This is for a down payment on a little place of my own. And this is to take us all out to a Welcome Home Cathy celebration at the Goldfinger Lounge. Wonder if that place still exists . . . hell, we had such a jol there in the old days . . . at the Goldfinger Lounge . . .

There is an altercation outside in the hallway.

GUPTA (*off*). No, no – not so close to where I live and breathe. You can smoke in the street and in the rest of the world where you think you're in charge, but not here!

HECTOR (*off*). They're my lungs, Gupta!

He enters with his cigarette.

God, that man's starting on me again!

GUPTA *enters.*

GUPTA. No, no, I'm not starting; I started when I met you three years ago. My air is here, Hector Prince. I pay for it. I like it clean and smokefree. What you people do to the ozone layer I cannot control, but this layer is mine. Why do you let this boy smoke on my staircase, Cathleen?

CATHY. Also my staircase, Gupta, until tomorrow. Hector, go and smoke in the sun outside, man!

HECTOR *exits.*

HECTOR. Fascista!

GUPTA. Now what does that mean? Coming from one of them?

CATHY. He's struggling here, because he wouldn't become one of
them!

GUPTA. You mean, ran away from a fully-laden table with five-star
room service? Well, my instinct still warns me, Cathleen, that
boy could be spying for their Embassy.

CATHY. Not that nonsense again! Who would now spy on me?

GUPTA. I would not allow even a caged South African bird in my
room in case it carried a bug.

CATHY. Gupta, you're a suspicious old bugger!

She laughs.
He has discovered all her money on the table.

GUPTA. And all this money lying naked? Are you senile now,
Cathleen September? Did I not educate you over the years to
protect your cash safely in the bank?

CATHY. Ja, which I did, but today I closed my account and
withdrew all my money for tomorrow.

GUPTA. Unpractical and careless in my eyes.

CATHY. But in my eyes my money looks so good and real, all piled
up and close enough for me to stroke it.

GUPTA. But why did you not organise travellers cheques? That is
the grown-up way to do it.

CATHY. Maybe, but when it comes to money, I'm still a child.

GUPTA. And if you get robbed?

CATHY. Who? You? Hector?

GUPTA. Your savings, dear Cathleen. The future.

CATHY. Ja, for each of these £10 notes, I get over R40 there. Hell,
I'm going home to Athlone a rich lady.

GUPTA. Not if the thief gets here first.

CATHY. Ag, stop fussing, man! You're worse than a nagging
husband.

GUPTA. That is the nicest thing you could accuse me of.

He studies the cakes keenly.

Ah, some lovely little cakes . . .

CATHY. Ja, shame, I'll really miss Hector with his damn cigarettes
and his funny opinions. He helped me to relax. Some old
horrible habits die hard. Sometimes when it would slip out, he

would say in his actor's way: 'And who's your Master?'

GUPTA. To have to call that boy Master?

CATHY. That very first time he wandered into the Taj Mahal and
ordered my curry, and then specially came 'backstage' as he
called it, to compliment the cook – and there I stood all hot
and sweaty and he said right out: 'Which part of Cape Town are
you from?' as if you couldn't tell from just looking at me, and
all I heard myself say was, 'Ag Master, I want to go home . . .'
We both cried. Shame.

GUPTA. Emotion in the kitchen is never good for the food.

Peeps at the cakes, hinting.

A nice little chocolate one in the corner here.

CATHY. Dearie me, I hadn't cried once here in the Northern
Hemisphere. I was happy that Hector Prince made me cry, at
last, from my heart.

GUPTA. We all know your curry makes all types weep, Cathleen.

CATHY. Maybe it was the curry. Ja, let's be English about it, Gupta.
No emotion. Just a stiff . . . what's it?

GUPTA. Stiff upper lip, yes. Discipline, self-control.

CATHY. My God, with a stiff upper lip all the Brits should sound
like Cape Coloureds without teeth!

They laugh at her demonstration.

With a stiff upper lip you can have a little chocolate cake if you
want one, hey!

Pause.

GUPTA. Cathleen, just now when you referred to me as a nagging
husband . . .

CATHY. You're a fusspot.

GUPTA. A fusspot, yes; but like a nagging husband? Surely not.

CATHY. No, not like a nagging husband. I lied. Just a blerrie
fusspot!

GUPTA. Ah. All lies are bad, Cathleen.

CATHY. Now don't nag, Gupta. Sometimes a small lie can be of
great help.

Pause.

GUPTA. So, you say you're happy about going home?

CATHY. I've never been happier in my life.

Pause.

No, really, I'm fine.

Pause.

GUPTA. So am I.

CATHY. Yes, you look happy.

Pause.

GUPTA. It's been six years, Cathleen.

CATHY. Over six.

GUPTA. Such dear and close companions.

CATHY. No man Gupta, man.

GUPTA. I will always be grateful to you. You found me that room upstairs.

CATHY. No man, it's okay Gupta.

GUPTA. Every day working together and me living just a headspace above you.

HECTOR (*off*). Smokeless Zone comin' in!

HECTOR *enters.*

HECTOR. Satisfied? I blew all my smoke into your neighbour's letterbox.

CATHY. Hector, for God's sake just act out something.

HECTOR. Gupta, this TV play I'm doing might interest you.

GUPTA. Highly unlikely. Cathleen, I must go to work now.

CATHY. Oh, yes, but . . .

GUPTA. I'll be back again at four.

CATHY. Just in time for tea.

GUPTA. Ah and some of the little cakes?

CATHY. But have that little chocolate cake, man!

HECTOR. It's an incredibly powerful courtroom scene.

CATHY. We can have tea and as many of the chocolate cakes as you like, Gupta. For old times sake.

GUPTA. I hate old times.

HECTOR. It'll only take a few minutes.

GUPTA. What is it this time? Another Afrikaan policeman?

CATHY. Yes, he does it very well.

HECTOR. This time it's a very complex character, Gupta.

GUPTA. Nice change from the last effort.

HECTOR. The one about Namibia? That sergeant was just a simple psychopath.

GUPTA. While this one is of course a complex psychopath?

HECTOR. Give me some feedback on the Namibian play. You saw it? .

GUPTA. Cathleen invited me to watch it with her.

HECTOR. It's so difficult for me to be objective.

GUPTA. That, I thought, was the problem.

> *Pause.*

HECTOR. I won't let him provoke me. I'll just come through the door like on page 40.

> *Puts the script in* GUPTA's *lap.*
> *He exits to passage.*

GUPTA. There is still so much left unsaid between us, Cathleen.

CATHY. God, if you make me cry here and now, I'll never stop and I want to look like a person when I get to Cape Town tomorrow, not a wet old Kleenex.

GUPTA. You know what I want to say and cannot . . .

HECTOR (*off*). Are you ready?

CATHY. Please, let the boy show off a bit. Help me to forget just for a minute, why I so much want to stay here near you . . .

HECTOR (*off*). Someone read the first line!

GUPTA (*reads*). 'The Court will Rise.' What nonsense is this?

CATHY. We rise, Gupta. Okay Hector we're up!

> HECTOR *enters, acting accordingly. They watch him amazed. He then explains.*

HECTOR. There's been an interdict against the Minister of Law and Order. Allegations against me of torture and the assault of young schoolkids in detention, you know, the usual.

GUPTA. The usual, yes.

HECTOR. I'm handcuffed and I'm shoved into the dock. Okay,

Gupta, read the Prosecutor.

GUPTA. With pleasure.

HECTOR. Cathy, be the high school student. He's seventeen.

CATHY. Bit young for me . . . 'Sipho Molifi'?

GUPTA. I think we should really have a heart to heart talk before you get onto your aeroplane, Cathleen.

CATHY. Read, Gupta!

GUPTA (*reads*). 'Sipho Molifi? You say you were interrogated by the accused for six days, beaten and made to do lengthy physical exercises? Please speak up . . .' Who speaks now?

CATHY. Hang on, man, I'm trying to see where I must read . . . (*Reads.*) 'They asked me why I had told the doctor that they assaulted me. That man . . .' That man?

HECTOR *indicates himself.*

'That man, he slapped me on my face . . .'

HECTOR. 'Not true!'

GUPTA. 'Silence in Court! Proceed!'

CATHY. Proceed? Oh me . . .
'He threatened to kill my parents and to kill me. He said they would cut a policeman's neck with a bottle and that they will say it is me who did it . . .'

HECTOR. 'Lies!'

GUPTA. 'Silence in Court! Proceed!' Is this all I say?

HECTOR. Shhhhh.

CATHY. 'They kicked me and slapped me and swore at me continuously.' All those f-words, I'm sure.

GUPTA. No f-words in my court. Proceed, Cathleen!

HECTOR. Don't wreck it now, Gupta.

CATHY. Okay, okay. 'On the sixth day, they put a sack over my head and prodded me with a rod. I did not see it, but it induced a sharp intense pain. I was screaming.' This they do to a child?

GUPTA. Yes, this is one of the ways in which it is done.

HECTOR. And when I wanted to put a silly old pillowcase over your head, you thought I was joking?

GUPTA. It could've been far worse in real life.

HECTOR. How come you seem to know all about methods of torture, Gupta?

GUPTA. I am aware of anything my fellow man could use against me to make me betray myself. And so because I cannot be astonished by evil, I am relatively protected against its surprises. But let me drag myself away from this 'stimulating entertainment.' Mere hungry mortals wait at the Taj Mahal with their Visa cards, to make our landlords' dreams come true.

HECTOR. Anyway, I don't have much to do in this scene – just look shocked and innocent.

CATHY. How can you be innocent after all they said you did?

HECTOR. But that's the whole point.

GUPTA. He is not innocent.

CATHY. They let you go free?

HECTOR. Good twist, hey?

GUPTA. Who is having the last laugh here?

HECTOR. It's not a comedy.

GUPTA. You flee the culture of death and bring its infection to your adopted cradle of freedom? Decent people also live here and we don't want to have to watch you play out your guilt on our television all the time. Do you see the trauma of my country being publicly flayed open for the commercials to enliven?

HECTOR. Yes. *Passage to India, Jewel in the Crown?*

GUPTA. I said: *my* country, not their colony.

HECTOR. God Gupta, I don't choose the flavour of the month. Yesterday it was India. Today it's South Africa. Tomorrow, who knows? I'm not going to waste my luck. Lots of work around, and with my British passport coming through any day from now . . .

GUPTA. Yes, something I was content to wait fourteen years for!

HECTOR. I'm on the shortlist.

GUPTA. But of course, you're young and clever.

HECTOR. Thank you.

CATHY. Don't start again, you two.

GUPTA. You're outwardly healthy. You can speak their language. Sound like one of them. Even pretend you are one of them. That's what they like, Hector Prince.

CATHY. Don't tease the boy.

GUPTA. Oh yes, and you're nice and white.

HECTOR. And you think that helps?

GUPTA. Unquestionably.

CATHY. Shame on you, Gupta!

GUPTA. No, shame on you, both of you. Your last day in the relatively normal decent society and you play-act death and lies and torture!

HECTOR. She's helping me with my work!

GUPTA. How much is study and how much nostalgia?

He exits.
Pause.

HECTOR. He doesn't like whites.

CATHY. Come on. Right from that first day when you asked to meet me at the Taj Mahal the two of you have . . .

HECTOR. He just tolerates me, but with an edge of contempt all the time.

CATHY. Well, I've never seen contempt.

HECTOR. I can't help my roots.

CATHY. Nor can he.

HECTOR. So why does he hold apartheid against me?

CATHY. Hector love, we don't hold you responsible.

HECTOR. I go out of my way to treat him like a decent human being and then he gives me his superior attitude.

CATHY. It's just his way.

HECTOR. From him of all people!

CATHY. Gupta is a highly-born man from a very good family.

HECTOR. You're joking. He's got such a fucking chip on his shoulder.

CATHY. He came here with nothing . . .

HECTOR. A whole packet of chips.

CATHY. . . . not even a trade.

HECTOR. Fish and chips!

CATHY. He worked his way up from the waiter to managing a

whole restaurant.

HECTOR. Call him whatever makes him happy.

CATHY wants to answer, but doesn't. Busies herself packing.

CATHY. My two brollies and my woollies. I won't need them from tomorrow.

HECTOR. He wouldn't allow me backstage to see you that first time.

CATHY. Hey hey hey! House rules: no customers in the kitchen!

HECTOR. He was bloody cheeky for a waiter!

CATHY. Tell the people under the bridge I put all my old TV magazines and *Woman's Owns* in this box in case someone wants them.

HECTOR. I hate being held responsible for what those Afrikaner bastards are doing to South Africa!

CATHY. Look through my cassettes in case you fancy some.

HECTOR. If I had my way, I'd raise a liberation army. Hey, you've got the latest Sting!

CATHY. God, I love that boy.

HECTOR. Can I have it?

She nods. He sorts through the cassettes.

I'd raise a liberation army, like during the Spanish Civil War. Have you heard of it?

CATHY. Ja, Hector, we saw the film together.

HECTOR. Now there was passion and commitment. Jesus Christ!

CATHY. What's it?

HECTOR. The Madonna Concert! Ladysmith Black Mambazo? Any excuse for a party, hey Cathy?

CATHY. Oh, but the rhythm is still in my blood, Master Hector.

HECTOR. 'Master Hector' again? Or just practising for where you're going?

CATHY. Hey, I'm going home as me, not as a maid, okay?

Pause.

HECTOR. You know I didn't mean it like that, Cathy.

Pause.

CATHY. So, you're marching to Pretoria.

HECTOR. Yes, imagine hundreds of thousands of exiles marching through Africa, with Miriam Makeba singing and Hugh Masekela playing his trumpet.

CATHY. All going home like me.

HECTOR. To build a future for everyone.

CATHY. Ja, like me! Well, let me know when you come, and I'll organise some cooldrink and fancy little cakes. But no bobotie!

HECTOR. We'll fight those Nazi fuckers on the steps of their Voortrekker Monument!

CATHY. All those f-words again! Help yourself to some cooldrink.

HECTOR. Revenge will be sweet . . . and all this money?

CATHY. Hey, hey, hey – don't scratch in my things, man Hector man!

HECTOR. Cathy, are you crazy to leave cash lying around here like this?

CATHY. I hid it away; you're leaving it lying around!

HECTOR. Anyone could steal it.

CATHY. Not just anyone comes to visit me. Mmmm, considering how long it took to save, it's not a fortune. My doctor's bills were more hungry than I thought.

HECTOR. That's what the National Health is for. Free treatment for your asthma!

CATHY. For the Brits, yes.

HECTOR. Take what you can, while you can – everyone does.

He sees the SAA travelbag.

You're not flying back SAA, are you?

CATHY. They gave me that bag for free!

HECTOR. After boycotting Outspan oranges and Grannie Smith apples for twelve years, you now go back in the belly of the beast?

CATHY. I'm going back to where the beast lives, so who cares how! On SAA I'll get a taste of Afrikaans, sort of being part of it before actually being there. They say the service is good.

HECTOR. But you know how well British Airways will treat you.

CATHY. We came over on BA in 77. My first trip on a plane; I nearly died with nerves. This big Jumbo jet with me and the kids at the back.

HECTOR. And Master and Madam in the front?

CATHY. You pay for the seat, you choose where you sit.

HECTOR. Typical.

CATHY. Practical, man, The kids were impossible. So I slipped some of Madam's valium in the orange juice and we all slept like logs, missing all the excitement of flying over Africa. The next day here at Heathrow, skoon valium-bedonnerd, suddenly there's this fashion parade on that rubber belt, with everyone clapping hands as my pink underclothes and my squashed hat went round and round, all hanging out of my broken suitcase. I was so embarrassed.

HECTOR. A hat? You?

CATHY. Of course, my family said I must have a hat, in case I have tea with the Queen.

HECTOR. Hats are optional.

CATHY. Promise you won't laugh.

HECTOR. I won't laugh.

CATHY. Promise!

HECTOR. Cathy, I swear!

CATHY. Okay.

> *She exits.*
> *Then reappears wearing a hat and a funfur. Poses.*
> *He hoots with delight.*

CATHY. No sis man, you swore! You can laugh, but I'm going to arrive in Cape Town wearing my hat and my funfur from Miss Selfridges.

HECTOR. In the Cape Town weather?

CATHY. Even if I melt from the heat, it's worth it. Just to see the expression on their faces. Aunty Cathy looking like Joanie Collins.

> *Pause.*

I still get postcards from the Sharp kids. They say their new maid is not a patch on me. Anyway they all hated the weather here.

HECTOR. Those fucking white liberals!

CATHY. . . . you must admit, though, the weather here is funny. The sky is always so low. Not natural. Gupta says it's the pollution and something to do with the ouzo layer.

HECTOR. Ozone layer, Cathy. Ouzo is a Greek drink . . .

CATHY. I know that now. God Hector, I was trying to make a little joke. I'm so depressed man – look around you.

HECTOR. You wasted all these years saving up to go home after those rich Yids dumped you here.

CATHY. . . . I must say, they make you feel very at home here, the English.

HECTOR. It's the only place to be.

CATHY. Ja, until you've dropped your defences and really feel yourself at home. Then they politely remind you that you're not 'actually' and that you'll never be 'really' . . .

HECTOR. Well, nothing would make me go back.

CATHY. How can you, after all those anti-South African things you said here?

HECTOR. I just told people what happened to me. I'm a political refugee, not a tourist.

CATHY. No, tourists don't so easily get passports!

Pause. He is offended.

But those terrible things I read in your script.

HECTOR. And you didn't believe me when I told you what they did to me?

CATHY. Well, I still can't understand it. All that hatred – and for what?

HECTOR. But that's what's so good about being here, Cathy. Here it's life you worry about, not death!

Her front door bell rings.

CATHY. Who's this now?

HECTOR. All the friends coming to say so long?

CATHY. You've been. Go and see. Maybe it's not for me.

He exits.

God, I don't have enough cooldrinks.

She puts her hat on the table. Sees the script, opens it and reads.

'They ordered me to remove my shoes and then stamped on my toes with the heels of their boots. They knocked my head against the wall . . . my nose bled . . .' No sis, man, I don't like this part.

Hector enters.

HECTOR. Cathy.

CATHY. Hey?

HECTOR. It's for you.

TREVOR JURIES *enters. Small travelbag, rolled blanket. He's been travelling.*

TREVOR. It's me, Aunty Cathy.

Pause.

CATHY. My God, what happened!

Blackout.

ACT TWO

The action continues.

TREVOR. It's me, Aunty Cathy.

Pause.

CATHY. My God, what happened!

TREVOR. I'll come back later . . .

CATHY. No, no . . . Trevor? Trevor, why are you here? Let me look at you properly! My God Trevor, I would never have recognised you.

TREVOR. We sent you a photo.

CATHY. Three years ago! You were only so big and look at you now? Trevor, is it really you?

She hugs him hard.

TREVOR. It's me, Aunty Cathy. Who's this?

HECTOR. Hector Prince.

CATHY. He's the actor.

TREVOR. You acting now, Aunt Cathy?

CATHY. No man, Trevor, this boy is the actor; I'm still just me. Hector, this is my sister Eileen's oldest boy, Trevor.

HECTOR. Hi.

Holds out his hand but TREVOR *has turned to her.*

CATHY. God, let me sit down . . .

TREVOR. I phoned the number Ma still had for you.

CATHY. The Taj Mahal Restaurant probably.

TREVOR. I can't talk into those answering machines.

HECTOR. Cathy doesn't work there anymore.

CATHY. The doctor says I mustn't stand all day.

TREVOR. Still in the kitchen, hey Aunt Cathy?

Pause.

CATHY. Hector love, do you fancy a cigarette?

HECTOR. No.

CATHY. Then go and smoke it outside.

HECTOR. Oh. Yes.

HECTOR *exits.*

TREVOR. Who's he?

CATHY. My friend.

Pause.

So. How are you, Trevor?

TREVOR. Okay, Aunt Cathy.

CATHY. You've really grown up.

TREVOR. Ja.

Pause.

CATHY. How's Eileen?

TREVOR. Ma's okay, Aunty Cathy.

CATHY. And your Pa? Is his heart better?

TREVOR. His heart's okay, Aunty Cathy.

CATHY. So everything's okay?

TREVOR. It's okay, Aunty Cathy.

Pause.
She glances at his bag and blanket.

CATHY. You brought the good weather with you.

TREVOR. It's horrible outside.

CATHY. That's called good weather here.

TREVOR. Not like home.

CATHY. You'll get used to it.

TREVOR. I don't care about the weather, Aunty Cathy.

CATHY. Well, you won't get a suntan here, that's for sure.

TREVOR. That's not what I came for.

CATHY. No, I don't suppose it is.

Pause.

He looks around.

TREVOR. Looks like someone's moving.

CATHY. Isn't your school still busy at this time of the year, Trevor?

TREVOR. I thought this place would be bigger, you know.

CATHY. Or have the school terms changed?

TREVOR. Just one bedroom?

He looks down the passage.

CATHY. This is your last year at school, Trevor?

TREVOR. I failed last year, Aunty Cathy.

CATHY. Not like you to fail.

TREVOR. We all failed.

CATHY. The whole class failed?

TREVOR. It was a boycott.

CATHY. So when the time came to write exams . . .

TREVOR. There were no exams.

CATHY. I remember.

TREVOR. Ma wrote?

CATHY. Here I see everything you do on TV. How could you allow yourself to fail, just in reach of your education?

TREVOR. Hell, Aunt Cathy, you sound just like Ma.

CATHY. And what did Eileen say? I can't imagine she was pleased?

TREVOR. It's all more important than just being pleased or not pleased.

CATHY. I can't see my sister or your father just letting you throw away your education and come here for a holiday! Or did you force them into agreeing not to give you a damn good hiding!

TREVOR. Don't come to me with words like that, man Aunt Cathy!

CATHY. So what are you doing here when you should be at school?

TREVOR. I thought you'd have a bigger place.

CATHY. Then why don't you just make my day and ask me for a bed to sleep in, because you've run six thousand miles away from home, and the first stop is old Aunty Cathy in London NW1!

TREVOR. I don't know anyone else here.

CATHY. Then talk to me, Trevor, and do it quickly and truthfully, or else I go down the hallway and phone Eileen in Athlone: 010.27.21.654.3321. Some explaining needs to be done.

She starts off.

TREVOR. Don't phone!

CATHY. Then talk.

TREVOR. It's a long story.

CATHY. It's also a long way. Do they know where you are?

He shakes his head.

They don't know where you are?
For God's sake, Trevor, look around you – where am I going to put you up?

TREVOR. I'm not fussy, Aunt Cathy.

CATHY. There's no room for you, and besides . . .

TREVOR. Back home we sometimes slept four to a room, or have you forgotten those times?

CATHY. No, I haven't forgotten, and so let me remind you that this is not back home! You could've phoned, dropped me a card – anything! Why all this mystery?

Pause.

Show me your passport.

TREVOR. I don't have a South African passport.

HECTOR *enters.*

HECTOR. I've smoked two; I'll get lung cancer if I have another cigarette.

CATHY. And when did you arrive?

TREVOR. This morning.

HECTOR. SAA?

TREVOR. Can we go out and talk, Aunt Cathy?

CATHY. Talk here. Hector is my friend. Hector, it seems this boy has run away from home!

HECTOR. You too? You're joking!

TREVOR. Why?

HECTOR. And they always thought running away from home was to the next town, not another hemisphere. Good for you! I first tried to get a job as an airline steward to get out, but they just turned me down. Said my qualifications were too good – a kak old B.A.Drama from the University of Cape Town.

TREVOR. Cape Town?

HECTOR. Originally, then I did two months in the Army.

TREVOR. Ah, another one dodging the call-up?

HECTOR. Political exile. It's okay, we're on the same side.

TREVOR. How come?

Pause.

HECTOR. Because of what they did to me in the Army. Eh, ask Cathy. I'm anti-apartheid, aren't I, Cathy?

TREVOR. 'Anti-apartheid'? Hell, I wish I'd thought of that – when my parents were treated like shit by you whites; when your family and friends aimed their guns at my family and friends and fired – even then I wasn't 'anti-apartheid'; I was just scared, man, fucking terrified!

HECTOR. Your aunt doesn't like those words.

CATHY. No, talk Trevor!

TREVOR. No, I'm just saying: it's easy for him here.

HECTOR. Really?

TREVOR. You can stand in front of the Embassy with a banner and then go for a safe beer. Where I come from, where he came from, banners mean jail, blood not beer.

HECTOR. I'd say it must be hard work having to act up a good riot for every TV camera that points your way.

TREVOR. Where've you been sleeping, whitey? There are no TV cameras around anymore!

HECTOR. Shame.

CATHY. But we still see those things here on the News.

HECTOR. That's old footage.

TREVOR. When did you leave?

HECTOR. Just after the State of Emergency.

TREVOR. Shame, you missed all the fun in the townships. You left when the fighting was still only up in Angola and Namibia?

HECTOR. That had a lot to do with my leaving.

TREVOR. But you were never forced into the townships with a gun in your hand, hunting down kids your own age?

HECTOR. My conscience forced me to leave!

TREVOR. Kids with stones in their hands!

HECTOR. Oh please, grenades in their hands!

CATHY. Let's have some cooldrink . . .

TREVOR. Ja, five million potential soldiers with two dozen handgrenades? Wake up, Liberal!

HECTOR. I won't be provoked.

TREVOR. Now the lid is just being screwed down, it's being soldered tight! And just when you whiteys think we have no way of letting off steam – bang! Bang!

CATHY. Bang?

TREVOR. Bang!

CATHY. What goes bang?

TREVOR. Bang!

CATHY. The Boere go bang? The world goes bang?

TREVOR. Bang! The next step is ground-to-air missiles. Take out a few domestic airbuses carrying fatcat civil servants to another committee meeting.

HECTOR. That's an old movie, Trevor.

TREVOR. Then some house-burning raids into your nice white suburbs to remind you people of democracy.

HECTOR. Yesterday's war. You can fight your battles at home now. It's all over.

TREVOR. What's all over?

HECTOR. There's a new South Africa.

TREVOR. Oh yes? Do we all now have the vote?

HECTOR. Hey?

TREVOR. The vote? Equal education? Can I live where I like?

HECTOR. No, but . . .

TREVOR. No buts. We suffer, you suffer. We die, you die.

HECTOR. Fifty years of Beirut.

TREVOR. Victims and victors.

HECTOR. Me and you.

TREVOR. Or you and me. Anything can happen when there's equality in hatred and violence.

CATHY. No more! God, what a horrible picture.

TREVOR. A true picture, Cathy!

CATHY. Ag rubbish man. How come Hector's parents in Rondebosch say things is now fine? And I'm Aunty Cathy to you, my boy!

HECTOR. Cathy, my parents wouldn't notice the world nuked from their verandah.

TREVOR. No, Hector's folks are right: Rondebosch is fine. It's us who must change their minds.

HECTOR. Oh, so you'll still go and chop up my parents, Trevor?

TREVOR. Not now that I've met you, no. I'll get one of the others to do it!

HECTOR. Equality for all?

TREVOR. Equality *in* all!

Pause.

HECTOR. Jesus! It's that . . . passion that I miss! That madness!

CATHY. It's pathetic!

HECTOR. You really make me want to go back, you know that? It's crazy.

TREVOR. Crazy people come back all the time. I'll give you a week there.

HECTOR. Hang on, I'm not the one who's leaving.

TREVOR. They won't arrest you for running away from the Army and telling the world all the usual shit that makes people's mouths water for more.

HECTOR. I won't give them a chance to catch me.

TREVOR. Because they'll ignore you. Or worse, now they'll welcome you back at the airport like a long-lost son of the Volk. You were confused, they'll say. Dankie Oom, you'll say.

HECTOR. Never!

TREVOR. Dankie Oom, You'll say! And you'll enter meekly into the new Laager with happy tears in your eyes, smell South African cigarettes in the air, hear Afrikaans make you feel safe and important. You'll see no more 'Whites Only' signs at the airport.

CATHY. Really?

TREVOR. Not good for business. You'll think, 'Gee whiz, it's not as bad as they said in London.'

CATHY. Not if most of the signs are gone!

TREVOR. You'll be on your favourite open beach within days, suntanning somewhere with blacks and coloureds too, because 'Gee whiz, it's not half as bad as they make out in the world.'

CATHY. Are all the beaches really open now, Trevor?

TREVOR. 'Gee whiz, what was the problem anyway,' you'll think.

CATHY. I wonder if my asthma will get worse out there.

TREVOR. Go home, Hector. And if you can, after just one week, look at yourself in the mirror and say: 'I once had a conscience.'

HECTOR. I still have a conscience!

TREVOR. If you can say that, we'll see you back here in ten days.

CATHY. So, where does your ma think you are?

TREVOR. It's not special not to know where your child is.

CATHY. So Eileen thinks you're in jail! Shame on you, Trevor.

TREVOR. Ma thinks I'm dead.

CATHY. Oh, now you're just a ghost, Mr Trevor Juries?

TREVOR. It's the best that way.

CATHY. I'm going to phone her right now. I'm cross – and believe me when I'm cross, I'm cross!

She exits.

TREVOR. The police leave her alone now.

Pause.

They don't wake her up three and four times a night looking for me . . .

CATHY *enters slowly.*

Pa had another heart attack because of that. Now at last the shock is over.

CATHY. But you're alive . . .

TREVOR. They can sleep at night now. They have a hero for a son.

CATHY. A dead hero?

TREVOR. I'll tell them differently when the time's right.

CATHY. She's your mother!

TREVOR. Everyone is in danger out there!

CATHY. I don't understand.

TREVOR. Aunty Cathy, you remember the Brandon family, with the three boys? Never mind . . . the oldest boy was chased down the streets one night by vigilantes . . .

HECTOR. Blacks collaborating with the System.

CATHY. I know, I know.

TREVOR. He ran to his parents' house. The door was locked. He cried and screamed and banged on the door, begging for them to open. But they didn't.

CATHY. His parents?

TREVOR. They had to protect the other children in the house.

CATHY. Protecting children from other children?

HECTOR. Did they get him?

TREVOR. His parents and brothers and sisters listened as they hacked him to pieces –

She tries to get up. He holds her.

– blood against the front door, under the carpet in the hall.

CATHY. I don't want to hear anymore.

TREVOR. It turns out the vigilantes had made a mistake.

HECTOR. Killed the wrong victim!

CATHY. I don't want to hear about the Brandon family! I want to know what this has to do with my family!

TREVOR. They'll all live longer out there if they think I'm already dead!

Pause.

CATHY. Not even a postcard to help her along?

TREVOR. That's why you must help me, Aunt Cathy.

CATHY. Why didn't Eileen tell me anything?

TREVOR. I've got to get involved from here, help organise things for the struggle there.

HECTOR. I'll help you! That's the thing about living here. You're free to make up your own mind, form your own opinions.

TREVOR. I've got opinions.

HECTOR. And, what's more, you'll have a chance to find out the truth about what is happening in South Africa.

TREVOR. I know, I've just come from there!

HECTOR. The Real Truth!

CATHY. It makes my stomach turn to hear all this.

TREVOR. It's war, Aunt Cathy!

CATHY. Ja? And once the comrades have killed all the collaborators and the vigilantes have killed all the radicals, who will remain to throw a party?

TREVOR. I want to stay here with you, Aunt Cathy.

CATHY. You want to bring your revolution into my home?

TREVOR. You've lost touch!

CATHY. No, I've learnt to touch! That's why I'm here and not there! I could've gone back – the Sharps offered me a ticket, Hector, but I said no. I wanted to take my chances here on square one with everyone else. Everyone has a chance here, Trevor; we can all sink or swim!

HECTOR. God, Cathy, there's a woman in 10 Downing Street who would pay you to repeat that on the BBC.

TREVOR. Those fucking Sharps! Don't pretend they're your friends!

CATHY. Yes! The Sharps showed me that there was a world outside my kitchen! They took me to Covent Garden and let me watch an opera in Italian. They showed me the races at Ascot – where I did wear my silly hat, Hector, and no one laughed! And even when I lost £5 on some silly horse that fell over its own feet, Dr Sharp replaced it that very night!

TREVOR. They could afford it!

CATHY. And every time there was a birthday in Athlone, they let me phone and say hello to you and your sisters and your ma and pa and talk over six thousand miles for as long as I liked. So don't you shout your slogans against my friends!

HECTOR. And when you go back now, will they still be your friends?

CATHY. Who knows. I'm not too proud to go and say hello.

TREVOR. Go back? What do you mean: go back?

CATHY. Go back.

TREVOR. Go back where?

Pause.

HECTOR. Yes, Cathy's going back.

Pause.

TREVOR. You're joking! Aunt Cathy? Tell me you're joking!

CATHY. No joke, Trevor. I'm going back to Cape Town tomorrow and there's nothing you can say that will stop me. Nothing!

TREVOR. Why?

CATHY. Why what?

TREVOR. Why are you going back to South Africa?

CATHY. Because.

TREVOR. What sort of answer is that?

CATHY. Because I have no answer!

She has a severe asthma attack. HECTOR *hands her her pump. She sucks at it. Calms down.*

Sometimes . . . it's like I can't breathe . . . a tightness in my chest . . . a banging, like my heart is being chased into my ears . . . There's a pain, then I panic.

TREVOR. Get some pills from the doctor.

CATHY. I'm not sick! It's just, like you, I also have a story to tell of a mad struggle, a war – but it's all in my head.

She points to her head.

I switch on all the lights and the TV and the radio to make it go away but it's still here. I try to find an ordinary name for this terrible Fear. So I call it 'Johnny', 'Jimmy' or 'Lancelot' . . . anything ordinary, other than Fear. Then I'm able to handle it, like any old Johnny, Jimmy or Lancelot.

TREVOR. You going back, I can't believe it.

HECTOR. Swopping Johnny, Jimmy and Lancelot for Jannie, Pietie and Stoffel.

CATHY. Believe it, Trevor, it's a fact. I've got my ticket in my bag – there's my bag. I've been sitting here on my own for too long, watching as the gutters of the Cape run red on the TV. I'm so scared I'll go home one day in a cardboard coffin with no windows to show me my mountain and my sea . . .

She is overcome.
Pause.

TREVOR. So what do I do now? What happens to me? Where do I sleep? How do I eat? It took me seven months to get here.

HECTOR. Seven months? How?

TREVOR. I don't know. It's crazy. We hid from security police near Port Elizabeth and then got chased across the country towards Botswana, but couldn't find a safe place in through the fences. Then Joburg and the Northern Transvaal. There were roadblocks everywhere. It was impossible to get into Mozambique. Then this crazy idea: formed an 'ethnic' popgroup with some white students who got us false papers and we just drove across the Limpopo into Zimbabwe. Crazy.

HECTOR. Crazy.

TREVOR. Then the horrible mix-up at the refugee houses outside Harare – thousands of our people saying they're waiting to go home, once the Boere finally retreat into their madness.

HECTOR. That's crazy.

TREVOR. Then Lusaka: tough grillings by the ANC, knowing there were spies among us working for the Boere. They took us in an open truck through jungle, then in an old aeroplane from Zaire. There were big tropical storms. Then we were in Ghana. Mosquitoes everywhere. I got sick. My friends were taken off somewhere else. And always, everywhere, those colour posters of dead blacks and fat whites watching rugby. Seven months of hell, Aunt Cathy, but it was okay, because I knew there was a place here for me, and a person!

CATHY. So, your revolution now depends on me.

TREVOR. How can you do this to us?

CATHY. Us? Welcome to the Planet Earth, Trevor Juries. Normal life, my boy, is also full of surprises. Hector, find me that spare toilet roll in Gupta's box. I want to blow my nose.

He does.
She blows her nose.

I'll cry in the Southern Hemisphere. Facts: You have no papers, no money, no education, no bed, no nothing.

TREVOR. No family.

CATHY. Wait till I go tomorrow, before you break my heart with that excuse. Hector, can you help this boy with some warm English clothes for this Indian summer?

HECTOR. I should have something that fits at the flat.

CATHY. Trevor, when last did you eat?

TREVOR. Lusaka.

CATHY. Hector, I've packed up the kitchen. Look in Gupta's box for the Post Toasties.

TREVOR. Ag no man, Aunt Cathy, Post Toasties is for children.

HECTOR. And there's no milk.

TREVOR. And there's no milk!

CATHY. Bleddy fussy too. Do you like Indian food?

TREVOR. I'm not mad about it.

HECTOR. What about a hamburger?

TREVOR. That I like. With chips.

CATHY. Just chips? What about ice cream and chocolates and jellybabies? Trevor, for a freedom fighter who so misses his war, thank God you've still got a schoolchild's taste in junkfood. Okay, I'll get you a hamburger. Wait here.

She puts on her outside shoes, gets her bag. HECTOR *is also ready to go with her. She stops him.*

. . . Both of you.

She exits.

The moment she leaves HECTOR *takes out his cigarettes.* TREVOR *helps himself to two. Drinks water from the jug, splashes water over his face and neck. Looks around the room.*

TREVOR. Kak little room.

HECTOR. It faces the sun.

TREVOR. What does that mean? What sun? Where is the sun?

HECTOR. Somewhere out there.

TREVOR *looks out of the window.*

TREVOR. And this window looks out on another window. Hey, whites living next door.

HECTOR. It's not exceptional here.

Pause.

Give yourself time to get used to your freedom, Trevor.

TREVOR. How can I get used to something I never had?

HECTOR. It took me forever and now that I realise what freedom is, it nearly frightens me to death.

TREVOR. Never mind, you can always run back to Cape Town when you flop here.

HECTOR. My agent's put me up for some good parts in a TV series and a film.

TREVOR. Go back home, man Hector. You can play Hamlet and be a star. The mother in the township who's just buried her children won't have time to sit and listen to your 'to be or not to be' – but then that's not the question.

Lifts clothes out of boxes.

Books, magazines, belongings – all this kak!

Throws them on the floor.

HECTOR. A lot has changed in seven months, Trevor. Why don't you just phone your parents and tell them you're safe?

TREVOR. Why don't you go and fuck yourself, whitey!

HECTOR *replaces the things in the box.*
TREVOR *finds his walkman.*

This yours?

HECTOR *nods.* TREVOR *listens.*

What's this tape?

HECTOR. It was sent to me from Cape Town. To make me homesick, I suppose.

Pause.

TREVOR. Is this what I think it is?

Laughs and takes off earphones.

You're stupid, listening to this.

He looks into the travelbag and sees the money.
Pause.
Then he is aware that HECTOR is watching him.
Pages through the script.

What's all this marked in yellow?

HECTOR. My character. It's a good part.

TREVOR. Why have I never heard of you? 'Hector Prince'?

HECTOR. My name was Henry King, but there's another Henry King in the profession so I had to change it.

TREVOR. I also never heard of Henry King!

HECTOR. This part may be my big break.

TREVOR. Hector Prince's Big Break? How do you remember all this?

HECTOR. Study.

TREVOR. Study this?

He reads.

'Black bastard. Four innocent people you killed!' Don't tell me you're studying to play a Boer!

HECTOR. It's a very complex character.

TREVOR. 'Black bastard . . .' Is that what they get you to say? *(Then says in recognisable character.)* 'Black bastard!' *(He reads.)* 'There was also a dead black man, splattered in so many bloody bits against the toothpaste adverts in the supermarket, that not even when they scrape him off that Colgate smile will he fill . . .' hey . . . 'will he fill an icecream cone'? *(He laughs.)*

HECTOR. That's what happened. It's based on fact.

TREVOR. Oh, you've seen someone's 'bloody bits' fill an icecream cone?

HECTOR. The violence is the issue.

TREVOR. The violence is the issue? Yes of course.

HECTOR. It's all centred round the Trial. This scene is just the start.

TREVOR. And what do you do to this Black Bastard?

HECTOR. He dies.

TREVOR. That's useful. Okay, show me how you do it?

Pause.

HECTOR. Hey.

TREVOR. Maybe it's something I can also do. I played the drums in that band. Quite fancy myself as one.

HECTOR. As one what?

TREVOR. A fucking actor, man Hector!

HECTOR. Okay.

TREVOR. So okay. I'm now also an actor!

HECTOR. Let's set this chair here. We'll need some rope.

TREVOR. You can hang yourself by your underpants.

HECTOR. Just to tie your hands. I don't want to mess with Cathy's things.

Looks around the boxes.

TREVOR. Use electrical cord.

HECTOR. There's a Brasso rag in the broom cupboard. Now you sit here. Keep the script to check my lines.

TREVOR. What's my name in the play?

HECTOR. It's . . . 'Sipho Molifi.'

TREVOR. Based on fact.

HECTOR. It seems he was in the crowd when the police cameras video'd him with a wooden AK-47 in his hands.

TREVOR. Part of his costume.

HECTOR. He was guilty of murder by association, or something.

TREVOR. Guilty of watching?

HECTOR. I don't know . . . look, it's really the Interrogation Scene that's important. Page 8.

TREVOR. Guilty of pretending.

HECTOR. You're in solitary confinement.

TREVOR. For how long?

HECTOR. About a week.

TREVOR. You lose track of time in solitary.

HECTOR. That's a good point, I'll tell the director.

TREVOR. Guilty of acting.

HECTOR. You've been beaten and given shock treatment, yes . . . suffocation: pushing your head under water . . .

TREVOR. No man, Hector man – how can I act and pretend my arms are tied and then hold a script in my hand? Can't you remember 'black bastard'?

HECTOR. I should by now.

HECTOR *takes the bin off.*

TREVOR *rearranges the furniture, clearing the centre of the room. Sets the chair. Sits in it.*
He remembers:

TREVOR. Take off your shoes . . . But Mr Swanepoel? Off with your shoes, boy . . . that's right. Now your T-shirt . . . illegal to have that slogan on your T-shirt, but never mind . . . take off your jeans . . . But Mr Swanepoel . . . It's just me and you. We'll sort all this out before the medics come and check if I'm treating you well. You feeling fine, hey? Hey? Ja Mr Swanepoel. Good. Now take off your things, black bastard.

HECTOR *enters with the Brasso rag.*

HECTOR. I really don't think we'll need to go this far.

TREVOR. 'It's just me and you . . . you and me . . .'

HECTOR. Hang on, you don't do anything yet.

He 'pretends' to tie TREVOR*'s hands.*

Right . . . 'Black bastard! Four innocent people you killed. A little girl who's having her birthday tomorrow, won't be having candles on her cake, because she's lying in the mortuary in little pieces, because of you, you terrorist animal!' Now squirm.

TREVOR. Why?

HECTOR. Maybe you're trying to get free. I need you to squirm so that I can say my next line which is: 'Shut up when I'm talking to you!'

TREVOR. But 'Shut up' means I'm trying to talk; stop squirming means I'm trying to squirm.

HECTOR. Oh . . . eh . . . well, pretend you've got a gag on. Then squirm and grunt or whatever.

He prepares himself:

'Black bastard . . . talk talk talk . . . little candles on her cake . . . I'll cut to the end of the scene, you terrorist animal!' Now!

TREVOR *squirms and grunts.*

Great! 'Shut up when I'm talking to you! Two old ladies were out buying food for their cat and an old dog called Rambo who will now not be fed or stroked . . . (TREVOR *starts laughing.*) . . . stroked ever again because of you, you communist madman!' No man, Trevor, come on – this is serious.

TREVOR. Rambo?

HECTOR. It's in the script!

TREVOR. What a load of shit, man. Kak!

> *He takes a box and throws it at* HECTOR.

Rambo? Here, hold this . . .

HECTOR. But . . .

TREVOR. No man, stretch out your arms and balance the box.
(HECTOR *does tentatively.*) Okay. 'Black bastard! Four innocent
people you killed!'

HECTOR. Go on, that's the feeling I'm looking for.

TREVOR. Shut up, boy! Just hold the box up nice and steady.

HECTOR. It's quite heavy.

TREVOR. But then you're used to heavy labour, black bastard. Pain
just happens in a brain, and if you have no brain, you have no
pain.

HECTOR. You try holding this.

TREVOR. Shut up when I'm talking to you!
(*Pushes him down into a squatting position.*)
Down. One Sound and I'll fill your mouth properly!
(*He moves to the table in search of a gag. Hovers around the travel bag
but doesn't open it. Finds* CATHY's *hat on the table. Picks it up.*) Two
white girls were driving their car from their home to the
bioscope to see a nice movie, when a stone hit their windscreen
and one girl was blinded and the other is still in a coma. I
wonder what it must feel like to see the light one second and
never again the next?

> *He takes out the hatpin and crouches close to* HECTOR.

Nasty people around who would take this pretty hatpin and
slide it into your open eye like a warm fork into jelly.

> HECTOR *winces and closes his eyes tight.*

HECTOR. Please man, I have a thing about my eyes.

TREVOR. Me too. You peep and I'll pop them! (*Pause.*) Open your
eyes.

HECTOR. No.

TREVOR. Open your eyes man, Hector man . . .

> *He does.* TREVOR *waves with his fingers.*

Hello Hector . . .

HECTOR. Jesus, don't get so carried away! The script says
blindfolded, not blinded! (*He puts the box down and rubs his*

arms.) It's like being in the Army again . . .

TREVOR. Okay.

HECTOR. What?

TREVOR. We'll stick to your script . . .

> *He uses a red scarf of* CATHY's *as a blindfold.*

HECTOR. It's all right.

TREVOR. Yes, it's fine, your director will be so impressed.
(*Ties the blindfold.*) Now sit in the chair . . . (*But he moves the chair away.* HECTOR *sits and falls on the floor.*)

HECTOR. Jesus.

TREVOR. You fell off the chair!

HECTOR. There is no fucking chair!

TREVOR. Let's pretend there's a chair. Okay?

> *Slowly* HECTOR *takes his position again.*

You want to hold the box as well?

HECTOR. No.

TREVOR. Nice and comfy?

HECTOR. Yes!

TREVOR. Good. Because we've got all the time in the world.
(*Pause. He sits. Eats a cookie. Eventually* HECTOR *looks round in the silence. Stands up straight.*) . . . We'll just sit around!
(TREVOR *goes to the travel bag. But again he doesn't open the zip where the money is. Eventually*):

HECTOR. I can't anymore.

> TREVOR *goes to him and gives him a little push.*

TREVOR. Then don't.

> HECTOR *falls back in the chair.*

HECTOR. I don't want to do this anymore.

TREVOR. What sort of an actor are you?

> *Pause.* TREVOR *moves away from the chair.* HECTOR *sits.*
> TREVOR *uses a belt of* CATHY's *and ties his hands at the back of the chair.*

All right, we'll go back to your script.

HECTOR. Okay, but no fooling around this time, Trevor.

TREVOR. Back to page 8.

HECTOR *is tied.* TREVOR *pulls his T-shirt up over his head.*

HECTOR. Hey . . . no man, don't fuck up my T-shirt.

TREVOR *gags him with the red scarf over the T-shirt.*

HECTOR *struggles, but* TREVOR *holds him down.*

TREVOR. I'm waiting patiently for you to say your lines . . .
whatever comes to mind . . . (HECTOR *struggles. Held down.*)
Pollution? What do you think of pollution? I love nature,
walking in the veld, smelling the fresh air, feeling God around.
Not like in here – stinks of kaffir in here! Fresh flowers and the
sounds of nature: birds and bees and the sea – and God. No
dirt, like where you live. Where you make noise. Where you
pollute! God and me? We hate plastic bottles and tins and bags
left by you who should know better . . . you collectors of
garbage and cleaners of drains. Like your mother who smells
like garbage and stinks like drains – who bows and scrapes and
says: 'Ja Master.' I'm Master, she's Rubbish! Your ma! Now, do
we make her mad . . . (*He takes out a cigarette and trails it over*
HECTOR*'s bare chest.*) . . . or do you tell us everything and
everyone will be happy. Your ma will be happy to carry out my
garbage and you will be happy to clean my drains and I will be
happy to walk with God in nature – and forget about this dirt
and stink and kak! (*He 'stubs' out the cigarette and stamps on*
HECTOR*'s foot.* HECTOR *screams and struggles up, still tied to the*
chair.) Hell sorry man Hector, I meant to pretend that . . .
(HECTOR *is pushed down so that his head goes into the bin with*
water.) . . . just pretend it's better. You got to trust me. It's just
me and you. You and me. We're on the same side, remember . . .
(HECTOR *comes up for air.*)

HECTOR. Jesus . . . are you fucking mad . . .

TREVOR. Will I be a good actor?

HECTOR . . . suffocating . . .

TREVOR. You're not very good.

HECTOR. Okay okay you've . . . you've made your point . . .

TREVOR. But it's all on page 8.

HECTOR. Okay, it's obviously not right in the script. I'll tell the
director to check the torture.

TREVOR. You think this is torture?

HECTOR. This is torture!

TREVOR. This is just chatting, man! You want me to show you

torture?

HECTOR. No!

TREVOR. But then you know what it's really like . . . after what they did to you?

HECTOR. After what they did to me . . . yes . . .

TREVOR. And that wasn't pretending, like now?

HECTOR. No . . . No! Untie my hands!

TREVOR *unties him. Pause.*

TREVOR. 'Cut to exterior.'

HECTOR. That means the scene is over!

TREVOR. 'He dies offscreen. Cut to exterior.'

Pause. HECTOR *puts on his shoes. Suddenly the doorbell rings repeatedly.* TREVOR *reacts tensely.*

HECTOR. Relax man . . .

CATHY (*off*). Come and help me here, for God's sake.

HECTOR *exits. Pause.* TREVOR *goes to the travel bag and takes the money. Hides it on himself.*

CATHY (*off*). Careful . . .

She enters with GUPTA *and* HECTOR. *They are helping* GUPTA *whose clothes are bloody. There is a bandage/*CATHY's *scarf across his eyes.*

And what's been going on here?

TREVOR. Page 8 of Hector's play.

GUPTA. You have visitors . . .

CATHY. No man, my nephew. I'll tell you later. Trevor, here's your hamburger. Sit down, Gupta.

TREVOR *takes it and eats hungrily.*
HECTOR *and* CATHY *help* GUPTA *onto the sofa.*

GUPTA. Ah, the nephew from Cape Town? Welcome to this blessed shrine of hospitality . . .

CATHY. Shut up, man. It was those damn football hooligans again.

TREVOR. Just looks like a knife cut to me.

CATHY. Shame, Gupta . . .

HECTOR. Can you see, Gupta?

GUPTA. As always more than you could imagine.

HECTOR. He sounds fine!

CATHY. Shame, Gupta, they also smashed the window, with the name of the restaurant gone. Thank God it was lunchtime.

HECTOR. Luckily no one there as usual.

GUPTA. Please do not discuss me like you would a pigeon run over by a bus.

CATHY. Shame, Gupta.

GUPTA. I never know what you mean when you say it, Cathleen. You see a small child laughing, you say 'shame'; you see a starving kitten, you say 'shame'; you see a car smash, 'shame!'

CATHY. But shame, Gupta, your face.

GUPTA. My arm is bruised and my head is rather painful. But I'm sure my eyes are not affected, in spite of the fact that they went for my glasses first and smashed them onto my nose.

CATHY. Your nose?

GUPTA. That is the issue, Cathleen, is the nose broken?

They look.

CATHY. Hector, what do you think?

HECTOR. I've got my flatmate's car here. Let's get him to Casualty.

GUPTA. It would really sadden me if it were broken, as I really like my nose. Not like you who had his nose remodelled on the National Health Service.

CATHY. Since when?

HECTOR. Listen to that crap! He sounds fine!

CATHY. But what did your nose look like before this?

HECTOR. Skew.

CATHY. Not yours, man, his! Hey, Gupta?

She peers under the bandage.

God, it looks like the same nose to me.

HECTOR. Did you phone the police?

CATHY. The police? Eh?

GUPTA. No, no, it's not that serious.

CATHY. Ag no, it's not serious, it's just a cut.

HECTOR. A cut? The man needs stitches. Compensation! The window is insured, phone the police!

TREVOR. Do you think the police would arrest a gang of white skollies because an Asian immigrant and a Coloured tourist complain of assault?

CATHY. I'm not a tourist.

HECTOR. The police here protect people.

TREVOR. Maybe on TV.

CATHY. We don't want to cause any trouble.

GUPTA. It could've been much worse.

CATHY. Ja, and then the police come and find you here with the wrong papers and then what?

GUPTA. Oh my goodness yes.

HECTOR. You say they were the same kids who sprayed those slogans on the walls last week?

He covers GUPTA *with a dressing gown from the box and* CATHY's *funfur.* GUPTA *is shivering.*

CATHY. Those little buggers. God, they need a damn good hiding!

GUPTA. I know where they live.

CATHY. That little racist with the red hair? He's the one who sprayed the yellow star on the restaurant's door.

HECTOR. So who said the Taj Mahal isn't Jewish!

CATHY. How must he know the difference? Hate is hate!

GUPTA. Paki go home! Paki go home! And I'm not even from Pakistan! (*He laughs but winces.*) Oh but it is very painful.

HECTOR. I'll drive you to the Hospital, Gupta.

GUPTA. No, no I'll be fine, after I've had some tea.

CATHY. Man forget about the tea. Take the cakes with you. (*Holds the cakebox, but he doesn't react.*) For God's sake, Gupta, don't be so pigheaded! (*Hands* TREVOR *the cakebox.*) Then pop into the chemist on the corner. Mr Golan will fix you up. I've closed my account there, but take some of this. (*She goes to the travel bag and her money.* TREVOR *is very uncomfortable.*)

GUPTA. The mob, as you well know, Trevor, is always led by the obvious, the loud, the crass.

HECTOR. Even in this free country!

CATHY. God, I can't find anything in this mess. (*She looks through the travel bag.*)

GUPTA. This is what you must find here, Trevor. An alternative to beating a man, because you have lost – be it a soccer match or the right to vote; or because he is black or Asian or white; or because you have ants in your pants, like your Aunty Cathleen.

CATHY. Where the hell did I put it? (*She goes to the boxes and searches.*)

HECTOR. Yes Gupta, and education is a pretty dependable condom against the disease of racism.

GUPTA. Very good. I wonder who said that?

HECTOR. You did.

CATHY. This is ridiculous, but Cathy, stay calm.

HECTOR. What is it?

CATHY. Nothing man, nothing.You two, go up to Gupta's room.

GUPTA. I can go.

CATHY. No, you can't! Get his pyjamas and his spare pair of glasses.

TREVOR. Hector can go.

CATHY. Both go! And when you get back from the chemist we'll sort out where you're going to sleep and how you finish school.

TREVOR. Like hell.

CATHY. Ja, like hell, and then we phone your ma and tell her you're safe. Now move!

TREVOR. Shit man, already she's nagging me like a mother.

He exits to kitchen.
HECTOR *realises her money is gone and comes to her at the travel bag.*

CATHY. And what are you waiting for?

HECTOR *exits quickly to outside.*

GUPTA. Children are such a blessing.

CATHY. To those who don't have them.

GUPTA. How would I have been now, surrounded by a child? It's not been my obsession, you realise, Cathleen. No, that fulfilment I neglected in my all-consuming passion to fit quietly into this strange society. But then is this a decent world in which to eventually unleash a child? Cathleen.

CATHY *is looking around the boxes.*

Where are you, Cathleen?

CATHY. I'm here, Gupta. I'm listening.

GUPTA. I remember how we as children still played with the bricks and window frames that littered the ground outside our old home in the valley near Chandigarh. Our lives were wrecked, our houses burnt, our elders shedding tears of anger, even hatred, but we didn't have the time to understand their pain. It was an adventure for us.

CATHY. Oh God.

GUPTA. We only saw the excitement.

CATHY. What am I going to do?

GUPTA. Be like a child, Cathleen. Just see the fun. Those hooligans did us a favour.

CATHY. Oh God, what am I going to do?

She takes the travel bag and sits next to him on the sofa. She unpacks the bag and carefully sifts through her magazine, her Stephen King novel, the Wet Ones, the track suit, the scarf . . . TREVOR *appears and watches her.*

GUPTA. The landlords have decided to convert the Taj Mahal into a wine bar on continental lines.

CATHY. Oh yes?

GUPTA. Yes, young Swedish barmaids with 'continental lines.' A little joke, Cathleen.

CATHY. I'm laughing, Gupta.

GUPTA. No place there for an old fool like me.

CATHY. Shame.

GUPTA. Shame again? Maybe. But some good friends have promised me a prospect or two.

CATHY. That's what I love about you, Gupta. Your crazy dangerous optimism.

GUPTA. I'm glad, Cathleen. That small lie will be a great help to me.

CATHY. It's the truth. Cross my heart and hope to die.

GUPTA. Cross your cheques and hope to live! It would be such a pleasure to assist you in paying the rent on this flat and contributing to the boy's education – if you decided to stay,

Cathleen.

Pause. She takes his hand. TREVOR *has second thoughts about the money but* HECTOR *enters before he can give it back.*

CATHY. This room faces the sun, you know.

HECTOR. I've brought your toothbrush and your pyjamas.

GUPTA. I will not go to the hospital! Never!

HECTOR. Calm down, Gupta! Listen, my flatmates have gone to the country for the weekend. You're welcome to stay over at my place for a day or two. Till you feel better.

Pause. GUPTA *gently touches his hand on his shoulder.*

GUPTA. You are inviting me to stay at your home?

HECTOR. If you like.

GUPTA. What an extraordinary and wonderful gesture, Hector. But I'll take a raincheck on that. My health is fine. And besides, I prefer my own room. (CATHY *gives a deep sigh and puts down the travel bag.*) Cathleen? Cathy? What is it?

CATHY. There's something I have to ask you boys.

HECTOR. Before you do, Cathy.

TREVOR. Here.

He quickly slips money into the cookiebox on table.

HECTOR. We put it in the cookiebox.

TREVOR. It was me.

HECTOR. Yes, it was Trevor's idea. To keep it safe.

CATHY. In the cookiebox?

TREVOR *goes to* CATHY.

TREVOR. It was a lot of money . . . I was hungry . . . I didn't want you to go.

Pause.

CATHY *hands* TREVOR *the cookiebox.*

TREVOR. There's only one left . . .

GUPTA. Only one left?

TREVOR. Who's going to have this last one?

GUPTA. Eh . . . you must.

TREVOR. Don't you like chocolate?

GUPTA. No, no, I cannot bear chocolate.

TREVOR. Ja. Chocolate is for children.

CATHY. Oh yes? Then I'll have it!

She breaks the cookie in two. Eats a piece. Then breaks the remaining piece in two: gives a piece to TREVOR, a piece to GUPTA. Holds up the empty little cakebox.

Another damn box for my collection.

Tosses it with the others.

Trevor, take Gupta's arm. For God's sake, the man's in a bad way.

GUPTA. Only by Olympic standards!

TREVOR and HECTOR help GUPTA up.

HECTOR. See you outside.

TREVOR and GUPTA exit.
CATHY stands shocked and upset.

Say Johnny Jimmy Lancelot, Johnny . . .

CATHY. . . . Jimmy Lancelot, Johnny . . .

She breaks down. HECTOR puts his arms round her.
Pause.

Trevor . . .

HECTOR. He's a good kid. Give him time. He's also mad . . .

CATHY. It runs in the family. I'm also worried about Gupta. He's so frightened of hospitals. What if he dies?

HECTOR. No one is going to die.

CATHY. How do you know?

HECTOR. Just . . . because!

Pause.

Cathy, there's something I must tell you . . .

CATHY. You don't have to. Just thanks for sorting it all out.

HECTOR. Couldn't imagine Gupta moving in with a 'fascist' like me.

CATHY. That's not what I meant.

Pause.

HECTOR. Remember those things I said about what happened to

me in the Army?

CATHY. The reasons why you're getting asylum here?

HECTOR. It wasn't that terrible. Bad yes, but not that terrible.

CATHY. I'm glad you're here safely, Hector, and not forgotten in some prison there.

HECTOR. There it seems the only respectable place to be.

Pause.

I'll write to you.

CATHY. Just think of me once in a while.

HECTOR. 'Once in a blue moon'?

CATHY. On the beach in sunglasses and a big hat, sipping ice-cold cooldrink and eating fancy little cakes.

Pause.
He hands her his walkman.

HECTOR. Take it and play it on the plane. Home's only twelve cassettes away.

CATHY. But your special tape's still in it.

HECTOR. Ja, play it before you leave.

CATHY. You know I can't stand Boeremusiek!

He kisses her goodbye.
Takes his carrier bag, packs his cassettes, etc., and exits.

You've left your kettle . . .

Pause.
She picks it up slowly.

Maybe I'll just hang onto it for a while . . . Ag no sis man, look at my fancy hat . . . Shame . . .

She pushes out the dents and puts it on firmly. Goes back to the money and counts it in three little piles:

Johnny . . . Jimmy . . . Lancelot . . . Johnny . . . Jimmy . . .
Lancelot . . . Gupta . . . Hector . . . Trevor . . . Ja never mind,
Cathy September, you'll relax in the Southern Hemisphere one day, when you retire.
(*Puts on her overall.*)
Now let's get this place back to normal.
(*Takes the walkman and puts on the earphones.*)
Hector Prince, if this is terrible Boeremusiek that makes me cry with longing, I'll go and hang myself in the lavatory. (*She picks*

up a box. Stops and listens.) What's this? I know this sound? I can smell it . . . the salt, the foam . . . the seaweed, the seagulls . . . the wind from the bay . . .

We hear the sounds of sea on rocks, gulls.

. . . it's . . . it's just like . . .

The sea crashes on the rocks.
She laughs with delight.
The sun shines on her face.

GLOSSARY

aandag attention
baas boss
bioscope cinema
bladdy, blerrie bloody
bliksem bastard, mess up
bobotie baked savoury mince
boetie little brother
bokkie sweetiepie
cherry girlfriend
china friend
deurmekaar mixed up
doos cunt, spoilsport
dop tot, drink
dwaal lost
Egoli, Joeys, Joburg Johannesburg
eina ouch
ek sê I say, I'm telling you
gat arsehole
goeters, goede things
goffel coloured
gogga insect
hardegat hard-arsed
Here, Jirra, Yere Lord God
hou jou bek keep your trap shut
indaba conference, problem
ja yes
jammie car
jislaaik, yislaaik! heavens!
jol joke, celebration
jong fellow
kaalgat bare-arsed, naked
kak shit, rubbish
kif good, all right
klaar finished, over
klap hit, strike
kop head
kraal corral
laager fortified enclosure
lahnie, larney white, boss, stuck up
lekker nice, fine

maat mate
man, manne guy(s)
moegoe dumbcluck, backvelder
moer hit, fuck up
moffie male homosexual
mooi nice, attractive
ou, ouk, oke, ouen, outie chap, fellow, person
panga machete
pasop be careful
poephol arsehole, idiot
poeslap sanitary napkin
pozzy place, hideout
robot traffic light
sat full, sufficient
score give
shame exclamation of sympathy
shebeen drinking den
sies, sis exclamation of dislike
skeef crooked
skelm rascal
skinner gossip
skollie delinquent
skop kick
skrik fright
skyf cigarette
sluk swallow
smaak like, enjoy
sommer just, rather
suka go away!
sukkel struggle
teef bitch
troepies army conscripts
tune tell
vasbyt hang on, hang in there
voetsek get lost
waai go
zol cigarette, smoke